LI

TH   KINS
—————————————

LIVING ACROSS AND THROUGH SKINS

Transactional Bodies, Pragmatism, and Feminism

Shannon Sullivan

INDIANA UNIVERSITY PRESS

Bloomington and Indianapolis

This book is a publication of

Indiana University Press
601 North Morton Street
Bloomington, IN 47404-3797 USA

http://www.indiana.edu/~iupress

Telephone orders   800-842-6796
Fax orders   812-855-7931
Orders by e-mail   iuporder@indiana.edu

© 2001 by Shannon Sullivan

The paper used in this publication meets the minimum requirements of American National Standard for Information Sciences—Permanence of Paper for Printed Library Materials, ANSI Z39.48-1984.

Manufactured in the United States of America

Library of Congress Cataloging-in-Publication Data

Sullivan, Shannon, date
Living across and through skins : transactional bodies, pragmatism, and feminism / Shannon Sullivan.
    p.   cm.
Includes bibliographical references (p.   ) and index.
ISBN 0-253-33853-0 (cl : alk. paper) — ISBN 0-253-21440-8 (pa : alk. paper)
1. Body, Human (Philosophy) 2. Ecology. 3. Pragmatism. 4. Feminist theory.   I. Title.
B105.B64 S85 2001
128'.6—dc21   00-058159

1 2 3 4 5   06 05 04 03 02 01

CONTENTS

Contents

ACKNOWLEDGMENTS

My warm thanks go to the following people for discussions over the last few years that helped shape the ideas in this book: Vincent Colapietro, Celeste Friend, Irene Harvey, Lee Horvitz, Bill McKenna, Phillip Mc-Reynolds, Ashley Pryor, Ben Pryor, Susan Schoenbohm, and Lori Varlotta. The following people graciously read and commented on earlier versions of individual chapters, for which I am grateful: John Compton, Dan Conway, Brian Domino, Susan Jarratt, Charlene Seigfried, and Emily Zakin. I am especially grateful to Del McWhorter for reading multiple chapters multiple times. I appreciate Silvia Stoller's critical response in the Winter 2000 issue of *Hypatia* to the article that became Chapter Three for helping me clarify the relationship of transaction and phenomenology. For their advice and guidance, particularly that which helped me navigate the publishing process, I am grateful to John Lachs, Charles Scott, and John Stuhr. I also happily acknowledge the work of my editor, Dee Mortensen, who made many fruitful suggestions that are incorporated in the pages that follow, and the skillful copyediting of Karen L. Lew.

The long-standing friendships I have with my sister, Jennifer Sullivan, and my college roommate Michele Howard have helped sustain me and, thus, my philosophical work over the years. I am grateful to my parents Alex George Sullivan and Bettye Sullivan for giving me their love and, just as importantly, an example of how to free-spiritedly question one's life, demonstrating the truth of Dewey's claim that the habits that constitute the self can be reconfigured at any age. Above all, I thank Phillip McReynolds, not only for carefully reading and insightfully commenting on the entire manuscript, but also for his love and support and the many philosophical conversations we have had while cooking and hiking, without which this book would not have been possible.

Earlier versions of two of the chapters were originally published in the journal *Hypatia*. Chapter Three is a revised and expanded version of "Domination and Dialogue in Merleau-Ponty's Phenomenology of Perception," published in the Winter 1997 issue, volume 12, pages 1–19. Chapter Four was originally published in a shorter form as "Reconfiguring Gender with John Dewey: Habit, Bodies, and Cultural Change" in the Winter 2000 issue, volume 15, pages 23–42. I am grateful to Indiana University Press for permission to reprint them here.

ABBREVIATIONS

References to the work of John Dewey are to the following volumes and are abbreviated in the standard form of initials for the series, followed by volume number and page number. Thus, for example, the first page of the first volume of the *Later Works* would be listed as LW 1:1.

EW   *John Dewey: The Early Works: 1882–1898.* Ed. Jo Ann Boydston. 5 vols. Carbondale and Edwardsville: Southern Illinois University Press, 1969–1972.

MW   *John Dewey: The Middle Works: 1899–1924.* Ed. Jo Ann Boydston. 15 vols. Carbondale and Edwardsville: Southern Illinois University Press, 1976–1988.

LW   *John Dewey: The Later Works: 1925–1953.* Ed. Jo Ann Boydston. 17 vols. Carbondale and Edwardsville: Southern Illinois University Press, 1988–1991.

LIVING ACROSS
AND
THROUGH SKINS

INTRODUCTION

Transactional Bodies after Dewey

This book presents an account of corporeal existence as transactional and explores some of the social, political, ethical, and epistemological implications of transactional bodies by engaging various pragmatist, feminist, genealogical, and phenomenological philosophers. I take the term "transaction" from American philosopher John Dewey and, following him, use it to indicate the dynamic, co-constitutive relationship of organisms and their environments. The term "interaction" suggests two independently constituted entities entering into an exchange or relationship with one another. In contrast, the term "transaction" reflects a rejection of sharp dualisms between subject and object, and self and world, as well as a rejection of the atomistic, compartmentalized conceptions of the subject and self that often accompany such dualisms. The boundaries that delimit individual entities are permeable, not fixed, which means that organisms and their various environments—social, cultural, and political as well as physical—are constituted by their mutual influence and impact on each other. This co-constitutive process does not merely happen once to establish static entities that never change; because the relationship between organism and environment is dynamic and ongoing, both organism and environment are continually being remade by means of shifts and changes in the other. Thus "transaction" designates a process of mutual constitution that entails mutual transformation, including the possibility of significant change.

To think of bodies as transactional, then, is to conceive of bodies and their various environments as co-constituted in a nonviciously circular way. It is to realize that bodies do not stop at the edges of their skins and are not contained neatly and sharply within them. Rather, as Dewey eloquently puts it, organisms live "as much in processes across and 'through' skins as in processes 'within' skins."[1] This does not mean that organisms transact in physical, chemical, or material senses only. While these are important examples of how transaction occurs, it is no less important that human transaction with the world takes place in social, political, and cultural senses as well. The suggestion that bodies and environments are transactionally co-constituted is not restricted to "natural" environments, as the word "environment" often is interpreted; "environment," in this case, includes the wide variety of cultural situations and surroundings that also make up the world.

While a more detailed presentation of what transaction means will have to wait until later, I want to set out here the advantages of thinking of bodies as transactional. First, thinking of bodies as transactional allows a nonreductive recognition of the significance of bodily materiality to human lived existence. One can acknowledge the importance, even the primacy, of corporeality to human life without opposing bodies to the mental, psychological, cultural, or other so-called nonmaterial aspects of human existence. The nonmaterial aspects of human life would not be possible without bodily materiality. In that sense, bodies are primary. The nonmaterial is not separate from, but includes or depends upon the material in fundamental ways. But because human bodies are constituted through transaction with their environments, to say that bodies are primary is not to dismiss the nonmaterial, nor to collapse the nonmaterial into the material. Human corporeality includes the mental, psychological, and cultural aspects of human life, which are different from, though related to, materiality.

Connected to this idea, or perhaps another way of looking at it, is that understanding bodies as transactional has the advantage of avoiding a variety of ways of formulating a nature-nurture dualism with respect to bodies. If bodies are transactionally constituted, then bodies are not lumps of passive matter imprinted with significance and meaning by an active culture. Nor are bodies sealed off from culture such that, at least on some level or in some respect, they remain untouched by culture. The latter notion suggests that a precultural body can be reclaimed and perhaps used to change culture; in opposition, the former implies that culture destroys or erases the naturalness of bodies when it comes into contact with them. Both notions share the problematic assumption that bodies are part of a nature that is originally "outside" or "prior" to cultural or social influence. And in this assumption, the transactional relationship between nature and culture, or between bodies and environments, is mistaken in two ways. Such a relationship is assumed to be unidirectional, whether from culture to nature or from nature to culture. The relationship is also assumed to be one between atomistic entities that existed prior to their relationship with each other. Both these mistakes can be seen, for example, in the environmental movement of deep ecology, which assumes a fundamental dualism between demonized humans and a romanticized nonhuman nature.[2]

Thinking of bodies as transactional means thinking of bodies and their environments in a permeable, dynamic relationship in which culture does not just effect bodies, but bodies also effect culture. This relationship is one in which bodies and culture are formed from the beginning, as it were, by means of mutual constitution. In Dewey's words, "[t]he epidermis is only in the most superficial way an indication of where an organism ends and its environment begins. There are things inside the body that are foreign to it, and there are things outside of it that belong to it *de jure,* if not *de facto;* that must, that is, be taken possession of if life is to continue."[3] Bodies and their specific environments are not capable of existing or flourishing apart from one another. Humans and nature each contribute to the constitution of the other because humans are a part of nature, not something set off apart from it. Instead of demonizing humans and romanticizing nature as untouched by them, the notion of transaction focuses on the ways in which humans and nature effect each other so that their relationship might be improved.

While bodies and environments are co-constituted, they nevertheless cannot be collapsed into the same thing. In an attempt to avoid nature-nurture dualisms and the atomism they include, one should not conflate nature and culture such that all talk of nature is forbidden. While nature and culture, bodies and environments, are not capable of being what they are apart from one another, this does not mean that they are identical to one another. To understand bodies as transactional is to understand them as something different from culture, even as they are culturally configured and even as they in turn configure cultures and environments. Thus, one can speak fruitfully of humans as distinct from trees, rocks, and rivers even as one recognizes the constitutive impact that each has on the other.

A further benefit of understanding bodies as transactional is that it avoids views of the body as a physical substance that is opposed to the mental substance of psyche or mind. It does so by conceiving of bodies as activities and, in particular, as composed of the predispositions to act in specific ways that Dewey calls habit. Thinking of bodies as transactional construes bodies as *patterns of behavior* or action that occur *across and by means of* or trans- various environments, hence bodies as transactional. Thinking of bodies as patterned activities that come to have complex and multiple meanings, which on Dewey's terms constitute "mind," undercuts mind–body dualism without positing a monism of either body or mind.

Indeed, thinking of bodies as constituted by habit avoids the entirety of substance metaphysics itself.

Another advantage of emphasizing bodies as activity is even more important, or, perhaps better put, it explains why it is crucial to move away from accounts of bodies as substance, whether dualistic or not. By focusing on bodies as activities, one can turn one's attention to what is it is that bodies, in conjunction with their environments, *do*. For example, conceiving of bodies as activities focuses on bodies' walking, dancing, and talking, instead of on arms, legs, and brain considered apart from the situations in which they are engaged. Turning to the effects of bodies' transactions in this way encourages the exploration of whether these effects are beneficial or harmful, whom they benefit and harm, and ultimately whether they should be embraced or transformed.

Thinking of bodies as transactional is additionally fruitful because it emphasizes the significance of the concrete, lived experience of bodies. Following Dewey's emphasis on tying philosophy back to the concrete particularities of ordinary, or what one might call "real" life so as to improve and enrich it, understanding bodies as transactional attends to the specificities of transactions between bodies and environments. One can examine what sorts of effects these transactions have on the lived experiences of people and whether attempts need to be made to change the patterns of those transactions. Let me be clear that my position here is not anti-theory; my account of bodies as transactional certainly presents a theory of corporeal existence. As is the case with all theories, however, and especially with theories about bodies, it is crucial that after abstracting away from the complexity and messiness of bodies, one return theory to concrete bodily life in order to test its fruits in lived experience. Thus, in conjunction with theorizing bodies as transactional, this book will focus on transactional bodies in concrete ways and address some of the various impacts that transaction has on people's lived situations and experiences, particularly those of women.

In that my understanding of transaction heavily emphasizes habit and lived experience, my account of transactional bodies has a strong phenomenological angle. I mean to connote Dewey's work with this suggestion even though the phenomenological side of his pragmatism often is not recognized.[4] By starting with organisms and environments in a dynamic, co-constitutive relationship rather than starting with the primacy of a single ego (whether bodily or not) whose relationship with the world is secondary, the phenomenology presented here is transactional instead of intentional. A transactional phenomenology presents feminists with an alternative to the phenomenologies of Maurice Merleau-Ponty and Edmund

Husserl even as it has some features in common with them, in particular with Merleau-Ponty's emphasis on bodily lived experience and corporeal habit.

Dewey's pragmatism constitutes a central thread in the reflections on and arguments concerning transactional bodies presented here. For this reason, my approach to corporeal existence could be characterized as pragmatist-feminist. By pragmatist-feminist, I mean a feminism that is informed by a general pragmatist sensibility, as well as by the work of Dewey in particular. By "pragmatist sensibility," I do not mean the colloquial sense of pragmatist: that of being practical or levelheaded. Rather, I mean the group of concerns and general way of approaching those concerns characterized by classical American pragmatists, such as Jane Addams, Charlotte Perkins Gilman, William James, Alain Locke, George Herbert Mead, and Charles Sanders Peirce, but especially Dewey. Pragmatism emphasizes praxis and the value of theory for praxis. It undercuts sharp dichotomies, such as those between body and mind, subject and object, theory and practice, ends and means, and nature and experience or culture. It sees knowledge as a tool for enriching experience; is pluralistic, experimental, fallibilist, and naturalistic; and rejects the quest for certainty while taking a meliorist attitude—an attitude that human action sometimes can improve the world.[5]

Charlene Haddock Seigfried's recent work is central to the recent development of pragmatist feminism.[6] As she believes, and I agree, feminism and pragmatism have much to offer each other. Pragmatism should be attractive to feminists because of the explicit connection it makes between values and categorizations of the world. In particular, pragmatism rejects any notion of a neutral, "God's eye" point of view, which feminists have shown to be covertly masculine. Facts and claims about those facts are always political and thus in need of examination to determine if the political reality they promote is one that should be endorsed. Also, pragmatism's emphasis on the concrete particulars of "real" life, instead of abstractions that seem to have no connection to lived experience, lend it to feminist discourse. Finally, pragmatism's style tends to be inclusive and collaborative, avoiding the hostile, "beat 'em up" attacks that characterize much of philosophy.[7]

Feminism also has important contributions to make to pragmatism. While pragmatism is pluralist and inclusive and emphasizes the importance of a multiplicity of perspectives, feminism reminds pragmatists that such pluralism itself proceeds from a particular perspective, with its own hidden assumptions and blind spots that are in need of critical examination.[8] Feminism provides pragmatism with analyses of some particular perspectives and aspects of lived experience, such as those of gender and sexuality, which classical American pragmatists rarely addressed.[9] A pragmatism that genuinely seeks to be pluralist and enrich life in as broad a way as possible must therefore be feminist, as well as other things such as antiracist and antiheterosexist.

My philosophical inclinations fit with pragmatism, feminism, and their intersections, so this book will take the tone and direction of pragmatist feminism. Nevertheless, I want to avoid a possible misunderstanding of the concept and term "pragmatist feminism." To me it does not mean that a theorization of bodies must discuss and draw from pragmatist and feminist philosophers alone. Readers should not expect this book to be solely on or about Dewey. While Dewey certainly is central and important to my reading of bodies, I do not consider this to be a book on Dewey, per se, nor is one of its goals a thorough presentation of or argument for Dewey's pragmatism. Rather, I want to think with Dewey about corporeal existence as I engage the work of feminist, genealogical, and phenomenological philosophy, particularly that of Carol Bigwood, Susan Bordo, Judith Butler, Eugene Gendlin, Sandra Harding, Maurice Merleau-Ponty, Friedrich Nietzsche, Lucius Outlaw, and Susan Wendell.

Mixing pragmatism with what is generally referred to in the United States as "continental" philosophy might strike some as analogous to mixing oil and water. Although for different reasons, many pragmatist and continental philosophers would agree that the two fields of philosophy do not blend well. In my view, however, pragmatism and pragmatist feminism continue, as well as transform in their continuance, Nietzsche's philosophy of joyful wisdom. By this, I do not mean that there is a direct causal or historical link between Nietzsche's philosophy and the development of pragmatism or feminism. Nor do I mean that Nietzsche would approve of pragmatist feminism if he were alive today. Rather, I mean that pragmatism, feminism, and pragmatist feminism in particular can be seen as pursuing the implications of the death of God. In its free-spirited, questioning approach to both life and philosophy and its emphasis on the perspectival nature of corporeal existence, pragmatist feminism explores what life can be like when one lives without the security and guarantee that absolute, certain foundations claim to provide. In a manner similar to that of the tightrope walker encountered by Nietzsche's Zarathustra, pragmatist feminism walks on a rope over an abyss without a safety net underneath and, moreover, does so in a joyful manner.[10] It might not always succeed in this effort; it may sometimes slip off the rope. The spirit of its endeavor, however, is consonant with that of Nietzsche's work, and thus pragmatist feminism joins with continental philosophy in taking up and transforming the legacy of Nietzsche's corpus.

Because genealogical and phenomenological philosophies play a large role in this book, the term "genealogical-phenomenological-pragmatist-feminist" might better describe my approach. Aside from unwieldiness of this term, however, using it is unnecessary because of pragmatism's pluralism. Just as feminism encourages cross-fertilization and boundary crossing to disrupt rigid compartmentalization, so does pragmatism. Thus pragmatist feminism need not, and indeed should not be understood to be a feminist approach to the work of pragmatist philosophers only. Instead, on my terms, pragmatist feminism crosses among and encourages the development of the intersections of the different, but often related, fields of genealogical, phenomenological, pragmatist, and feminist philosophies. Understood in this way, "pragmatist-feminist" is the most accurate description of my theoretical approach to corporeal existence.

I should add that it would be disingenuous for me to deny that I want to convince philosophers who are not sure what to make of Dewey of the value of his pragmatism. Philosophers in general, and feminist, genealogical, and phenomenological philosophers in particular who are unfamiliar with Dewey's philosophy—and this is a great many of them, as far as I can tell—should take another, or perhaps even a first, look at his pragmatism. If understanding bodies as transactional is fruitful for feminist and other philosophical work, then given the centrality of both human corporeality and the concept of transaction to Dewey's thought, Dewey's pragmatism should be seen as a rich resource for a variety of philosophical projects, feminist and otherwise.

One final possible point of misunderstanding to deflect—one that I hesitate to bring up as it might not have occurred otherwise—brings me back to the particular term "transaction." Because of the economic connotations of the everyday use of the word, some readers might prefer "interaction" to describe the dynamic, mutual co-constitution of organism and world. And perhaps, given the problems for pragmatism caused by William James's infamous use of the term "cash value" to talk about meaning, there is good reason to avoid a term whose everyday usage can suggest monetary matters. Even granting these legitimate concerns, however, I think it important to use the term "transaction" to avoid the atomistic connotations of "interaction." As Dewey decided when he switched terms, I believe that "transaction" works better than "interaction" to disrupt the notion of two separate entities that come into contact with one another. In case the term "transaction" has triggered concerns about commercialism, however, I want to make clear that Dewey did not, nor do I use the term to apply to, represent, or be a metaphor for economic exchange.

To begin, some detailed explanation of what Dewey means by transaction is needed. It is no exaggeration to claim that the concept of transaction is key to every aspect of Dewey's philosophy, including his aesthetics, ethics, social and political philosophy, metaphysics, and epistemology. Rarely, however, has it been made explicitly central to the work of theorists influenced by his pragmatism.[11] My focus will be on an in-depth discussion of transaction as it pertains to bodies, exploring in particular the importance to Dewey's understanding of bodies of the concepts "body–mind," organism, and habit. For my purposes here, transactional bodies are conceived as activities that are grounded in physicality, while they maintain the possibility of mental characteristics, and that exist by means of the environmental situations with or within which they take place.

The idea of bodies being constituted in and through their transactions with their environments implicitly raises the question of the existence of non- or prediscursive bodies; that is, bodies understood as fundamentally prior to or outside of cultural, political, and social meanings and norms. This question has been at the heart of recent disagreements between poststructuralists and phenomenologists, who generally seek to theorize bodies in very different ways. While Carol Bigwood and Eugene Gendlin, in particular, have emphasized bodily lived experience by conceiving of bodies as atomistically sealed off from the cultural world, Judith Butler has affirmed the discursiveness of bodies in a way that neglects the concrete aspects of bodily existence. By reading Butler, Bigwood, and Gendlin through the lens of transaction, the importance of both recognizing the discursivity of bodies and attending to lived bodily experience can be acknowledged.

Because of its extensive attention to lived bodily experience, the phenomenology of Maurice Merleau-Ponty provides an account of meaning-creation and communication with others that seeks to demonstrate why human existence is neither atomistic nor solipsistic. While Merleau-Ponty's emphasis upon the role that bodies play in the reciprocal relationship of self and other is well placed, his account of bodily intersubjectivity is troubling from a pragmatist-feminist perspective because it appeals to the notion of an anonymous body when explaining how bodies communicate. The anonymous body problematically understands common meaning as the imposition of one person's meaning on another. Merleau-Ponty's phenomenology of projective intentionality fails to explain how corporeal beings can create a genuinely common ground between people that is nondominating. This is where the notion of transaction can aid phenomenology. By questioning the role that bodies play in Merleau-Ponty's work and developing an alternative to its account of communication, an understanding of bodies as transactional enables thinking of meaning-creation as socially constituted through an appreciation of the differences of others. It also provides a conception of communication as a transactional circle in which all parties involved in a situation jointly constitute its meaning.

How bodies create meaning has implications for the constitution of gender, and Dewey's notion of habit is crucial to understanding gendered existence, including the possibility of its reconfiguration. Thinking of corporeal existence as composed of habit recognizes that the gendered and other habits that structure a person *are* that person. Habit makes human existence possible, as well as constrains it to the particular forms of existence that constitute it. Reading habit in conjunction with Judith Butler's notion of performativity shows how an organism and its cultural and other environments can be altered even though they might reinforce each other in ways that can make substantial change seem unlikely. The sedimentation of habit does not preclude transformation because the different contexts in which particular habits occur can promote their reconfiguration. Because the relationship between individual habits and the environments in which they are performed is transactional, even relatively fixed habits can be changed.

Somewhat surprisingly, given his comments on women, the thought of Friedrich Nietzsche contributes fruitfully to a pragmatist feminist investigation of how humans might transform their bodily habits. Nietzsche emphasizes bodies in an attempt to cure his readers of their guilt and bad conscience. In my view, when Nietzsche urges attention to one's body as part of a cure, he means bodies literally, rather than merely metaphorically. His emphasis on bodies is part of a practice of "somaesthetics" (that is, bodily practices aimed at improving corporeal experience), which he would have his readers adopt. A somaesthetics that utilizes Nietzsche's work is potentially problematic for pragmatist-feminists because of Nietzsche's misogyny. However, even though Nietzsche's attitude toward women is extremely negative, his conception of bodies makes possible the development of a transactional somaesthetics that undermines the misogyny in his philosophy. Nietzsche's work points to ways to develop specific guidelines for transforming bodily habits that counter his sexism.

Because human life is bodily, it is limited and shaped by humans' various physical, social, psychic, and cultural particularities. Rejecting the notion that humans can attain a "God's eye" point of view does not mean, however, that one must accept judgmental relativism. Feminists, pragmatists, and others need standards by which to judge practices and institutions as better and worse; these standards, however, need not and should not be objectivist ones that attempt to occupy a "view from nowhere." Because Sandra Harding has done important work developing an alternative to traditional notions of objectivity, her version of feminist standpoint theory provides the beginning of a counterattack to patriarchal view of bodies and knowledge. But Harding's work needs to be taken even further to produce what I call a pragmatist-feminist standpoint theory. While Harding proposes to do away with the need for truth, feminism requires instead an account of truth as flourishing transactions between organic bodies and world. Combining Harding's feminism with a transactional notion of truth produces a standpoint theory that includes standards for judging better and worse that do not fall prey to objectivism.

Finally, one of the particular reasons that feminism needs nonobjectivist standards for political and moral judgment is that transactions between human organisms and world have been and continue to be racist. When applied to a world of various races, the concept of transaction suggests that races are dynamically co-constituted in such a way that their particularities are preserved, rather than lost. Because the preservation of distinctiveness through transaction applies to all races, white as well as nonwhite, a concern about transaction might arise that thinking of whiteness as preserved necessarily entails the support of white supremacy. In my view, however, conceiving of the distinctiveness of whiteness as preserved is a valuable part of understanding race as transactional. The concept of transaction carves out conceptual space for each race that is needed if its members are to address their past and present racism in antiracist ways. Nowhere is this needed more than in the case of whiteness.

Although transaction preserves distinctiveness and particularity, distinctiveness and particularity need not suggest an atomistic understanding of bodies and their environments. Transaction is characterized as much by connection and continuity as it is by distinctiveness and particularity, and thus distinctiveness and particularity cannot be understood apart from connection and continuity. From an atomistic point of view, the combination of these characteristics probably seems impossible to achieve. Likewise, focusing on bodies' environments to understand "bodies themselves" probably seems wrongheaded from an atomistic point of view. These approaches are only wrongheaded, however, if one considers the distinctiveness of bodies and their environments to be fundamentally unrelated and thus irrelevant to each other. If, to the contrary, bodies and their various environments are dynamically co-constituted, then each is crucial to and connected with the other. This means that the best way to understand and improve bodily existence is to concentrate on the environments and situations that effect bodies and, reciprocally, that the best way to attempt to change the world is to transform a body's transactions with it. Bodies and their habits should not be treated as substantially sealed off from the physical and social worlds in which they are engaged because doing so hinders attempts to envision how the relationships between bodies and world might be transformed. The project of thinking about the world and the place of bodily existence in it should be at the heart of philosophy. Thinking of bodies as transactional will best enable feminist, pragmatist, and other philosophers to turn their attention to this task.

Living Across and Through Skins
Bodies in Transaction

What does Dewey mean by transaction, particularly with respect to bodies? Central to transaction are its undercutting of the dualism of organism and environment—or, of humans in particular, self and world—and its rejection of the atomism that accompanies such a dualism. Two notions are especially important to an understanding of bodies as transactional: the related concepts of "body–mind" and organism, and the concept of habit. By conceiving of bodies as body–mind and as organism, Dewey rejects the idea that humans are made up of two separate mental and physical substances that somehow coexist. In contrast to accounts of self as substance, including that of monism as well as that of dualism, Dewey claims that the human organism is characterized by activity, which has physical and mental aspects to it. An organism's activity, in turn, is characterized by a particular style. In an organism's transactions with the world, patterns occur, which is to say that organic activity is characterized primarily by habit.

By transaction Dewey means an active and dynamic relationship between things such that those things are co-constitutive of each other. I use the term "things" here to indicate broadly that transaction is a feature of many, various entities, not merely physical things. While Dewey often uses the word "interaction" to describe the constitutive "back and forth" between things, the term does not capture the relationship between things that Dewey intends.[1] Because the term "interaction" can suggest a process by which things that exist apart from each other come into contact and exchange with each other, it can imply a positing of those things as fundamentally, ontologically separate. In so doing, it tends to cast the dynamic exchange of things as a relatively superficial process that has little constitutive impact on what those things are, rather than as a thoroughgoing process that effects the constitution of the things themselves.

Put another way, the idea of interaction conceives of entities as in an exchange that is relatively static, as previously and fully formed prior to interactions with others, and therefore as not significantly effected by those interactions. For this reason, in his later work and using the specific example of an organism and its environment, Dewey describes interaction as "assum[ing] the organism and its environmental objects to be present as substantially separate existences or forms of existence, prior to their entry into joint investigation."[2] In contrast, the term "transaction" indicates dynamic entities that are continually undergoing reconstitution through their inter-constitutive relations with others. Again, in the instance of organisms and their environments, one can see what Dewey means by transaction: "Organisms do not live without air and water, nor without food ingestion and radiation. They live, that is, as much in processes across and 'through' skins as in processes 'within' skins."[3] The epidermis is not some sort of rigid border that guards the organism "inside" the skin from foreign elements "outside" it. Organisms, such as humans, are not "located" within the epidermis in an isolated, self-contained way; they are instead constituted as much by things "outside" the skin as "within" it, as well as by the skin, or site of transaction, itself. The commonplace process of being nourished by eating food is merely one possible example of how organisms are constituted through their transactions with the world. As Dewey claims, "there is no absolute separation between skin and the interior [or exterior] of the body. No sooner is the distinction drawn than it has to be qualified."[4]

The example of organisms living in processes that reach across and through skins illustrates the dynamic quality of transaction without suggesting a formlessness in which entities are in such flux that they have no stability, order, or identity. That organic processes take place between organism and environment in such a way that rigid boundaries between the two are blurred does not mean that the organism can have no form or distinction or that it does not exist as this particular organism and not another. In its rejection of a static ontology, the notion of transaction does not reify flux or complete dissolution of identity. Put another way, the concept of transaction no more supports a process metaphysics than it does a substance metaphysics. Instead, as Dewey claims, transaction invokes something like "a stability that is not stagnation but is rhythmic and developing."[5] Moreover, this stability is something that the process of transaction can bring about by and for itself. In Dewey's words, "[o]rder is not imposed from without but is made out of the relations of harmonious interactions that energies bear to one another. Because it is active, order itself develops."[6] The dynamic order of transaction is not something that comes from without, imposed upon transaction. Nor is it something that transaction imposes upon something else external to it. Because the passive and active voices can suggest these two misunderstandings, we might say, following Charles Scott's discussion of the middle voice, that in transaction, order orders.[7] This phrase captures the sense that the order of transaction develops out of its own movement. Rejecting the sharp dichotomy of the fixed and unchanging versus the fleeting and evanescent, as well as rejecting the understanding of order as artificially imposed, the notion of transaction attempts to describe how change and continuity, and activity and stability can go hand in hand.[8]

In the effort to avoid positing radical isolation and separation between things, as the notion of transaction seeks to do, one might be tempted to make the equally bad mistake of collapsing two separate things into one ontological whole. But such a collapse is merely the flip side of the same atomistic coin: it assumes that if things are not utterly different and isolated, they must really be the same thing. And if they are really the same thing, then all things that are different from other things must be different in radically isolated and separate ways. The total elimination of distinctions between things is merely one half of the dualism of atomistic isolation and indistinguishable sameness and does not further an understanding of how things can be simultaneously related and different. In its rejection of the fundamental separateness of things, the notion of transaction does not eliminate all distinctions between those things by collapsing them into each other. Understanding things as transactional is to understand them neither as completely different and separate nor as completely the same and merged into one. Rather, it is to understand them as formed through a constitutive "back and forth" between each other. Such a dynamic "back and forth" requires that there be two different things, but it does not translate into atomism because of the constitutive permeability between those things.

A few food metaphors may help illustrate the distinction I am trying to draw between an atomistic view of things, a distinction-erasing view that collapses things into one another in its attempt to avoid atomism, and a transactional view of things. The familiar metaphors of the melting pot and the tossed salad are nontransactional conceptions of the relationships between individuals and the society to which they belong. The melting pot metaphor corresponds with what I have called the distinction-erasing view. It demands that all differences be melted away with the result that everything thrown into the pot is the same. The melting pot is like a fondue into which cubes of different cheeses are thrown, with the end result being a complete dissolving of the individual cubes so that the fondue is made possible.

The way in which the melting pot metaphor often has functioned in the United States does not match what is promoted by the metaphor's meaning. The metaphor of the melting pot has been used not to produce a genuine fondue, but to force all the different kinds of cheese into being one of those cheeses: American cheese. That is, the melting pot metaphor has functioned to promote the assimilation of ethnic minorities into Anglo-Americans. Because of the way it has served in the United States to preserve the interests of one particular group over others, rather than to completely erase all group distinctions, the melting pot metaphor corresponds to the distinction-erasing view to only a limited degree. Nonetheless, the melting away of all differences, as opposed to the preserving of particular traits, illustrates the distinction-erasing view.

Corresponding to the atomistic view of things, the tossed-salad metaphor sometimes emerges as a response to and rejection of the damaging disregard for differences and particularities that the melting-pot metaphor promotes. Rather than the idea of throwing individual things into a pot with the end of dissolving their distinctions, the tossed salad conceives of individual things being thrown together in the same bowl in such a way that the individual things are merely juxtaposed with each other. In a tossed salad, the lettuce, cucumbers, and carrots may all be in the same bowl together, but their being in the same bowl does not alter their existence in any significant way; the lettuce, cucumbers, and carrots remain the very same vegetables that they were before they were thrown together. Unlike with the melting pot, in the tossed salad, the distinctions and differences of all the various things thrown into the bowl are preserved. Such preservation of differences and particularities is achieved by conceiving of the individual things in the bowl in an atomistic way. Only because the vegetables do not affect each other in any thoroughgoing way are their distinctivenesses preserved. For all its differences from the melting pot, however, the tossed salad is similar to it in that they both fail to provide a way out of the atomism that characterizes metaphysical dualism.

In contrast to both the tossed salad and the melting pot, a stew can provide a metaphor for transaction and thus a way of thinking of difference and continuity together. In a stew, the potatoes, onion, carrots, and spices neither melt into one another as do the individual ingredients of a fondue, nor do they remain isolated and separate, as do the ingredients of a tossed salad. Rather, as they are in the pot together, stew ingredients intermingle in such a way that each helps constitute what the others are. For example, and to oversimplify by focusing on two ingredients only, the flavors of the carrot and onion in a stew impact each other such that the carrot is no longer a carrot, but an onion-y carrot, and the onion is a carrot-y onion. A mutual interpenetration of the vegetables takes places by means of the intermingling of their flavors, making all of the vegetables something different from what they were before they were in the stew. This transformation does not mean that the vegetables have been collapsed into one another or into some sort of formless mush (unless the stew is overcooked). Rather, the carrot is still distinct from the onion and vice versa—an onion-y carrot is not the same as a carrot-y onion, after all—but at the same time that they are distinct, they permeate one another in a constitutive way. Their distinctions and difference are not atomistic; they coexist with the connections and continuities between them. When a stew is finished cooking, each vegetable in the stew has helped make the other vegetables in the pot what they have become. In this way, the vegetables are co-constitutive of each other, but they also remain vegetables with their own distinct, but transformed and thus not isolated identity. As Lawrence Hatab has explained, the relationship captured by the metaphor of a stew is that of "an intermingling of identity and difference that is not reducible to any one identity, a mere aggregate of identities, or a merging of identities."[9]

While the melting pot incorporates the notion of transformation of individual identity, it can only do so by eliminating, in the process of transformation, any sort of continuity or connection with what that individual identity was before. And while the tossed salad has the advantage of preserving individual identity and distinction, it lacks any sort of account of how individuals are or might be in a dynamic relationship with one another. The metaphor of stew, however, helps us conceive of difference and continuity as related, rather than opposed. In that way, the stew demonstrates what I mean by transaction and how the notion of transaction takes us beyond the dualism of atomism and its flip side of ontological collapse.

Of course, all analogies and metaphors have their limitations, and the metaphor of stew is no exception. Stew can misrepresent transaction in a significant way. Before going into the stew, the vegetables exist as separate and isolated and only enter into a transactional relationship with one another after being put into a pot. But the notion of transaction does not assume separate, isolated things prior to their transformation by other things. Rather, the things are constituted by their various transactions in the first place. Things are always already in transaction; that is how they come into being as the things they are. There is no "pretransactive" phase, as the metaphor of stew might suggest. An improved stew metaphor would recognize the transactive quality of vegetables even before they were put into a pot. And because vegetables come into existence by means of transaction with the soil and air, perhaps the stew metaphor does not, after all, depend heavily on a sharp division between the vegetables' nontransactional, pre-stew existence and their transactional, stew existence.

Another problem with the metaphor of the stew, however, is that the vegetables in the stew are passive rather than active. The vegetables come into relation with one another through no doing of their own. They are not in any significant sense actively engaged with the "world" of the stew and the other vegetables in it. Instead, being components of a stew is something that is imposed upon them from without by the activities of the cook and the heat of the stove. But the conceptual point of transaction is precisely that it is an *active*, co-constitutive relationship between things. The things in a transactional relationship are not what they are because they are passive recipients of the impact of something else. They are what they are because of their active relation with their environment. That is, while they are indeed impacted by other things, this impact does not occur passively; instead it happens because of the active way the things respond to impact. While the carrot and onion exhibit some activity in their taking up of the nutrients of the soil when in the ground, they are wholly passive once in the stew pot. Because of this passivity, stew is still a flawed metaphor for the activity of transaction. While I will use the stew metaphor because of its strength in conveying a nonatomistic, nonreductive relationship of identity and difference, I do not want to suggest that transaction is a passive process whose movement is generated by a nontransactional source outside it.

Dewey never used the metaphor of a stew. But his explanation of his distaste for the melting pot metaphor and his reservations about the alternative metaphor of an orchestra shed further light on the notion of transaction. Around the time of World War I, American intellectual Horace M. Kallen proposed the metaphor of an orchestra to illustrate a theory of cultural pluralism that resisted melting pot and other societal models that promoted conformity of various immigrant groups to Anglo-American values.[10] Kallen argued that, just as in an orchestra each instrument has its own distinct sound and plays a distinct role in producing the beautiful music of the whole symphony, each individual or ethnic group in society has a distinct contribution to make to the larger harmony of the overall culture. Dewey wrote to Kallen that he liked the orchestra metaphor, but he qualified what he meant by liking it:

> I quite agree with your orchestra idea, but upon [the] condition we really get a symphony and not a lot of different instruments playing simultaneously. I never did care for the melting pot metaphor, but genuine assimilation *to one another—not to Anglosaxondom*—seems to be essential to an America. That

each cultural section should maintain its distinctive literary and artistic traditions seems to me most desirable, but in order that it might have more to contribute to others. I am not sure that you mean more than this, but there seems to be an implication of segregation geographical and otherwise [in the orchestra metaphor].[11]

Dewey's concern with Kallen's orchestra metaphor was that it might turn out not to be a stew, but rather a tossed salad in disguise. For the orchestra to be merely a collection of instruments playing at the same time would be for each of those instruments to be isolated and separate from one another, not impacting each other by means of the music the other is playing.

Dewey is clear that in his rejection of an atomistic understanding of the orchestra metaphor, he does not prefer the melting pot metaphor in its place. The melting pot includes assimilation, which might have the potential of being transactional if it were assimilation of each member of the whole to one another. The character of its assimilation, however, is such that all differences and distinctions are dissolved in a set of allegedly neutral values and standards that are instead the values and standards of one group only. As Dewey wrote around the same time that he considered the orchestra metaphor, "[t]he theory of the Melting Pot always gave me rather a pang. To maintain that all the constituent elements, geographical, racial and cultural, in the United States should be put in the same pot and turned into a uniform and unchanging product is distasteful."[12] In contrast to both the erasure of variety and difference promoted by the melting pot ("Anglosaxondom") and the isolation suggested by the orchestra ("segregation"), Dewey desires a stewlike "assimilation" of ethnic groups to one another so that each is enriched by its transactions with the others. A jazz band might better represent this relationship than an orchestra. In a jazz band, each player riffs off the other, and the whole group comes to be more or less harmoniously co-constituted by means of listening to and actively taking up the parts of the other players, rather than by being orchestrated by a conductor who follows a preset score.[13] A jazzlike transformation of ethnic groups in the United States would produce connections and continuities among them, but not by means of enforcing a predetermined commonality or score ("Anglosaxondom") onto them. The groups themselves might effect such a common ground or common life by creating it out of their transactions with each other.

While Dewey usually resists the idea of a preset score for transaction, he appears to endorse it when he suggests that there are core democratic values in America that have priority over the values of its various ethnic groups.[14] Continuing with the orchestra metaphor, Robert Westbrook claims that Dewey "was willing to put the orchestra in the hands of a conductor—the democratic state and the public schools at home and a democratic organization in the world at large—which would, if necessary, constrain group autonomy in order to foster, even impose, the conditions of democracy."[15] But the notion of transaction does not necessarily include, and in fact can be used to resist, static, preformed ideas of what the results of particular transactions should be. Transactions often develop in unexpected ways that force the reworking of prior assumptions about their outcomes and effects. No completely preset score or unquestionable conductor—even that of the ideal of democracy—can be seen as directing the music of transaction.

Misreadings of Dewey's notion of transaction as a melting pot instead of as a stew often result in Dewey's being criticized for not allowing for "real" (read: atomistic) individuality. As is Michel Foucault, Dewey sometimes is accused of emphasizing the role of societal and cultural influences upon the individual to the extreme point at which the individual as something distinct from those influences is eliminated. One could say that Dewey is criticized for providing a melting pot view of culture in which all individuality is erased. But this criticism sets up a false dichotomy in which the only alternative to tossed salad atomism is the loss of the individual in the melting pot. Dewey responds to this false dilemma using a metaphor of a garden: "[t]o gain an integrated individuality, each of us needs to cultivate his own garden. But there is no fence about this garden: it is no sharply marked-off enclosure. Our garden is the world, in the angle at which it touches our own manner of being."[16] While "old-style" individualism implies that a garden can exist separate from the air, sun, and water around it, Dewey points out that a garden will die apart from these elements. Even stronger, far from being threats to the integrity or coherence of the garden, the air, sun and water are crucial to the existence of the garden as the particular garden that it is. The garden metaphor demonstrates how individuality is transactional. As individuals, each human organism is her own "garden," in need of cultivation to be the particular individual that she is. But the activity of cultivating oneself as an individual cannot be done apart from the world with which one transacts. One's individuality is one's own in that it can be distinguished from that of another. At the same time, however, it is able to come into being only because of the way in which the world, including other human and nonhuman organisms, permeates and in turn is impacted by it.

The work of feminist philosophers Elizabeth Spelman and Susan Wendell is useful for illuminating further the notion of transaction. In *Inessential Woman: Problems of Exclusion in Feminist Thought*, Spelman argues that the "ampersand problem" in feminist thought occurs in analyses of gender and race that attempt to understand gender and race in isolation from each other.[17] The result of treating aspects of a person's identity as separate is an inability to see the effects that each of these aspects has on the other. In addition, because gender and race have been understood as independent of each other, when the links between them *are* considered, those links are conceived as external to the constitution of gender and race itself. Thus when considering both gender and race in women's lives, feminists often produce what Spelman calls an "additive analysis" of identity, which piles gender and race on top of each other, and in so doing fails to understand the ways in which gender and race interlock in women's lives.[18] Additive analyses of identity have helped sustain a white, middle-class, heterosexual bias in feminist theory, even as feminist theory has sought to examine the effects of sexism and racism, sexism and classism, or sexism and heterosexism. Precisely by treating these various "isms" as things to be added together, feminist theory implicitly has understood sexism as something that occurs to women who do not confront racism, classism, and heterosexism in their lives. By adopting additive rather than transactional analyses, feminist thought has often excluded and been inapplicable to the lives of most women.

Dewey complains of a fallacy often found in philosophy, that of "the breaking up of a continuity . . . into two separate parts, together with the necessity which follows from the breaking-in-two for some device by which to bring them together again."[19] It is precisely this fallacy that is exposed in feminist theory by Spelman's rejection of ampersands and additive analyses in favor of what could be called a transactional understanding of identity. A good deal of feminist work is confronted with the ampersand problem—that is, of constructing links between aspects of identity like gender and race that misconstrue the transactional relations between those aspects—because it starts with the breaking up of identity into ontologically separate parts. But one's identity is not built out of discrete blocks. Gender, race, and other characteristics of one's identity interpenetrate and co-constitute each other such that a white woman's experience of sexism in the United States will be very different from that of a black woman. As Spelman claims, while both experience sexism, "they are affected in different ways, depending upon the extent to which they are affected by other forms of oppression," such as racism.[20] It is not that black women have a burden of oppression provided by their race in addition to that of sexism but that they have a different kind of burden of sexism because of white privilege.[21] This is not to say that one cannot make functional distinctions between gender and race in particular contexts and for particular reasons, but that gender and race should not be understood as existing substantively prior to or independent of each other. Like the vegetables in a stew, one's gender helps constitute one's race, and vice versa, in a dynamic relationship.

Susan Wendell's account of disability also provides a helpful illustration of transaction.[22] In *The Rejected Body: Feminist Philosophical Reflections on Disability,* Wendell argues that disability is "socially constructed," by which she means that "the biological and the social are interactive in creating disability."[23] According to Wendell, the biological and social are "interactive" with respect to (dis)ability in two important senses. First, social factors "interact" with bodies to create their health, illness, and levels of functioning. And second, social arrangements can make almost any biological condition that was not a disability into one by making that condition relevant to a social situation, and vice versa.[24] With respect to social factors that impact the health of bodies, one only need think of pesticides. Pesticides have improved crop yield, but they often are poisonous when ingested. The social factors that require farmers to produce more food at the lowest possible cost and at maximum profit transact with bodies that consume food to constitute their level of functioning. With regard to social arrangements and biological conditions, architecture comes to mind. Buildings with stairs but no ramps make transporting oneself with one's arms via a wheelchair, instead of one's legs via walking, into a disability. The biological condition of legs that do not move becomes a disability when a society makes that condition relevant through its construction of buildings only for people who can move their legs.

Wendell often uses the word "interaction" in her account and she sometimes speaks of striking a balance between body and society in one's understanding of the creation of disability.[25] These terms and descriptions should not be allowed to mislead her readers, as they might, into thinking that Wendell conceives of body and society as atomistic, separate entities that come into contact with one another. In contrast to the descriptions of the relations between body and society as "interactive" or "in balance," the term "transactional" best captures Wendell's account of disability, which she defines as constituted through the interpenetration of a person's body and his or her social, as well as physical, environment. According to Wendell, it is not the case that a person's disability is "purely" physical or biological and thus that it is fully "there" prior to a society's consideration of it. On this mistaken account, one would only see that bodies create the society around them but not that society helps constitute the bodies that they are. One would realize that human bodies construct buildings but not that buildings also fashion people as abled and disabled depending on the degree to which building structures correspond to human capabilities. On this approach, a society can do better and worse jobs of accommodating disabilities, but accommodation is the extent of a society's involvement. It is never a question of how a society helps make a particular physical or biological condition into a disability in the first place.

In contrast to an atomistic view of disability, Wendell argues that "the question of what abilities are [considered] basic, like that of what abilities are [considered] normal, is to a significant extent relative to the environment in which the abilities are exercised."[26] If a particular social, cultural, or physical environment assumes that transportation with legs is a normal ability, then relative to that environment, transportation with arms and a wheelchair is constituted as a disability. Likewise, if the environment in which abilities are exercised prioritizes a fast pace of life, as most of the United States does, then those who are not strong or healthy enough to maintain such a pace often are unable to participate in public life because the environment is not structured to allow for different paces.[27]

Bodies and social factors do not exist independently and then come into contact with each other to affect and create bodies' health or illness. One might try to make the case that they are fundamentally independent by claiming that, as in the pesticide example, a person's body and its level of health exists prior to the ingesting of pesticide. In that way, one does seem to have an instance of bodies and society merely interacting or, at best, an instance of people contributing to the makeup of society only, and not also vice versa, through the creation of pesticides. But to make this claim is to overlook that a person's body prior to its ingestion of pesticide was constituted in part by social factors. To take just one possible example, a fetus develops by means of the nutrients provided by its mother, the quality and availability of which are profoundly affected by social factors in the mother's life, such as poverty, overwork and stress, as well as by the pesticides in the food she consumes. Social factors are always already in transaction with bodies to create their levels of ability and disability, just as bodies create the societies, including pesticides and their use, that help make them the (dis)abled bodies that they are.

Another interesting and important way in which bodies and societies co-constitute each other emphasizes that disability is not something "belonging" to a body conceived as existing apart from its environment. Societal norms and standards, often reflected in physical and institutional structures, establish the line between ability and disability, thereby marking off and creating a distinct category of disability with the very establishment of that line. To take my earlier example, if in a given society, buildings and walkways were built with ramps and not stairs and aisles, and passageways were made amply wide, then transportation via wheel-chair would not be a disability. The condition of needing a wheelchair is relevant to the social situation of shopping in a department store because the department store has stairs but no elevators or ramps, narrow aisles, narrow bathroom stalls without handrails, and merchandise placed at a height over three feet. The social arrangement of department stores makes the biological condition of needing to sit to transport oneself relevant to the situation of shopping. With a different social arrangement—easily accessible elevators, wide aisles, wide bathroom stalls, and merchandise placed no higher than three feet—the biological condition of not being able to move one's legs need not be relevant to the situation of shopping, nor need it function as a disability in that situation.

All of this is not to deny that physical factors are involved in disability or to claim that only societal factors are relevant to the constitution of bodies as disabled. Affirming the transactional status of disability is not to say that one must believe, for example, that all people are able to use their legs in the same way. That some people can use their legs in more ways than others does not yet constitute a disability, however, for it is a situation that requires legs to be used in a particular way, and thus it is a situation that makes how one can or cannot move one's legs a (dis)ability. Even what counts as movement of the legs is itself situational or contextual. What is problematic about reducing disability to merely a biological "fact" is not only that it leads one to overlook the situational aspect of disability. It also is that overlooking the transactional constitution of disability perpetuates oppression in many people's lives because, as Wendell claims, "it masks the social functions and injustices that underlie the assignment of people" to the category of disabled.[28] With different social arrangements, many people currently considered and made disabled by societal norms and ex-pectations would not have to be so.[29] By treating disability as a biological given that cannot be changed, one is not prompted to ask why norms have been set up as they are and why resources have been distributed in the ways that they have so as to create these particular disabilities.

When one comes to regard disability and ability as products of the transactions of body and society, one can see how everyone's (dis)ability depends upon resources from their various environments that help them function and develop opportunities for themselves. When understood as transactional, the category "people with disabilities" possibly is not worth retaining. As Wendell suggests, the term is "too specific to identity those in need of resources and too general to identify what kinds of resources are needed."[30] When disability is viewed transactionally, the question then is no longer one of who is dependent (= disabled) and who is independent

(= abled). It has become a question of what different resources do people with different physical conditions need to function effectively, why are resources distributed the way in which they currently are, and who has the authority to make decisions about the distribution of those resources. Attention is directed to the ways in which humans transactionally have made and might remake the particular society in which they live.

For all the importance of transactional bodies to Dewey's pragmatism, Dewey does not use the term "the body" very often. This apparent oddity makes perfect sense, however, when one realizes that Dewey does not think that bodies can be understood as entities unto themselves, isolated from either mind or the world around them. When Dewey speaks explicitly of bodies, he prefers to talk of "body-mind," and most often he chooses to discuss bodies more obliquely by means of the term "organism." While "body-mind" is the more narrow term, used for the particular purpose of addressing the mind-body problem in philosophy, both terms designate bodies as transactional, that is, as constituted by and constitutive of their various environments, mental, social, cultural, and political, as well as physical and natural. Additionally, both terms mark the heavy emphasis of Darwinian evolutionary theory upon Dewey's philosophy, as they indicate human animals' continuity with nonhuman animals and, more broadly, the physical world in general.

Dewey uses "body-mind" to question assumptions upon which the so-called mind-body problem is based, in particular, the assumption that a sharp division exists between minds and bodies. In contrast to much of traditional philosophy, Dewey describes mind as continuous with and emerging out of physicality, even as it is distinguishable from it. The physical and the mental are not two radically different things that somehow correspond or are in need of connection. According to Dewey, they instead are ways of designating different types of transactional relationships that different sorts of organisms have: a more narrow level of transaction had by all organisms (the physical) and a broader level of transaction had by more complex organisms like humans (the mental).[31]

With Elizabeth Spelman, one could say that Dewey rejects additive analyses of psyche/mind and body. To make sense of this claim, we must back up to consider inanimate bodies and their differences from and similarities to animate bodies, both those with and without mind. For Dewey, whether inanimate or animate, all bodies are "physico-chemical" and all bodies exhibit "bias" in that they respond to their world in a selective manner. The difference between the inanimate and animate is not that the inanimate is more properly considered to be physico-chemical nor that the animate includes something added to the physico-chemical from without. The distinction to be made between the two instead "lies in the *way* in which physico-chemical energies are interconnected and operate," that is, in the different ways that inanimate and animate bodies transact with the world.[32] While it exhibits bias, an inanimate body does not transact with its world in such a way as to preserve itself, as animate bodies do. For example, while iron is "biased" in that it will react with water but not air in becoming iron oxide, it does not attempt to modify its transaction with water so that it avoids turning into rust. If it did so—that is, if it exhibited such *organiz*ation in response to the world—then it would be *organic:* a living body, which would be called an *organism*.[33] Because the physical is often identified with the inanimate, Dewey needs a different word to designate a physical thing that actively organizes itself. He chooses "psycho-physical" not to indicate that the physico-chemical has been left behind or that two ontologically separate things, the physical and the psychic, are juxtaposed, but to mark the different sort of transaction with the world that organisms display. That is, Dewey's distinction between the physico-chemical and psycho-physical—as well as the physical and mental, in general—is functional, not substantial.

In charting the transformation from the physico-chemical to the psycho-physical, Dewey retools the philosophical problem of understanding psychic existence such that it is not one of understanding a mystery, but rather one of attempting to understand a highly complex event.[34] As I see it, the problem of understanding how the psychic can emerge from the physical is analogous to that of understanding how hurricanes develop. Meteorologists do not currently comprehend, and indeed, may *never* comprehend or be able to explain all the various conditions that must come together to produce a hurricane so that they can save lives by predicting hurricanes' paths with precision and, perhaps, even by redirecting them. But the problem of understanding them is not one of solving a mystery of how air pressure and wind currents, considered as something divorced from hurricanes, can relate to hurricanes. Instead it is a matter of investigating the complex organization of the event that is a hurricane in an attempt to comprehend the transactions of meteorological phenomena that make it up. Likewise, psychic existence occurs when the organization of physico-chemical things becomes sufficiently complex. No one today understands all the various conditions under which such complexity occurs, and indeed, we may never understand exactly *how* the psychic sometimes comes to emerge from the physical. Nor does Dewey claim to provide an explanation for such emergence. There is no problem of understanding *that* the physical and the psychic are related, however, because they are not two ontologically separate substances that are in need of connection.

Dewey's explanation of physico-chemical and psycho-physical things as nonreductively continuous does not yet address the mental, as distinct from the psychic. On Dewey's account, the psycho-physical is not the mental. Organisms only come to be marked by mind when psycho-physical existence becomes complex enough for it to be aware of meanings, which is more than just to have feelings. One can have feelings without knowing that one has them, as many nonhuman animals do. To make sense of feelings, rather than just have them, requires the capacity of language, which allows humans and some other animals to discriminate, identify, and communicate such that meaning is generated.[35] Once organisms possess and respond to meanings, psycho-physical existence has become sufficiently complex to have a mental life as well.

Again, there is another important distinction to mark, this time with regard to the difference between mind and consciousness. For Dewey, mind is the cultural fund of meanings embodied in some organic life; consciousness is the awareness had by an individual organism of those meanings. Mind is much broader than consciousness for organisms are never consciously aware of all the meanings that inform their actions and beliefs. As Dewey states, "[t]he greater part of mind is only implicit in any conscious act or state."[36] Mind is the context and backdrop for the immediacy and focus of consciousness; the sharp focus of consciousness shades off into a field of increasing obscurity that is mind. Mind is the stock of meanings that humans and some other animals take for granted in their everyday doings, most of which they are never consciously aware. In contrast, consciousness can be understood as the portion of the cultural fund of meanings—mind—that is currently undergoing examination and transformation at a particular time.[37]

For Dewey, mind, including consciousness, is not something radically divorced from the physical. Rather, mind marks a particular way for some physical bodies who are organisms to transact with the world. As Dewey claims, "[t]he distinction between physical, psycho-physical, and mental is . . . one of levels of increasing complexity and intimacy of interaction among natural events," not one of levels marked by radical shifts in kind.[38] Or, put another way, any so-called difference in kind between the physical, psycho-physical, and mental is a difference of degree when that degree has become sufficiently large.[39] The mental is connected to, even rooted in the physical, which can be seen in the makeup of the mental itself. *Contra* Kant, mental structures are not *a priori;* they are evolutionary products of human animals' experiences and activities. As Dewey explains,

> Every thought and meaning has its substratum in some organic act of absorption of elimination of seeking, or turning away from, of destroying or caring for, of signaling or responding. It roots in some definite act of biological behavior; our physical names for mental acts like seeing, grasping, searching, affirming, acquiescing, spurning, comprehending, affection, emotion are not just "metaphors."[40]

Because it involves mental life, which allows for greater direction of transaction, the human animal's transaction with its world is more complex than that of the piece of iron, the plant, or the squirrel. Having a greater say in how one's transactions change the world—and thus also oneself as one continues to transact with the changed world—is extremely important to the flourishing of human animals. This greater say is made possible by mind and consciousness. Dewey's account of the connected relationship between the physical and the mental does not dismiss the tremendous difference that mind and consciousness make to both the makeup and the felt experiences of organic life. Nor does his description of the relationship between the physical and mental as continuous posit a reductive relationship between the two, as some feminists have claimed that such descriptions must.[41] To posit a transactional relationship between the physical and mental is to grant the qualitative impact mental life makes upon human existence, but in such a way that understands mental life as an outgrowth of some of the physical world that is organic. The mental is not an entity foreign to the physical whose relationship with it is to be thought of as quasi-magical, if not downright conceptually impossible.

How then does this discussion of physical and mental existence relate specifically to bodies? While Dewey's analyses of the physical, psycho-physical, and mental are put forth to undercut the mind-body dualism that has plagued much of traditional philosophy, Dewey does not at any point place the body in relation to the various levels he has outlined. In the absence of Dewey's comments on the body, it might be tempting to equate the body with the level of the physico-chemical, and indeed to do so would not be entirely incorrect since bodies are physico-chemical and since Dewey explains mind as growing out of the physico-chemical. But it is significant that Dewey does not lump the body together with the physical in his discussion of the physico-chemical, psycho-physical, and mental. One indication of this significance is that just before explicitly explaining what he means by body and body-mind, Dewey comments on the terminological obstacles to his capturing what it is he is trying to explain.[42] An implication of this remark is that Dewey deliberately leaves the term "body" out of his discussion up to this point because of the danger that with the use of the term, his explanations of the physical, psycho-physical, and mental will be collapsed by his readers into the familiar substantive dualism of body and mind.

An even more interesting reason for Dewey's avoidance of the term "body" is that no one of the levels Dewey describes neatly sums up what the body is. The body cannot simply be equated solely with the physico-chemical. This suggestion is supported by Dewey's description of what he means by "body" and "mind" in the term "body-mind," as well as what he means by the entire neologism itself:

> body-mind simply designates what actually takes place when a living body is implicated in situations of discourse, communication and participation. In the hyphenated phrase body-mind, 'body' designates the continued and conserved, the registered and cumulative operation of factors continuous with the rest of nature, inanimate as well as animate; while 'mind' designates the characters and consequences which are differential, indicative of features which emerge when 'body' is engaged in a wider more complex and interdependent situation.[43]

Here Dewey makes clear that "body" and "mind" are not in a dualistic relationship and, furthermore, that the term "body" in "body-mind" is not simply equivalent with the physico-chemical, as sharply distinguished from the mental. Dewey conceives "body" and "mind" as being on different ends of a continuum. They emphasize different aspects of human life, as well as possibly that of some other animals, rather than designate unconnected and unrelated "parts" of them. On this continuum, "mind" marks the meaningful qualities and consequences that organic acts come to have as a result of an organism's complex relationships with the world. As distinguished from those new qualities, "body" marks the biological or organic activities that persist throughout the emergence of meaning, even as the activities are transformed by the meaning they take on. On this conception of body and mind, the physico-chemical does not neatly map up with any point on the continuum. The physico-chemical cannot be quickly collapsed into "body," as if "mind" was not intimately connected to the physical as well. What Dewey's unconventional definition of mind and body achieves is the disruption of the dualistic question of whether mind or body is *the* physical or is the more physical. Such a question misconstrues the nature of organic, mental life because it attempts to divide the active organism ("body-mind") into separate and fundamentally unrelated substances of the physical and mental, rather than think of the organism in terms of different functions or activities.

An example of persisting organic activities ("body") in relationship with their meaningful qualities ("mind") provided by Dewey may help make his abstract definition of "body-mind" clearer.[44] A child who has been burned may shrink from a flame, but she also may come to respond to the flame by playing with and investigating it, for example by poking sticks or paper into it. In the playful investigation of the fire, the organic act of avoiding being burned, shared by humans and other animals, continues. However, the child's activities involving the flame can become more than the avoidance of being burned because of humans' abilities to develop meaningful accounts of it. Fire can come to mean a source of play or warmth and comfort. When what the fire is changes through the attribution of meaning(s) to it, the relationship between fire and human has been reconstituted such that new consequences, other than just being burned, can emerge from their transaction.[45]

In this example, "body" represents the act of avoiding being burned and "mind" designates the meanings that the child's transaction with the fire comes to have. The body—that is, the organism's act of avoiding being burned—does not disappear just because mind—that is, meanings being attributed to the fire—is also present. Body is the activity out of which mind emerges. But understanding bodies as a kind of substratum of minds is not to posit a unidirectional relationship between body and mind in which bodies are not impacted by that which grows out of them. Just as the child's relationship to the fire is transformed by the emergence of the fire's meaning, the occurrence of mind transforms the bodily activity out of which it emerged. Different activities with regard to the fire such as playing with or cooking with it—which is to say a different body—are now possible because of the different meanings that fire has accrued. In that way, a transactional relationship between body and mind exists, in which each effects the other. In human activity, organic activities can give rise to meanings, and those meanings in turn can transform the activities in which humans are engaged, which new activities will likely give rise to yet other, new meanings, and so on.

Two important points emerge from the example above. First, the categories of the physical and the bodily do not neatly correspond. A body is not so much a thing, as it is an act—an act made possible, to be sure, by the physicality of the organism performing it, but not identical or reducible to the organism's physicality. Just as walking is possible only because of the existence of legs but is not the same thing as legs, so too is a body conceived of as activity possible only because of physicality at the same time that it is not reducible to its physicality.[46] In addition, the physical and bodily do not neatly correspond because mind too, like body, is made possible by the physicality of the organism. Since mind is a feature of organic events and the organic includes the physical, then like body, mind includes and is dependent upon, but is not reducible to the physical.

Second, body is not only in transaction with mind; it also is in transaction with the world. Body, as well as body-mind, is not a sharply distinct unit existing in isolation from its environment(s). As Dewey explains the transactional relationship between body, mind, and society, "mind can be understood in the concrete only as a system of beliefs, desires and purposes which are formed in the interaction of biological aptitudes with a social environment."[47] As the act of withdrawing from or avoiding fire, body is not a thing existing prior to its engagement with the fire, but rather *is* that act, that engagement itself. This understanding of body as act is one of the best illustrations of Dewey's claim that philosophers would find many of their problems simplified if they refrained from using nouns because nouns imply a static structure that too often is misleading.[48] As an activity, bodily life is better designated with the gerund "bodying" and with "body" used as a verb instead of a noun.[49] Rather than being a static substance or a lump physical thing, bodily life is an organism's response to the world considered apart from the multiplication and combination of that response's meanings (= mind) that communication with other organisms makes possible. Likewise, mind is not a static structure or entity, but instead is a particular characteristic of some organisms' actions of responding to, or "bodying," the world.

Organisms' bodying generally occurs in patterned, rather than random ways. Bodying is constituted by habits, which are an organism's acquired styles of activity that organize the energy of its impulses. Dewey is deliberate in his use of "impulse" instead of the more common "instinct" because "instinct" implies that an organism's energies come already packaged into necessary and definite organizations with given meanings.[50] While impulses can be organized and have meaning, by themselves they are merely "blind dispersive burst[s] of energy" that are "loose [and] undirected" and that only gain their purpose and meaning from the habits that organize them.[51]

Just as it is important not to conflate impulse with instinct, it is also important to challenge many of the negative meanings that are commonly associated with habit. As Dewey develops it, habit is something much broader and richer than mere repetition or routine. Habit is "an acquired predisposition to *ways* or modes of response."[52] Habit is not so much the recurrence of particular acts but is instead a style or manner of behaving that is reflected throughout one's being—that is, throughout the way one goes about thinking, as well as acting, a point to which I shall return shortly. Far from being something evil to be eliminated from the self, habits "constitute the self."[53] They constitute one's identity as the particular self that one is, and they are the means by which one engages and transacts with the world. For example, when I sit, I respond to the chair I sit on with a particular posture, that of slumping slightly and curving my shoulders forward. This posture is a readiness to comport myself in a particular fashion whenever I am presented with a situation involving sitting. As a manner by which I respond to and engage with my world, it is part of my bodily constitution of self.[54]

As constitutive of the self, habits are both will and agency. Habit is how one is powerful and efficacious in the world. Two of the many possible examples of the way in which habits provide agency and will can be found in locomotion and language use. The habit of walking—of balancing and propelling oneself by means of the flexing and adjusting of countless muscles as one moves one leg in front of the other—enables a person to take on and accomplish various tasks, such as going to class or meeting a friend for coffee, that require transporting oneself from one place to another. The habit of using a particular language, such as English, enables a person to accomplish various tasks that require communication with others. Both of these habits are so deeply engrained in most adult humans that it is difficult even to see them as habits at all; they are just something that one does and is not conscious of doing. But this is precisely the way in which agency via habit functions: as something so familiar and commonplace that it scarcely comes to conscious attention. As long as habits are functioning smoothly, they do not produce consciousness—which is not to say that they cannot then be mental habits, to recall the distinction between mind and consciousness. The familiar, deeply engrained nature of habits such as locomotion and language often only becomes something of which one is conscious when they are interrupted. When one breaks a leg or travels to a country where one does not understand the language spoken, one is less able to smoothly engage with the world and one begins to realize how much one depends upon habits of walking and communicating to function.

Dewey argues that it is because habits involve "mechanization" that a person does not have to focus consciously on coordinating the use of her muscles or structuring her sentences and choosing her words, which enables her to effectively engage herself in the world by means of walking and talking. While "mechanization" sounds abhorrent to contemporary ears, we must hear the term in the way Dewey used it in 1925, which is to say that it should not be confused with routine or robotic activity, nor opposed to organic life or spontaneity. For Dewey, "mechanization" is precisely what makes possible the complex and delicate activities of life, including its improvisational and creative aspects. Instead of being construed as automatism or reduced to repetition, Dewey's "mechanization" should be thought of as an enabling structure that comes about through the familiarity provided by repetition and that is constitutive of the organism. For example, the expert violin player is able to play with the subtlety, emotion and power that she does because she does not have to rethink with each note where the various notes are located on her strings. Her playing is "mechanized" in that violinist's knowledge of how to hold the bow on the strings and where to move the bow to produce the desired sounds is so familiar to and deeply engrained in her that it happens "naturally" or "automatically." It is with and only with this backdrop of knowledge of the violin that the violinist is able to improvise creatively. Mechanized habits of violin playing are not opposed to the violinist's spontaneity, but rather are the structures that make improvisation possible. Without such habituation or "mechanization," "each act has to be consciously searched for at the moment and intentionally performed," and the result is that "execution [of those acts] is painful and the product is clumsy and halting."[55]

Three aspects of Dewey's understanding of habit are important for understanding transaction, particularly as transaction pertains to bodying. First, as the examples of locomotion and language use suggest, habits are characteristic of patterned behaviors of thought, as well as of physical activity. By claiming that habits pertain to both mental and physical activities, I do not mean that habits neatly divide into two separate realms that reinstate a mind-body dualism. In fact, the point is just the opposite: Dewey's analyses of habit function to undercut such a dualism, much in the same way that his conceptions of organism and body-mind do. Habits operate in all aspects of an organism's life, mental as well as physical. Although the predispositions that are habit are so familiar to and thoroughly a part of one that they function subconsciously, they are not, as a result, opposed to thought.[56] Rather, habits—particular ways or modes of responding to and transacting with the world—are just as crucial to the operation of mental as they are to physical activity. Just as walking could not and does not take place in a smooth and efficacious manner until one's muscles have gained the bodily habits associated with locomotion, thinking could not take place if it habits of thought were not learned.[57]

To claim that, like physical activity, thought functions by means of habit not only eliminates a sharp mind-body distinction, it also insists that much of thought is not conscious. Certainly conscious thought exists, but it is only a small fraction of the thinking that humans do. Habits, both of the body and thought, are that which fund conscious thoughts and ideas. A way of thinking that is not ingrained in habit is ineffective and will be betrayed by methods of thought that are so ingrained.[58] This point comes out most clearly through an example of bodily posture. One might assume that my failure to sit up straight is a failure of reason or "will power," but Socrates was wrong when he said that to do the good, all one needed was knowledge of it. Conscious knowledge of what is good posture is not sufficient for the attainment of good posture. By itself, it *will* help me sit differently for a while, but differently as "only a different kind of badly," as Dewey says—namely, awkwardly overarching my back in order to over-compensate for my tendency to slump.[59] After a brief spell of exaggerat-edly stiff and straight poor posture, I will likely revert to my usual slouch. The key to achieving good posture is not to consciously think my way to good posture but to find an act that keeps me from falling into my usual bad posture and that initiates the development of a new, improved pos-ture.[60] That is, I must find a way to alter my habits if I am to eliminate my bad posture.

The habits that are more likely to be capable of change are those that are formed with an eye for further transformation, rather than those that are formed as fixed grooves into which one settles. Since thought is often sub-conscious, the distinction to be drawn here is not between thought and habit, but between two types of habit: the intelligent and the routine.[61] Habits, which are subconscious, are involved in all aspects of an organism's life, no matter whether the particular psycho-physical activities in question involve thought. The question to be asked about habits does not concern their alleged opposition to thought. Instead, one should ask: does an organ-ism's particular habits allow it to adapt to changing circumstances and en-vironments, or are its habits rigid and inflexible, resulting in the enslave-ment of the organism to old ruts? Again, it is important to remember that these ruts can occur just as easily and often in thinking as they can in physical movement. What is important in the case of all habits is that, ide-ally, habits be formed with the recognition that new situations and environ-ments will require their modification. When that happens, instead of con-stituting stuckness, physical and mental habits can be fluid and dynamic because formed in light of future possibilities.[62]

Another aspect of Dewey's notion of habit, important for the under-standing of transactional bodies and that I want to emphasize, is that hab-its are not "inside" the organism, nor are they private or personal in the sense of existing in isolation from an organism's surroundings. Habits are formed in and through an organism's transaction with its various environments. In that way, they are similar to physiological functions, even though physiological functions are involuntary and habits are acquired. Both habits and physiological functions require that organism and environment work together. For example, respiration involves air as much as it does lungs; walking involves the ground as much as it does legs; and digestion involves food just as much as it does stomach tissue.[63] The cooperation between organism and environment in these physiological functions is characterized by the mutual reconstitution of organism and environment. When the body takes in air from its environment, the oxygen in the air is integrated into and transforms the body by oxygenating its red blood cells. The body in turn releases a transformed product, which is less oxygenated air, back into the environment. The less oxygenated air transforms the environment, admittedly very slightly in the case of one person, by making the ratio of carbon dioxide to oxygen in the air higher.

The key points in the example of respiration are that both environment and organism are required for the physical operation of respiration and that both environment and organism are reconstituted through that activity. The same is true for habit. Of both physiological functions and habit more broadly, one could say with Dewey that "[t]hey are [just as much] things done *by* the environment by means of organic structures or acquired dispositions," as they are things done by the organism by means of its environment.[64] An organism is not primary in the transaction between it and its environment, nor is the environment for that matter. An organism does not "own" either its physiological activities or habits. Of course, people often speak of habits, as well as physiological activities, as if they belong to a particular organism, and there are good reasons for doing so. Namely, it is more likely that an organism will take responsibility for the particular transactions it has with its environments.[65] But, as Dewey cautions,

> [t]o convert this special reference [to habit as belonging to an organism] into a belief of exclusive ownership is as misleading as to suppose that breathing and digesting are complete within the human body. . . . [W]e must begin with recognizing that functions and habits are ways of using and incorporating the environment in which the latter has its say as surely as the former.[66]

The analogy Dewey draws between habits and physiological activities is particularly suggestive of the ways in which habits are formed in response to one's physical environment. For example, my habit of slumping exists as a predisposition to respond to sitting in physical objects such as chairs and sofas in a particular way. But Dewey's use of physiological analogies should not be taken to mean that cultural, social, and political environments are unimportant to the formation of physiological and other habits, for they too play a large role in habit-formation. In fact, an individual's habits cannot be understood apart from her various cultures' customs, or as Dewey calls them, "widespread uniformities of habit."[67] This is because individuals come to have the particular habits they do by being embedded in cultures and societies whose customs and institutions exist prior to the individual and the formation of her habits.

The relationship of cultural customs and individual habits can be illuminated through comparison of habit with Michel Foucault's concept of discipline. Dewey's understanding of habit and custom both resonates with Foucault's analysis of the ways in which bodies are disciplined, as well as supplements Foucault's work in at least one important respect. While Dewey does not use the term "discipline," he like Foucault emphasizes the ways in which various cultural, institutional, and other nonindividual and nonpersonal structures actively constitute organisms. In addition to this, Dewey's understanding of habit explicitly provides a way to focus on forms of discipline at the level of the organisms effected by them. Seen from the perspective of the individual subject, a perspective that Foucault's work tends not to address explicitly, the lines of cultural and institutional power relations that crisscross and thereby constitute an individual's body can fruitfully be understood as habits.[68] Understanding power relations as habits allows exploration of the operation of modes of discipline at a more personal level than does Foucault's work, including the ways in which the incorporation of discipline as habit can be a positive tool for the transformation of modes of discipline. Such an understanding of power relations from the point of view of the subjects constituted by them is consonant with Foucault's work but not given enough explicit attention by it.

As Dewey construes it, the classic chicken-versus-the-egg dilemma is a question of the relationship between a society and its individual members. And on that question, his position is clear: the chicken (a society or culture) precedes the egg (any particular individual in a society or culture).[69] When an individual is born, she develops her habits through transactions with the people who care for her. As Dewey says, an infant's caregivers "are not just persons in general with minds in general."[70] They are members of particular cultures whose customs are reflected in their habits to different and varying extents. Cultures, along with their particular predispositions and styles, preexist any particular individual and thus delimit the types of habits that the individual initially forms. This is precisely why cultural customs endure over time. While to an extent customs exist because individuals face similar situations and respond to them in similar ways, "to a larger extent customs persist because individuals form their personal habits under conditions set by prior customs."[71] One's personal habits are at least initially formed by the incorporation of larger, cultural habits.

That the chicken comes before the egg does not mean, however, that the egg cannot modify the chicken.[72] While it is true that a human organism is a cultural being, humans also respond to their cultural environments in the process of their ongoing enculturation, and some of those responses can bring about significant change. My claim is not that all transactions between organism and environment significantly change the environment or the organism, or that transaction necessarily brings about significant change. Many times, the reconstitution of organism and environment through their ongoing transactional activity serves only to deepen the grooves of the transactions that came before. Because organism and environment are continually being remade through their transactional relationship, however, significant change is possible.

Let me say a bit more about the remaking of organism and environment through transaction. In one important sense, transaction means that organism and environment are constantly changing. Each time I act in accord with a particular habit of mine—say, that of deferring to a man in conversation—I contribute to cultural constructs of white, middle-class, southern femininity that, in turn, feed into the ongoing composition of my personal habits. Both my habit of deferral and the construct of femininity are remade in my act—not in the sense of making them up from scratch, but in the sense that I reinforce them, build them up, turn them into even stronger structures than they were before. Habits and cultural constructs are not static things that exist once and for all. Their existence is dynamic; one might even say they are alive. They continue to exist because, and only because the transactions between people and cultures give them life.

Change of this sort occurs in all transactions, which means that not all transactional change is significant. My deferring to men in conversation may reconfigure my individual habits and Western cultural constructs of femininity, but only in the sense of making them stronger than they were before, not in the sense of radically altering what femininity, whether personal or cultural, is. In the case of many transactions, the more things change, the more they stay the same. I call this kind of change "monotonous change" to signal that change does occur, but not the sort of change that makes for significant transformations that undercut prevailing personal and cultural patterns, rather than reinforce them.

In addition to providing monotonous change, the transaction between organism and environment makes possible significant change in which organism and environment are not merely reinforced. Significant change is possible because, as Dewey says, an organism's "undergoings are not impressions stamped upon an inert wax but depend upon the way the organism reacts and responds."[73] The undergoing, or "taking in" of culture is not something preestablished apart from an organism's response to it. Undergoing itself is constituted in part by the way that an organism "gives back" or responds to cultural customs. The manner by which an organism is constituted by its culture is effected by the particular ways that the organism responds to its constitution. Even though cultural customs precede and delimit individual habits, the relationship between cultural and individual habits is not necessarily one of repetition. It instead can be one in which cultures and individuals reconfigure one another in significant ways through their responses to each other. As Dewey states, "[w]e are not [necessarily] caught in a circle" in which cultural customs can only determine individuals habits, which then in turn must reinforce those customs. Rather "we [can] traverse a spiral in which social customs generate some consciousness of interdependencies [of cultural customs and individual habits], and this consciousness is embodied in acts which in improving the environment generate new perceptions of social ties, and so on forever."[74]

Returning to the relationship of habits and impulses, impulses should not be understood as more truly or properly bodily than are habits, nor, in a corresponding fashion, should habits be seen as aligned with culture in ways that impulses are not. The relationship of habits and impulses cannot be interpreted adequately as an instance of culture-nature dualism. Such an interpretation is found in an understanding of impulses and habits that takes impulses to be bodily expressions that stand outside of or apart from the habits, provided by cultural environments, that organize those impulses. On this model, culture would be seen as stamping itself upon the noncultural impulses of the body via its habits.

Dewey's own description of impulses as temporally prior to habits can lend itself to an atomistic, dualistic understanding of habit and impulses. Dewey claims that while impulses are not primary in conduct, they are primary in time. Babies are born with impulses but not habits and thus must acquire the habits that organize their impulses into meaningful activity. In that sense, Dewey views habits as secondary to impulses. In the sense of activity and conduct, however, Dewey states that impulses are secondary to habits. The meaning of a person's activities is not initially given with or in her impulses, but is acquired through transaction with the environment. As Dewey claims, "[i]n conduct the acquired [habit] is the primitive. Impulses although first in time are never primary in fact; they are secondary and dependent."[75]

By describing impulses as temporally prior to habits, Dewey implies that there is at least some stretch of time, even if it be a very brief moment in a newborn's life, in which impulses exist in a self-contained way, separate from the habits that will later impose themselves upon the newborn's impulses. But even though Dewey's example of a newborn suggests that impulses are encountered in experience as ontologically separate from habits, his description of the temporal separation of impulses and habits should be read as a functional distinction only. The temporal primacy of impulses is not something that is ever encountered "in fact," as Dewey himself goes on to claim.[76] From the moment of birth, and indeed even in the womb thanks to the sonogram and other technologies, a human organism's "spasm[s]" and "blind dispersive burst[s] of wasteful energy" that are its impulses are in transaction with the cultural habits that preexist the individual.

Admittedly, from the assumption of what the "internal" or "subjective" perspective of the newborn herself seems to be, a newborn does not yet understand or experience her impulses as meaningful in the ways that adults around her do. Nor are a newborn's impulses yet arranged into the smoothly efficient predispositions that characterize fully formed habits. In these senses, one can agree with Dewey that a newborn's impulses are temporally prior to or separate from their organization via cultural habits.[77] At the same time, however, from a perspective "outside" the newborn's felt experience, a newborn's impulses are always already being given meaning by those who care for her, and thus her impulses are always already in transaction with cultural habit. In addition, recent research in developmental psychology indicates that newborns are born with at least some minimal organization to their impulses, suggesting the existence of habits at birth provided by humans' evolutionary development, which is cultural as well as "natural." For example, newborns demonstrate intersensory coordination between seeing and hearing, and vision and touch, as well as exhibit hand-mouth and hand-face coordination.[78] In these regards, impulses cannot be thought of as substantively distinct from habit. The transaction of a newborn's impulses with the cultural habits embodied by her caregivers starts immediately upon, and even prior to birth. This is so even though it will take a few months or years for a newborn both to experience her bodily activities as meaningful and to more extensively organize her impulses into fully functioning patterns. Furthermore, since the newborn cannot speak to us about the nature of her "subjective" experience, the precultural dimension of her experience is something that adult cultural beings can only discursively posit. The precultural or prediscursive status of the newborn's subjective experience must itself be thought of as a cultural, discursive product, that is, of the discursive positing of something that is prediscursive.[79]

Impulses can indeed provide fresh energy and direction for habits, and, as Dewey said, "it goes without saying that original, unlearned activity has its distinctive place and that an important one in conduct."[80] Yet that freshness and distinctive place are not independent of habit; it is when impulses are engaged to reconfigure habits that they can have a transformative impact upon an individual.[81] Or, better, since habit is the organization of impulses themselves, the "original" material of impulses has its import and impact not apart from their organization, but through their *re*organization. Habits and impulses should not be understood as substantively separate, as Dewey's description of the temporal priority of impulses might suggest. Habits are not something foreign or external to impulses. They are the patterns of impulses themselves once they have achieved meaningful organization. Habit is not an agent that implements or directs the organization of impulses into patterned activities. Habit *is* the patterned organization of impulses.

In addition to treating habits and impulses in an atomistic and dualistic way, a second problem with the understanding of habits and impulses as corresponding to culture and nature/body, respectively, is that habits are just as "properly" or "truly" bodily as are impulses. Habits just *are* the predispositions of corporeal beings. They are the ways in which an organism transacts with its world, which is to say that they are the styles and patterns of the activities of bodies, not something cultural understood as over and against them. A woman's habit of crossing her legs when she sits in a chair is a predisposition of her bodying in its response to objects like chairs and activities like sitting, as it also is a pattern formed in conjunction with cultural customs about "proper" bodily comportment for women. Even in the case of habits of thought, which might seem less closely related to the movements of bodies, habits are corporeal. Thought is not independent of, but instead is predicated on bodily existence, even as cultural constraints and meanings shape it. Treating habit and impulse dualistically as instances of culture and body misunderstands both what impulses and habits are and the transactional relationship between bodies and environments.

Bodies exist by means of a co-constitutive relationship with their environments, which is why human organisms live as much across and through skins as within them. To conceive of bodies as atomistically sealed up within themselves or as existing as a lump physical thing is to misunderstand them. It is to neglect the tremendous role that situations, physical surroundings, cultural meanings, and other seemingly nonbodily factors play in their constitution and well being. It also is to make bodies seem passive and to place human bodies, in particular, in opposition to mind and meaning, none of which human bodies are. In contrast to these conceptions, a notion of bodies as transactional construes an organic body as a collection of activities characterized by habit and grounded in physicality that is constituted by its relationships with its various environments. For human bodies in particular, this means that bodies give rise to and participate in the meanings provided by their transactions. As transactional participants in meaning, human organisms often help secure existing habits and cultural customs, but they also are capable of transforming them.

Discursivity and Materiality
The Lived Experience of Transactional Bodies

One of the legacies of Michel Foucault's genealogical work on bodies is an ongoing disagreement, often found between philosophers working out of poststructuralism and those working out of phenomenology, whether a pre- or nondiscursive body exists. To grasp what is at stake in this issue, one can examine the different accounts, which are associated with it, of the enactment of political resistance to oppressive cultural norms. On the one hand, anatomical differences often have been used to justify the social and political oppression of some groups over others, such as men over women, white people over people of color, the "civilized" European over the native "savage." For this reason, poststructuralists sometimes argue that appeals to the "natural" body, understood as untouched by cultural and other meanings and thus capable of being a source of liberation from one's culture, can only backfire. Resistance to oppressive normative standards is not likely to be achieved by positing a natural, noncultural body if the way in which the body is delineated as natural is itself a product of culture. In such a case, rather than to transform culture, appeals to a body outside of cultural influences, meanings, and understandings tend to have an effect opposite of that which is desired: they further secure, rather than undermine, the cultural, social, and political status quo.

On the other hand, phenomenologists sometimes claim that there must be a nondiscursive body if there is to be any way of formulating political resistance against normative standards. If cultural norms totally imprint a body in their disciplining of it, if they "go all the way down," as it were, then resistance to them appears to be impossible. On this view, the result of the lack of a pre- or nondiscursive body is the enslavement of human existence to whatever oppressive normative standards currently exist. To avoid a cultural determinism in which the materiality of bodies ironically becomes immaterial, some phenomenologists argue that the notion of the fully discursive body must be rejected for an understanding of bodies that holds that at least some aspects of them are non- or prediscursive.

Let me draw attention to the term "discourse." While I have used the term as roughly synonymous with cultural meaning, the definition of "discourse" often is unclear in theoretical writing on bodies that uses it by conflating it with other, related terms. Such conflation obscures discussions about the existence of the pre- or nondiscursive body. Terms such as "language" and "discourse" have different meanings and originate out of different contexts, which should discourage easy interchangeability between them. Language in its Lacanian sense of a transcendental, grammatical structure that is the condition for the possibility of human experience must be distinguished from language in its everyday, evolutionary sense of verbal and written gestures that developed in human animals for the sake of communication. From both of these meanings of language, the term "discourse" must be distinguished. In its more narrow sense, discourse means something like speech, but in a broader, Foucauldian sense it means the entire interlocking web of cultural, societal, and other meanings, most of which are contained not in speech or grammar, but in institutions, buildings, habits, etc.[1] The Foucauldian sense of discourse is similar but not identical to the term "culture," and both Foucauldian discourse and culture are broader than the everyday, evolutionary sense of language as well as different in kind from a Lacanian sense of language.

These terminological distinctions will help minimize confusion when examining the issue of the discursivity of bodies. They also provide a clarifying backdrop for my claim that the disagreement over the non- or prediscursive body is about much more than a body's relationship to mere speech. The heart of the matter is the more substantial issue of whether there is anything bodily, material, or natural to be found apart or outside of the wide range of discursive formations. Whether discourse is the best word to indicate a web of meaning instantiated in different kinds of cultural and societal institutions is debatable because it often is taken to indicate matters of language or speech only. Dewey would use the word "mind" instead, but this term carries even more unhelpful connotations in its standard usage than does discourse. The word "genealogy" is an attractive alternative to discourse because genealogy indicates a complex fund of meanings without privileging language.[2] Nonetheless, because the term "discourse" dominates the discussions about the nature of bodies that I wish to engage, I will continue to use it. At the same time, however, I will recast the term, framing the issue of discursivity in terms of transaction and demonstrating how doing so produces a fruitful understanding of the relationship between bodies and their cultural and other environments.

Discourse is not homogeneous and undifferentiated. Many different, sometimes overlapping discourses exist. The question at stake here is not whether an *extra*discursive body exists, if "extradiscursive" means falling outside of some discourse(s) in particular. Extradiscursive bodies do exist in that bodies are engaged in and thus gather their meaning from some discourses and not from others. But to be extradiscursive is not to be prediscursive or nondiscursive, which two terms I use synonymously, because it is not to fall outside of all cultural and societal meaning or discourse as such. Because the disagreement about the discursivity of bodies concerns the possibility of human bodies existing outside of the realm of human meanings as such, I focus here on the non- or prediscursive, as distinct from the extradiscursive, body.[3]

Excellent work already exists on Foucault's particular contribution to the issue of the discursivity of bodies and their implications for political resistance.[4] Instead of providing more discussion of Foucault, I propose using the notion of transactional bodies as a means by which to understand and improve upon contemporary positions in the disagreement about the relationship between discursivity and materiality. The works of Judith Butler, Carol Bigwood, and Eugene Gendlin are especially fruitful for understanding bodies in this way: Butler because hers is perhaps *the* main account of the discursivity of bodies in feminist philosophy, and Bigwood and Gendlin because their positions are good contemporary representatives of the type of phenomenological case made in favor of the nondiscursive body.[5] Understanding bodies as transactional will reveal that the discursivity of bodies is compatible with attending to bodily lived experiences, including the possibility and need for corporeal resistance to oppressive societal norms. The disagreement over whether a non- or prediscursive body exists ultimately is redirected here to questions about the particular ways in which bodies transact with the world.

Writing about Butler's *Gender Trouble* and using "culture" as a synonym for "discourse," Carol Bigwood argues that Judith Butler's construing of gender as a fluid cultural configuration has disconnected gender and bodies in such a way that they are denaturalized into purely cultural phenomena. When Butler claims that gender is a stylized repetition of acts that creates the effect of a body's natural sex, Bigwood worries that Butler "leaves us with a disembodied body and a free-floating gender artifice in a sea of cultural meaning production."[6] Bigwood claims that Butler's position produces this problematic account of bodies and gender because it has completely abandoned nature in favor of purely cultural determinants in its account of how gender is constructed.[7]

Although Bigwood claims that she does not charge Butler with falling into a nature/culture dichotomy, more accurate is to say that Bigwood does not charge Butler with falling into a *particular* form of this dichotomy, the form that posits nature as a precultural given.[8] Bigwood does charge Butler with privileging culture over nature and body and thus merely turning on its head, but not overcoming, the dualistic hierarchy of nature over culture. As Bigwood asserts, while Butler is right that "there is no 'pure' body or untouched nature prior to culture, . . . her solution to the myth of a purely natural state prior to culture is merely to posit a 'pure' culture that is always already there, . . . [which] is also a myth."[9] Worried that the effect of poststructuralist philosophy is to make bodies disembodied, Bigwood argues that Butler's "constructivist" view casts bodies as virtually limitless in the types and numbers of cultural configurations that they can take on. Bigwood agrees that bodies are malleable, but she claims that Butler has made the mistake of construing bodies as so fluid that she makes bodily organizations and meanings completely contingent upon culture. According to Bigwood, on Butler's account bodies cannot be the source of any restriction on or limits to the possible cultural meanings and configurations to be taken up by them.

In contrast to Butler's position, Bigwood argues for a " 'natural-cultural' model of the body" based on Merleau-Ponty's phenomenology of corporeal existence that undercuts nature/culture dualisms by going beyond notions of bodies as fixed by nature and as being fully culturally inscribed.[10] On this model, gender would be neither wholly determined by nor completely separated from bodies. By using a phenomenological rather than a poststructualist approach to bodies, Bigwood claims that "we can find a way of affirming sexual difference while allowing for its inevitable indeterminacy and open possibilities for historical and cultural variation."[11] The notion of indeterminacy is important here: Bigwood does not argue that bodies fix gender in any particular way. But she does claim that bodies allow for an affirmation of sexual difference because, even though the givenness that they provide is indeterminate, it provides a continuity between bodies and gender. The virtue of using Merleau-Ponty's account of the body, in Bigwood's opinion, is that it allows feminists to "recover a noncultural, nonlinguistic body that accompanies and is intertwined with our cultural existence."[12]

At times, Bigwood's description of the indeterminate constancy of bodies sounds transactional. On Bigwood's account, bodies are "in" the world not in the way that water is in a cup, but in a way that it is "of" the world. Bodies are not external to the world but are part of the world in their orientation toward and tasks in it. Thus the relationship between body and world is dynamic rather than static. As Bigwood claims, "[t]he phenomenological body is not fixed but continually emerges anew out of an ever changing weave of relations to earth and sky, things, tasks, and other bodies."[13] Bodies are "woven" together with both natural and cultural things, which is to say that they are constituted by their changing relations with the natural and cultural things that surround them. According to Bigwood, such a model of corporeal existence suggests that "we exist simultaneously in cultural and natural ways that are inextricably tangled."[14]

Even in these moments, however, and certainly in the claim that bodies provide a givenness that accompanies cultural existence, Bigwood's account operates with a tossed-salad understanding of bodies in which body and culture are conceived as fundamentally distinct. For Bigwood, while bodies and cultures are "woven" together, "inextricably tangled," and "intertwined," they still are conceived as separately existing things that come into relation with one another. The fabric metaphor is telling in this respect. As Nancy Tuana has argued, fabric metaphors are something of an advance over traditional nature-culture dualisms in that they bring into joint operation that which was held to be radically disconnected.[15] They do not make a significant departure from the tradition, however, because on their terms, nature and culture are still conceived as additive. Like the threads of a piece of cloth, nature and culture combine with each other as originally separate strands. For Bigwood, therefore, body and culture are not transactionally constituted as are the ingredients in a stew. They instead are tossed together in a way that does not transform them ontologically.

The dichotomy between nature and culture in Bigwood's position becomes even more apparent when she argues that an advantage of a phenomenological account of the body is that it counters human beings' usual, insufficient attunement to things. According to Bigwood, the problem with humans' usual attunement to the world is that it allows one "to discover the familiar cultural presence in things, but not to disclose the nonhuman element that is an essential part of the thing's presencing."[16] Bigwood contrasts culture with the nonhuman in such a way that culture becomes synonymous with the human, both of which are set against nature, which is understood as nonhuman. For Bigwood, natural existence is that type of existence that is outside of human/cultural control. Renaturalizing the body, then, means to recognize that some aspects of bodily existence, including some form of gendered existence, are independent of human influence.

Here lies the heart of the issue for Bigwood and thus the underlying reason that she argues for the recovery of a nonculturalbody: control. For Bigwood, the main problem with doing away with the notion of a nondiscursive body is not so much that humans then are left alienated from nature, as she at times suggests; it is that a position that rejects the nondiscursive body suffers from hubris: it presumes that humans have fully under their control things that, in fact, they do not control. To renaturalize the body reminds us that all is not in one's control and gives humans a proper sense of humility in the face of the nonhuman world, of which the human body, strangely, is a part. As Bigwood states, to posit bodies as outside of culture is to ensure that human beings do not "presume that our given situation (including that of gender) is fully within our control."[17] It is not to claim that biology fixes human existence, but rather to claim that "the way life articulates itself has as much to do with the response of other nonhuman beings, with the currents of the earthly and skyly environment, and with temporal contingencies, as it does with our subjectivist cultural wills."[18] This point is made again in the specific example of the experience of Bigwood's pregnancy, a description of which is woven throughout her article: "[a]lthough a woman has much flexibility in taking up the pressing but indeterminate directives given by her mothering body, she is not like a subject in control of a growing object inside her."[19] Whether in the case of pregnancy or other examples given by Bigwood, such as gazing at artwork or lingering in a forest, Bigwood's main point is to remind her readers of the "upsurge of existence [that is] beyond our control."[20]

It is important to recognize the way in which control and discursivity are connected in Bigwood's account because only then can they be disentangled. Bigwood implicitly claims that to posit a discursive body is to posit complete human control over all things, and in particular over nature and bodily life. According to her, only by recovering the nondiscursive body can a person remind herself that she is not always in control. But understanding bodies as discursive does not imply total control if discursivity is read through the lens of transaction. To understand bodies as discursively constituted through their transactions with the world is to acknowledge that merely existing in the world is to have effects upon it. These effects can vary tremendously. They may be small or large, beneficial or detrimental; they may just as likely further entrench as transform various cultural and societal standards. More to the point, they are not always things that people intend, and even when people intend them, their effects on the world often turn out to be different from what was planned. Thus, to acknowledge that human organism and environment exist transactionally is not to claim that humans can effect any and all sorts of change to the natural world and bodies. What such an acknowledgement does do, however, is urge people to pay attention to the types of effects they have on the natural world so that they might learn to redirect the effects they help bring about.

It is here that the issue of control is most relevant, although only if "control" is not understood as an abbreviation for "absolute control." Human organisms often need to guide their transactions to improve the world around them. But to claim that people should seek greater control of their transactions does not mean that they have a relationship of one-way domination over nature or bodies because the direction of influence goes as much from environment to organism as it does from organism to environment. To understand bodies as transactional is to see physical and other environments as possibly having as much control over bodies as bodies have over environments, although there is not always a balance in the relationship between them. Recognizing the cyclical relationship of control between organism and environment allows humans to ask how they might transform for the better the various impacts that organism and environment have on each other without assuming that human organisms have total control.

Understanding bodies as transactional, one need not hold that rejecting the notion of a nondiscursive body necessarily means positing absolute human control. But does the notion of a discursive body sufficiently allow for resistance to oppressive cultural norms? Another theorist working out of a phenomenological tradition, Eugene Gendlin, answers this question in the negative.[21] Gendlin argues for a nondiscursive body understood as having a determinacy that is productive of discursive meaning but that is not itself discursive. According to Gendlin, only with such an understanding of bodies can oppressive societal structures be transformed.

Gendlin attempts to make his case for the body's determinacy by demonstrating how Merleau-Ponty's emphasis on perception encourages us, *contra* Merleau-Ponty's intentions, to think of bodies as mere perceivers, divided off from the world that they perceive via their senses. Arguing that bodies are not separated from the world in this way, Gendlin claims, "[o]ur bodies don't lurk in isolation behind the five peepholes of perception." Rather, "[o]ur bodies *are* interaction in the environment."[22] As interaction, bodies sense in their entirety the situations in which they are embedded, a sensing that enables action that is much broader than the mere five senses allow. According to Gendlin, bodily sense explains why bodies are not exhausted by discourse. Sentient bodily interaction is primary and prior to discourse, and although bodily sense can and does function through discursive means, it always exceeds it.[23] Gendlin represents this bodily sense with ellipses to indicate the way in which it is prior to and cannot be fully captured by language. The " ... " is the bodily sense that is a person's situation, which is to say, her interaction with the world.

Gendlin uses the term "language" instead of "culture" or "discourse" to represent that which cannot capture bodily sense. Yet his claim about bodily sense is much stronger than this terminology suggests. Gendlin explicitly equates language with "concepts, history, culture, and politics," and in doing so, he makes clear that he intends the term "language" to cover all that the other terms do.[24] His claim is that the " ... " cannot be fully captured by language and thus is broader than it might first appear. It is a claim that, to at least some degree, felt bodily sense always lies outside of discursive meaning.

Gendlin argues that one's felt bodily sense is determinate, by which he means that it includes many different alternatives for action within the world. His claim is not that the " ... " is exhaustive of all the different possibilities one has for action, but that the " ... " contains information that is formed enough to help determine one's next move in a situation but that it is not, or not yet, capable of being, put into language.[25] As a guide for one's interactions with the world, the " ... " exceeds the determinate forms that language, words, and concepts can provide. For that reason, Gendlin claims that bodily sense is a source of novelty. Because the information that bodily sense provides is both excessive of language and formed in a determinate way, it can "generate something new" and "very demandingly imply something that has never existed before."[26]

Recent neurological research confirms Gendlin's claims about the power of knowledge articulated by felt bodily sense and thus might also appear to confirm his claims about the nondiscursive body. As University of Iowa College of Medicine neurologists found, for most human beings, one's body allows one to make advantageous choices in uncertain situations before one's overt reasoning is able to do so and before one is able to express in language the situation or one's choices in it.[27] This bodily capacity was tested by means of a gambling experiment in which some players had prefrontal brain damage and others did not. The significance of prefrontal brain damage is that it eliminates the unconscious emotional signals that are crucial to the ability to make good decisions. These signals were measured in the experiment by means of the body's anticipatory skin conductance responses, or SCRs, which are the skin's ability to transmit electricity.

In a game of chance that simulated the uncertainties, risks, and rewards of real-life decision-making, all players were given four decks of cards and $2000 and were asked to play so that they lose the least and gain the most money. Turning a card over always resulted in an award: $100 in decks A and B and $50 in decks C and D. But it sometimes also resulted in a penalty: large for decks A and B, small for decks C and D. Playing mostly from decks A and B resulted in an overall loss; playing mostly from decks C and D resulted in an overall gain. The players had no way of predicting when a penalty would result, no way of calculating with precision the net gain or loss from each deck, no knowledge of when the game would end, and no initial knowledge of the patterns of penalty and reward for the four decks just described. After twenty card turns, players were asked everything they knew about the game up to that point and how they felt about the game. After sampling the decks and before any losses, all players preferred decks A and B and had no significant anticipatory SCRs. After encountering a few losses, by card ten, in decks A or B, undamaged participants began to generate anticipatory SCRs to decks A and B and to avoid those decks. They did this even though their responses to the questions about their knowledge, asked at card twenty, indicated that they had no conscious understanding of the patterns of gain and loss associated with the four decks. By card fifty, all undamaged players had anticipatory SCRs when contemplating turning a card on deck A or B, claiming to have a "hunch" that these decks were disadvantageous and reporting that they "disliked" them. By card eighty, undamaged players had attained conceptual knowledge about the decks and could explain why, in the long run, decks A and B were to be avoided. In contrast to the undamaged players, players with prefrontal brain damage never generated anticipatory SCRs, never expressed any sort of hunches about the decks, and never began to avoid the decks associated with large losses.

The data from the experiment support an argument for the existence of a felt bodily sense that is prior to both conceptual knowledge and language in its everyday sense. The knowledge about the game that players eventually could articulate in language was informed by and in some sense secondary to the knowledge articulated by their bodily sense. The experiment also suggests that Gendlin is right that one's bodily " . . . " remains primary even after the information it provides is put into language. Although three of the six patients with prefrontal damage reached the conceptual phase and could correctly describe which were the good and bad decks, those patients continued to choose disadvantageously. In contrast, the three undamaged players who did not reach the conceptual phase still made advantageous choices. The experiment as a whole thus suggests that a bodily sense about a situation can precede one's ability to put that situation into words and into conscious knowledge.

What the experiment does not do, however, is demonstrate that one's bodily sense occurs outside of discourse. While it supports the weaker claim that one's felt bodily sense cannot always or easily be articulated in language understood in its everyday sense, the experiment does not contribute to the stronger claim that one's bodily sense is prior to all discursive meaning. One's bodily attraction or aversion to particular cards is formed *in response to* the card game and thus can only be understood by reference to the cultural and societal meanings of winning, losing, and competing and to the meaning of money contained in the game being played. The felt bodily sense illustrated in the experiment is constituted in and through its relationship to the situation of gambling. It is not formed apart from them. Of course, the fact that one's bodily sense is formed in and through transaction with the world does not then mean that it is any less powerful or important. In fact, just the opposite: the fact that one's bodily sense is formed through transaction with the meanings that make up the situation at hand is precisely why one's bodily sense is able to be informative, powerful, and helpful.

Gendlin makes the stronger claim that the bodily " . . . " is prior to discourse, but he can only do so if he equivocates on "language." While Gendlin begins his argument by defining language broadly as "concepts, history, culture, and politics," he then appears to shift the term's meaning, using language more narrowly in its everyday sense in the course of arguing that some bodily experiences cannot be put into words.[28] Or, rather, without assuming such a shift in the term "language," his claim that one's felt, bodily " . . . " is prior to language does not hold up.

The problematic nature of Gendlin's position can be seen in the example that Gendlin uses to illustrate the determinate prediscursivity of bodily sense. In this example, Gendlin asks you, his reader, to imagine walking home at night and coming to sense that a group of men is following you.[29] Gendlin claims that in such a situation, you do not merely perceive via the five senses that you are being followed. For example, you have not merely heard footsteps behind you. Instead, included in your bodily sense of the men behind you is simultaneously your hope that you are not being followed, your alarm, all your past experiences in similar situations, the various options that you have at this point, such as running, shouting, and fighting, and. . . . Gendlin trails off with ellipses to indicate that in such a situation, your felt bodily sense includes far more than any list could encompass. It exceeds any description of the situation that language can provide, which on Gendlin's explicit terms is to say that your bodily sense falls outside of discourse. In particular, the " . . . " includes an implied next move that you will make in the situation, a move that is contained in the various determinations of your " . . . ," which functions to establish what that move will actually be. According to Gendlin, the " . . . " is not dependent upon discourse to take on determinate form. Bodily sense contains information about the situation prior to the casting of the situation into discursive meaning.

Rather than demonstrate the prediscursivity of human bodies, however, Gendlin's example of a felt bodily sense of being followed serves to demonstrate how the " . . . " is discursively constituted. To the extent that Gendlin's example works, it does so primarily because of the meaningful configuration of masculinity and femininity. While the reader's gender is left unaddressed by Gendlin's use of the second person, the gender of the people who are following you and of whom you are fearful is built into the example: the people are men, not women. Given that, generally, masculinity is discursively constituted as forceful, aggressive, and active and femininity as passive, nurturing, and weak, fear is more likely to be evoked in Gendlin's readers by the thought of men rather than women following them. Because women suffer from sexual assault in greater numbers than do men, fear also is more likely to be evoked in readers who are women. The meaning of gender—and race, class, and sexual orientation, even though Gendlin does not mention them in connection with either you or your followers—makes it such that the bodily sense evoked in the example is likely to be fear rather than curiosity, calmness, joy, or aggression.

Gendlin's account of bodily sense as prediscursive treats the meaningful outcome of transactions between bodies and cultures as a product that precedes the process of transaction itself. Dewey explains the relationship of meaning and "bare things" as such: "[s]ince . . . all things have a phase of potential communicability, that is, that any conceivable thing may enter into discourse, the retrospective imputation of meanings . . . to bare things is natural; it does no harm, save when the imputation is dogmatic and literal."[30] Dewey may not be right that it is natural, in the sense of unproblematic, for people to treat meaning loosely as a possession of a "bare thing" prior to its transactions with other things; he is correct, however, that it is problematic to impute pretransactional meaning literally to the nondiscursive body. Doing so does harm to the understanding of the relationship between bodies and discourse because it fails to see that the bodily " . . . " comes to have meaning in and through, not apart from, its transactions with its situations.

Gendlin rightly insists on the need to recognize and appreciate felt bodily sense, which is more than just the sum of five, discrete senses. To divide the body up into five senses and then ask how each of them works in a given situation overlooks the intricate and complex way in which bodies as a whole are engaged in a situation as active bodying.[31] Gendlin also rightly tries to undo the dualism between dumb body and thinking mind that has plagued Western conceptions of the body, and his attempts to do so are supported by recent developments in neurological research. And, finally, Gendlin rightly reminds us that many felt experiences probably cannot be fully captured in language, understood in its everyday sense. None of this, however, must commit us to an understanding of bodies as nondiscursive. We can think of bodies as discursively constituted at the same time that we can acknowledge the existence of and the powerful information provided by a felt bodily sense that is nonlinguistic.

Rejecting the notion of a nondiscursive body does not have to rule out the possibility that humans can challenge and resist normativity. This is Gendlin's primary concern when he speaks of the bodily " . . . " as a source of novelty. On Gendlin's terms, humans' capacity for creative challenges and responses to the world is made possible only because their bodily sense exists in a determinate way outside the boundaries of meaning. For Gendlin, if bodies are discursive, humans are incapable of generating responses to their world that are not already determined by the world's configuration of them. As David Michael Levin expresses a similar concern, the natural body of felt experience is the source of an emancipatory potential that has the capability of remaking and improving the world. If the natural body is completely conditioned by its discursive environment, however, one has no source of new and fresh challenges to the current order of things.[32]

Just as earlier it was important to recognize how the issues of discursivity and control are intertwined, here it is important to note how Gendlin's account risks conflating discursivity and repetition of the same. That bodies are transactionally co-constituted with the world does not mean that one cannot effect significant changes in it. Indeed it is precisely because bodies are transactional that such change is possible, albeit neither certain nor guaranteed. Although environments constitute bodies, that constitution is not a mere constraint on bodily being. It also is that which makes up the very "tools" that can enable people to be effective in their dealings with their environments. For example, my being constituted as an English-speaking body does not *just* constrain the ways I think and speak, although it does do that. In cultures where English is spoken, my speaking English is an ability that helps me achieve whatever particular changes I am trying to make in that society. And, of course, the same ability to speak English can be a disability in another society that does not speak English at all. That bodies are transactional and thus have effects on their environments does not then mean that one necessarily brings about significant change through one's transactions. Sometimes the effect that transaction has is to further sediment and solidify existing habits and customs, producing monotonous change. But transaction need not do so. It also can be a source for change because the co-constitutive relationship between individuals and their environments means that the effects one has on one's environments in turn can impact the constitution of many other individuals in those same environments.

I have not used terms such as "novel" to describe what sorts of changes bodies might effect through transaction because that term tends to imply a radical break with the present to bring about something completely different to it. But change tends not to be revolutionary in this way. The new comes about through a modification of the old—that is, in and through a relation with the old.[33] One does not stand outside culture in an atomistic way. Change therefore must come through reworkings of some cultural context, from within that context, not from without. These reworkings are new in that they alter what existed before, but they are not new in the sense of being utterly novel or radically divorced from what preceded them.

In many places Gendlin's account of corporeal existence is close to one of transaction. For example, Gendlin insists that the plant's "body does not first exist and only then interact. Rather, its growth and life processes consist of environmental interaction."[34] That they are constituted through their interaction with their environments is just as true of humans as it is of plants. That humans are sentient does not change the fact that humans are their interactions with their world. As Gendlin claims about humans, "[o]ur own living bodies also *are* interactions with their environments, and that is not lost just because ours also have perception."[35]

Yet, at the same time he argues that bodies are constituted through interaction with their environments, Gendlin states that one's bodily " . . . " stands outside of and even prior to one's cultural environment. One might think that Gendlin could consistently make this claim because he restricts the environment to the physical environment, leaving aside the problem of understanding the physical environment as atomistically separated from cultural, social, and political environments. But Gendlin explicitly refers to human bodies' sensing of their "human situations" as well as of their physical environment; thus this cannot be the basis for his claim that one's bodily " . . . " is prior to culture.[36] Gendlin's main point about the priority of a bodily felt sense therefore undercuts whatever other claims he makes about the transactional constitution of bodies. Bodies may be interactive with their environments, but for Gendlin "interaction" does not mean transaction because, on his view, bodies stay separate from the culture around them in a fundamental way. Body and culture are like the ingredients of the salad that are tossed together, but never impact each other in a fully constitutive, stewlike way. Ironically, by adopting a tossed-salad account with his description of the bodily " . . . " as prediscursive, Gendlin has locked bodies behind the "peepholes of perception" that divide bodies from the world, which was precisely the account of corporeal existence that he set out to undermine.

Judith Butler's account of bodily materiality is promising because, unlike that of Bigwood and Gendlin, it does not operate with an atomistic conception of corporeal existence. Before turning to the details of her position, I will address Butler's use of the term "language." Because Butler works out of a psychoanalytic tradition, her use of the term presumably indicates the structures for the condition of the possibility of experience, including linguistic experience in its commonsensical meaning. On the other hand, Butler also uses the terms "language" and "discourse" fairly loosely and interchangeably. In *Bodies That Matter*, for example, "language" is used to suggest both discourse and the transcendental conditions for the possibility of discursive meaning itself, but generally not to indicate the everyday sense of language. My discussion will be limited to Butler's analysis of the relationship between language and materiality understood as the relationship between discursivity and materiality. What I say might also fruitfully apply to the relationship between materiality and language in its psychoanalytic sense, but I will leave that to others to decide.

Butler's account of the relationship of language and materiality in *Bodies That Matter* provides some basis for the criticism that she does not eliminate the dualism between culture and nature, but rather neglects the latter by privileging the former. Even though Butler explicitly rejects linguistic monism, one of the particular ways by which she undercuts divisions between language and materiality seems merely to replace bodily with linguistic materiality. Arguing that her position does not entail that bodies are simply linguistic stuff, Butler claims that rather than exist in opposition, language and materiality are "fully embedded in another, chiasmic in their interdependency."[37] Instead of providing a transactional account of the relationship of bodies and culture at this point, Butler appeals to the materiality of language itself to explain this interdependency. According to Butler, language and materiality are enmeshed because language itself is material—for example, it can be heard and seen—although it is not exclusively so.[38] Butler claims that the materiality of language means not that language and materiality have been collapsed into one another, but that they are indissoluble. Language and materiality cannot be reduced to one another, nor does either ever fully exceed the other.[39] Neither identical nor completely different, language and materiality can never be fully distinguished from each other even though they are not the same thing.

While these last three sentences bring out the transactional aspects of Butler's account, her goal when explaining the interdependency of language and materiality does not appear to be to illustrate the transaction between bodies and language. It instead seems to be to emphasize the material dimensions of language when it is spoken or written. To explain her position on the relationship of language and materiality, Butler shifts away from questions of discursivity, as well as from questions of language in its Lacanian sense, by using "language" in its everyday, empirical sense of something written and spoken. She argues that if language itself is material, even as it functions by means of a set of larger nonmaterial relations, language is not foreign to the bodies it helps constitute. This means that when language is used to refer to bodies, language does not "contaminate" bodily materiality with some sort of immateriality, forever removing the body's materiality from one's grasp. The materiality of language allegedly ensures that as one uses language to gain access to bodies when speaking and writing about them, one is dealing in and with materiality all along.

Yet the claim that language itself is material in its written and spoken forms does not satisfactorily explain how bodily materiality has not been lost in Butler's account. Butler is right that writing and speaking are material in that they can be seen and heard. But it is not immediately apparent, and Butler does not explain how the materiality of writing and speaking are relevant or similar to the materiality of bodily matters such as bleeding, eating, and snoring. I am not suggesting that bodily matters such as these are nondiscursive, but rather that even though they be discursively constituted, the ability to hear and speak words does not tell one much about the materiality of bodies. To appeal to the materiality of language when pressed on the issue of the materiality of bodies has the effect of claiming that bodily materiality is not something that should or can be addressed in an account that recognizes the discursivity of bodies.

Butler's appeal to the materiality of language as an explanation of how one might approach the issue of bodily materiality shifts the issue of materiality from bodies to that of language in a way that does not clearly address bodily existence. The claim that the materiality of bodies is constituted through the materiality of language seems to avoid the materiality of bodies by means of an appeal to a linguistic materiality that was never at issue. Butler's point that language itself is material does not mean that when one addresses the issue of linguistic materiality, one is talking about the same thing as bodily materiality, even granting bodily discursivity. Rather than indicate that the materiality of bodies has not been lost in the indissolubility of bodies and language, Butler's appeal to the materiality of language through an equivocation of language can seem like an equivocation on the term "materiality" that overprivileges language at the expense of bodily physicality. While claiming not to be a linguistic monist, Butler's explanations of why she is not one can have the ironic effect of making her seem precisely what she denies being.

Butler's work fortunately offers other resources, which when read as presenting an account of bodies as transactional can best demonstrate why Butler's position is preferable to one that posits a nondiscursive body. To read Butler in this way, one must understand her account in conjunction with a particular implication of the notion of transaction for epistemology: the rejection of what Dewey calls the "spectator theory of knowledge."[40] The spectator theory of knowledge assumes that knowers are observers of a world that exists ready-made and the observation of which makes no difference or changes to it. The spectator theory of knowledge conceives of self and world in an atomistic way, as items in a tossed salad that are brought into conjunction with each other but that in no way contribute to the other's constitution. In contrast, to understand bodies as transactional means that the knowing organism and what it knows are intimately related in a stewlike way and thus are always in a dynamically constitutive relationship with each other. Rather than conceive of organisms as passive spectators, a transactional account takes knowers to be active participants in the world that is transformed through the act of knowing. As Dewey claims, "the spectator theory of knowing may, humanly speaking, have been inevitable when thought was viewed as an exercise of a 'reason' independent of the body."[41] Once one acknowledges that the human knower is a corporeal being and not "a little god outside" of the world, however, one must recognize that humans impact, transform, and constitute the world through their knowing of it.[42]

Butler's aversion to the nondiscursive body should be understood as following from her rejection of a spectator theory of knowledge, rather than as constituting a project of "grammatological creationism," as it has been colorfully called.[43] When Butler insists that one cannot posit a nondiscursive body without that positing itself being a discursive practice that effects the body that is posited, she is not claiming that positing brings bodies into existence by means of some kind of bizarre linguistic creation. She is insisting instead that human beings are not passive spectators of a ready-made world who can observe and record it without making any impact upon it. The nondiscursive body is not something ready-made, standing atomistically outside discourse waiting to be observed. Because human organisms are in a transactional relationship with the world, the way in which they understand bodies has constitutive effects on the bodies that are comprehended. We can see Butler rejecting the spectator theory of knowledge when she insists that "[t]o claim that discourse is formative is not to claim that it originates, causes, or exhaustively composes that which it concedes; rather it is to claim that there is no reference to a pure body which is not at the same time a further formation of that body."[44] If humans are not passive spectators of their world but instead impact it through their transactions with it, there is no way to conceive of a nondiscursive body without that conception affecting the intelligibility of the body itself.

Butler argues that "it is not that one cannot get outside of language in order to grasp materiality in and of itself; rather, every effort to refer to materiality takes place through a signifying process."[45] Her point is that the very act of grasping materiality through designations of it transactionally contributes to the constitution of the "it" that is known. One may concede, as Butler does, the "undeniability" of sex and bodily materiality, but when doing so, one must understand that "the discourse in and through which that concession occurs . . . [is] formative of the very phenomenon that it concedes."[46] Put another way, the materiality of human bodies may be undeniable, but its undeniability is, at best, only half the story. It does not yet tell us what it means to affirm a particular formulation of materiality, for there is no impartial, neutral formulation to be had. Nor, as Butler claims, does it tell us "what interpretative matrices condition, enable and limit that necessary affirmation."[47]

Here we can see the benefits of reading Butler through the lens of transaction. In her account of the discursivity of bodies, Butler explicitly emphasizes one half, so to speak, of the transactional relationship between conceptions of bodies and bodies that are conceived, the "half" in which conceptions are constitutive of that which is conceived. But it important to remember the other "half" of the relationship as well, which the term "transactional" captures better than does "discursive." The second half is that the bodies that are discursively constituted are also actively constitutive of the political and other discourses that constitute them. Like the co-constitutive relationship of the carrot and onion in the stew, discursive meanings and the bodies posited by those meanings are in a transactional relationship. This means not only that the understanding of bodies as male and female helps make those bodies be male and female; it also means that the resulting male and female bodies have constitutive effects on the world that composed them as male and female. Sexed bodies are not merely the products of political, social, and other demands that they be male or female. They also are actively productive in their environments by means of the ways that they live the impact of the demands made on them. This is true of bodies as "had," or nonreflectively lived, as well as of bodies as consciously known or posited, a point to which I shall return later. Whether "had" or known, bodies are both produced by and productive of their various environments through their transactions with them.

The point of emphasizing that humans are not little gods hovering outside the world but are constituted in and through their transactions with it is not only that one is not a passive spectator of the world; it also is that one's perspectives on and transactions with the world are not neutral. From the rejection of the spectator theory of knowledge follows an acknowledgment of partiality and bias as inescapable parts of corporeal existence. As Dewey claims, "[t]his interaction [of humans with their world] is subject to partiality because the human factor [in contrast to the divine, as traditionally conceived] has bent and bias."[48] Dewey quickly adds, however, that "partiality is not obnoxious just because it is partial."[49] To long for a world in which humans are not partial is implicitly to wish to return to a conception of humans as passive, uninvolved spectators of their world. Humans do not have a "God's eye" point of view, and to accept this is to accept the limitation and bias that accompany human existence.

What *is* problematic about partiality is when the result of some act or choice, either conscious or nonconscious, is treated as a preexisting, impartial given that is not the product of "bent and bias." As Dewey argues, "[s]elective emphasis, choice, is inevitable whenever reflection occurs. This is not an evil. Deception comes only when the presence and operation of choice is concealed, disguised, denied."[50] When partiality and selective emphasis are recognized for what they are, one can better avoid the philosophical fallacy that occurs so often in theoretical work: treating the outcomes or products of a process as fixed realities that precede the process itself.[51] Such hypostatization is problematic because it ignores the process that is the context and history for its eventual outcome. In doing so, hypostatization fixes as eternal and unchanging something that not only is a product of ongoing change, but that also is a candidate for further transformation. What Dewey calls *the* philosophical fallacy is a profoundly conservative practice of completely hardening something that is still somewhat malleable.

It is precisely the issue of partiality and the danger of hypostatization that accompanies it that concern Butler when she challenges the spectator theory of knowledge as it applies to bodily materiality. Butler rejects the customary understanding of sexed matter as a biological given and gender as a malleable cultural overlay because to accept such a sharp distinction between sex and gender is to hypostatize sex in the service of a heterosexual imperative. To conceive of the sexed body as prior to its signification "produces as an *effect* of its own procedure the very body that it nevertheless and simultaneously claims to discover as that which *precedes* its own action."[52] As a way of resisting hypostatization, Butler emphasizes the plasticity of matter, arguing that it is "*a process of materialization that stabilizes over time to produce the effect of boundary, fixity, and surface we call matter.*"[53] With regard to sex in particular, to see matter as a process is to refuse to see sex as a biological given that precedes the cultural processes that result in gender. Sex as a fixed, biological given is the sedimented effect of the ongoing process of materialization itself. Instead of being prior to gender, sex itself is an effect of gender. Like gender, sex is a normative cultural sedimentation that regulates bodies.[54] Bodies do not come ready-made as male and female and then have an "artificial" femininity or masculinity imposed upon them by culture. The designation of bodies into two sexes is itself a product of gender, which attempts to support its sharp binary of feminine and masculine with the biological "fact" of the mutually exclusive categories of male and female. The damaging effect of the hypostatized division and creation of sex is to reinforce a rigid cultural requirement of heterosexuality.

As Butler argues, "the matter of bodies [is] indissociable from the regulatory norms that govern their materialization and the signification of those material effects."[55] Once one realizes the indissolubility of materiality and its norms, one can see why it is doubtful that feminist appeals to a body understood to be apart from discourse will serve feminist aims. In attempting to ground feminist theory and practice on such a conception of bodies, "[w]e may seek to return to matter as prior to discourse to ground our claims about sexual difference only to discover that matter is fully sedimented with discourses on sex and sexuality that prefigure and constrain the uses to which that term can be put."[56] The question of the nature of the materiality of bodies cannot be separated from the question of which bodies are important in political, social, and even ontological ways. The attempt to think of bodily materiality as prior to or nonconstitutively outside of the cultural or social is already to make a political claim. This is because such an attempt assumes that the sexed nature of bodily materiality is never problematic. To posit an allegedly neutral body that is not the product of some particular selective emphasis is itself a selective emphasis with regard to bodies that has particular effects and goals.

Reading Butler's position with an understanding of bodies as transactional shows how she provides a valuable argument that humans are not passive spectators of the world. The way in which one understands and experiences the world has political and other effects that should not be accepted as hypostatized givens. Rejecting a fixed, static notion of materiality, Butler's goal is not so much to provide a negative answer to the question "is there a nondiscursive body?" as it is to steer feminists and others away from wrestling too long with such a question. As Butler claims, her purpose is to call the presupposition of materiality into question, which "is to free it from its metaphysical lodgings in order to understand what political interests were secured in and by that metaphysical placing, and thereby to permit the term to occupy and to serve very different political aims."[57] Butler's strategy is to attempt to change the subject when pressed on the question of nondiscursive bodies because she does not think that the question is a fruitful one for philosophers, feminist or otherwise, to continue to pursue. When theorists stop dwelling on questions about the ability of bodies to stand outside of discourse, they can then redirect their energies where they should be, that is, into examining and transforming, if needed, the effects of current discourses about and attitudes toward bodies.

Yet Butler risks undermining her project of redirecting attention to the transformation of bodies by largely neglecting to examine the concrete particulars of the ways in which bodies are transactionally constituted.[58] With her language of "positing," she also implies that she is interested only in the known body, as opposed to the had or nonreflectively lived body. Reading Butler's work in conjunction with a rejection of the spectator theory of knowledge not only demonstrates why Butler is not a linguistic monist, but also reveals how her account is restricted to an epistemological approach to bodies.[59] While the term "posit" might be stretched to include both the had and the known body, it lends itself more to the known, suggesting a neglect of the lived. If Butler's goal is to redirect feminists to the effects of current discourses on bodies, she needs to focus more concretely on those effects, including the ways in which they impact bodies as had, not just known.

The lack of concrete, practical spaces and the neglect of the had, lived body in Butler's work help explain why her position is often mistaken to be a declaration of linguistic idealism. At times Butler does mention the lived experiences of bodies' dying, eating, sleeping, feeling pain and pleasure, and enduring illness and violence.[60] These experiences are introduced briefly, however, for the mere purpose of reinforcing Butler's theoretical claim that the fact of them does not address the question of what it means to discursively posit them. That is, such experiences are not brought up for examination themselves. Butler is not wrong to claim that the positing of the ill or painful body is a positing of a particular sort of body for particular reasons and with particular effects. But she rarely examines the lived effects of that positing, which requires looking at concrete situations and experiences to find out the effects of various positings on bodies, both had and known.

Butler is not guilty of promoting a linguistic idealism of the body, and thus those who criticize her on this point have misconstrued her project. Nonetheless, her critics are not entirely off base with their claim that Butler's position omits something of importance about bodies. What is omitted is not the prediscursive body, but the concrete experiences of lived bodies. The positing of a nondiscursive body is itself a discursive phenomenon, but the discursivity of bodies does not have to preclude concrete acknowledgments and analyses of bodily transactions, including the non-reflectively lived experience of bodies. Embracing bodily discursivity does not have to entail the sacrifice of attention to the experience of bodies, and appealing to lived experience is not necessarily to attempt to get "behind" culture to a nondiscursive ground.[61] Thus, when I urge that bodies be understood as transactional bodying, I urge both that the discursivity of bodies be acknowledged and that room be made for discussion of the concrete, had experiences of lived bodies.

Two important examples of feminist philosophy that have done this can be found in the work of Susan Wendell and Susan Bordo. Both Wendell and Bordo recognize the discursivity of bodies as they carry out projects that concretely examine lived bodily experience. In her discussion of illness and disability in *The Rejected Body: Feminist Philosophical Reflections on Disability*, Wendell explores the ways in which the vocabulary and conceptualizations used to describe and understand bodily experiences produced by Western biomedicine often are limited in their capacity to understand and describe those experiences.[62] Wendell's point is not that there is a culture-free, nondiscursive bodily experience that needs to be freed from the constraints of modern science; rather, it is the opposite: precisely because scientific discourse, among other types of discourse, is formative of humans' experiences of their bodies, its limitations are experiential.

We can see the experiential effects of discourse in the example of different scientific conceptions of the body provided by Wendell. She quotes eighteenth century medical logs that summarize female patients' reports of their bodily suffering as feeling like "womb fear, womb anxiety, . . . a cold womb that was open too wide, . . . a womb cramp manifesting itself mostly in the mouth and in the tongue and rendering the latter useless for speaking."[63] Wendell suggests that, due to their incorporation of eighteenth-century medical conceptions of how female bodies functioned, these women may not have merely described, but also experienced their bodies in very different ways than did women in the late twentieth century. In addition, variations in bodily experiences do not occur only when comparing different points in history. For people in the current time period, different bodily experiences may be possible depending on which conceptualizations of corporeal existence are culturally available. Because "different conceptualizations might lead to different experiences of the body" and because Western biomedicine is not good at handling patients' experiences of pain, Wendell thinks that it might be worthwhile to explore conceptualizations of bodies other than the ones with which Western medicine functions.[64] To that end, Wendell suggests how traditional Chinese medicine might produce for her a different experience of her illness than does Western medicine. While Chinese medicine would explain Wendell's illness as an imbalance of energy that is *chi*, Western medicine calls her illness chronic fatigue syndrome (or myalgic encephalomyelitis) and explains it as an immunological abnormality.

Wendell's example of illness does not function to claim that Chinese medicine is truer than Western medicine, or vice versa, in that Chinese medicine copies or represents the nondiscursive experience of bodies more accurately than does Western medicine. Nor does her example deny that the experience of one's body based on Chinese conceptions of *chi* might have limitations of its own. Rather, it suggests that different conceptions can produce different experiences and, more specifically, that some non-Western conceptions might provide a range of possibilities for felt bodily experience that enable ill people to cope with chronic pain much better than do the concepts provided by Western medicine.

In her *Unbearable Weight: Feminism, Western Culture, and the Body*, Susan Bordo examines, in particular, the discursive formation of women's experiences of their bodies in relationship to food.[65] In that book, and in her more recent "Bringing Body to Theory," Bordo makes clear that her use of gender as a category of analysis is not due to a covert positing of a nondiscursively gendered body on her part.[66] Bordo's work demonstrates that even though gender and other cultural configurations are discursive formations, they have powerful effects on the ways in which women and others experience their own bodies. Bordo argues that the discursive formation of the body as an alien enemy that confines the soul or mind and that threatens attempts at control is constitutive of anorexics', and to a lesser degree, most women's lived experience of their bodies.[67] In addition, Bordo insists that one not lose sight of the concrete effects that gender has in human life because of the concrete difficulties of subverting or transforming gender binaries. As Bordo claims, "[d]ualism . . . cannot be deconstructed in culture the way it can be on paper."[68] Deconstructing dualism in "real" life is far more difficult and will take much more effort than deconstructing it in scholarly writings. For that reason and not because gender is nondiscursive, the category of gender continues to be important to attempts to understand lived, bodily experience. One must recognize the discursivity of gendered bodies not to neglect lived, bodily experience, but precisely so that one might better understand and slowly transform it.

Wendell's and Bordo's accounts also help demonstrate why one need not understand bodies as nondiscursive to deal adequately with issues of control and creativity. At the same time that Wendell emphasizes what she calls "the social construction of disability," including the experience of disability itself, she is sharply critical of the various versions of the myth of control over the body in which North Americans tend to believe. These myths usually serve to increase the suffering of those who, due to disability or illness, do not have "proper" control over their bodies. Indeed, the title phrase of Wendell's book, "the rejected body," serves precisely to refer to those bodies or aspects of bodies that resist human control and thus that are despised, feared, and ignored.[69] As Wendell suggests, pain is transactionally constituted by and capable of transformation through the "complex physical, psychological, and social context" in which it occurs, but this does not mean that people in pain have total control over their pain and can wish it away.[70]

Just as Wendell's examination of the lived experience of bodies that are disabled disentangles discursivity and total control, Bordo's analyses of women's bodily experiences demonstrate how understanding bodies as discursive need not preclude the possibility of resistance to cultural norms. For Bordo, it is precisely by exploring the concrete ways that bodies are discursively constituted that one is able to assess "the concrete consequences of actions" so that one might gauge "in what direction(s) they are moving (or reproducing) the institutions and practices of society."[71] Bodily experiences and practices related to things such as food are transactionally constituted, but this does not mean that they cannot move the institutions, practices, and norms of our society in slightly different ways. As Bordo argues, "[t]he fact that resistance is produced out of a hegemonic order does not preclude it from transforming that order, any more than the fact that we are our parents' children precludes us from living lives very different from theirs."[72] For example, even as anorexics' bodily experiences are discursively formed by Western culture's fear and loathing of bodies in general and of women's bodies in particular, they also might be a form of resistance to cultural expectations that women be sexually available to men and embody the ideal of female domesticity.[73]

This is not to claim that anorexia is the best way to resist cultural norms of femininity nor to deny that anorectic practices function to support women's powerlessness at the same time that they attempt to challenge it. Rather it is to demonstrate that critical attitudes toward one's culture are possible even though, or rather precisely because, organism and environment are transactionally constituted. Such transformation will not be easy or occur in large, revolutionary ways, nor is it guaranteed to occur at all. Indeed, Bordo is very aware of the ways in which transaction can reproduce hegemonic orders. But by bringing to attention the concrete ways in which harmful transactions operate, Bordo demonstrates how one can call into question their "naturalness." By making the familiar seem strange, such a calling into question is already the beginning of a slight alternation of those transactions and of the possibility of further transformation of them.

Understanding bodies as transactional means that there is no body in itself that one can get to apart from its various cultural and social environments. Bodies are not isolated physical objects existing outside or prior to their meanings. To undercut dualisms between organism and environment, and between self and world, is to understand bodies as always already constituted by the social, cultural, and political meanings that are found in the environments in which they live. Framing the notion of discursivity in terms of transaction does not entail the loss of the "real" body. Instead, attending to the effects of transaction is precisely the best way by which one can recognize and do justice to bodily existence. Holding that bodily activities are shaped by transactions with their environments is valuable to philosophy in particular, and to life in general, because such an understanding of bodying encourages people to ask whether, when, how, and for whom those transactions are beneficial.

THREE

Communicating with Another

Transaction and Merleau-Ponty's
Phenomenology of Corporeal Existence

Many of the characteristics of Maurice Merleau-Ponty's phenomenological account of human existence are valuable both for feminism and for philosophy at large. These characteristics include the primacy given to bodily existence; the attention paid to the nonreflective aspects of human life; the importance of situation for understanding human engagement with and in the world; the crucial role that habit plays in corporeal existence; and the emphasis placed on lived experience.[1] Merleau-Ponty's phenomenology is noteworthy particularly because it gives import to the intersubjectivity of bodily existence. For Merleau-Ponty, bodily existence is projective, and projection is part of an intersubjective relationship between corporeal subject and world. Through his account of projection, Merleau-Ponty seeks to undercut dualisms of self and world, and mind and body, and thus to undermine the Cartesian solipsism and atomism that have plagued Western thought. For all these reasons, feminists, pragmatists, and others should appreciate Merleau-Ponty's account of bodily existence.

However, his notion of projective intentionality, combined with the assumption of the body as a neutral commonality shared by all people in the same way, prevents Merleau-Ponty from breaking completely free of a problematic understanding of bodies as atomistic, solipsistic, and domineering. As feminist critics have noted, Merleau-Ponty's appeal to a nongendered body produces an account of corporeal existence that is androcentric, rather than neutral.[2] As is less often noted, Merleau-Ponty's account of human existence based on projective intentionality tends to construe a person's being-in-the-world as a solipsistic activity of imposing her intentions, value, and meanings onto objects and others in the world. By solipsistic, I mean here ethical rather than metaphysical solipsism.[3] Projective intentionality does not necessarily assume literally that only one self exists, but it tends to operate with the assumption that the beliefs, values, desires, and intentions of only one self are of any importance. The ethical solipsism of projective intentionality and the assumption of an anonymous body make Merleau-Ponty's account of corporeal existence troubling from feminist and pragmatist perspectives. Instead of being an account of the dynamic, co-constitutive relationship between self and other, the model of intersubjectivity offered by Merleau-Ponty tends toward that of a subject's monologue with itself that includes a domineering erasure of others in its projective "communication" with them.

According to Merleau-Ponty, projection is the normal function of human beings and is centrifugal. Projective existence throws out its own background, which is the backdrop of a meaningful world against and in which one lives.[4] The centrifugal power of projection is in contrast to centripetal movement, which operates against a given, rather than projected background. To illustrate centripetal movement, Merleau-Ponty draws upon the case of Schneider, a man whose occipital lobe was damaged by shrapnel in World War I. The studies of Schneider by psychiatrists in the 1920s interest Merleau-Ponty because they reveal how changes in Schneider's physiology resulted in changes to his lived existence. After he is injured, Schneider does not inhabit his world normally. He "spins" his existence in such a way that the givenness of his world is a force directed in toward the center, at which he is stationed and in which he is constrained. The meaning of his world is that which presses in against him, rather than that which is thrown out by him. Instead of existing such that he spins out the backdrop that is the fund of the meaning in his life, he accepts and is restricted to the meaning that is given to him by the world.

Merleau-Ponty claims that Schneider's centripetal existence can be seen in his sexuality, specifically in the way he engages—or, rather, does not fully engage—in sexual encounters. When in an erotic situation, Schneider is incapable of "maintaining it or following it through to complete satisfaction," as is evident when his "half-fulfilled desire vanishes" if "orgasm occurs first in [his] partner and she moves away."[5] According to Merleau-Ponty, the ultimate meaning and result of Schneider's erotic situation are things that are given to him by his world. Rather than take up an erotic situation and follow it through to its fulfillment in his own orgasm, Schneider accepts and thus is restricted by the meaning that his partner has given to it.

Merleau-Ponty claims that Schneider's lack of projective powers means that for him "the world exists only as one readymade or congealed, whereas for the normal person his projects polarize the world, bringing magically to view a host of signs which guide action."[6] The "normal" person has projects by which meaning is constituted in her world. For most people other than Schneider, the world and its meaning are constituted to a large degree by the selective emphasis generated by a person's particular interests, desires, and needs. In the blooming, buzzing confusion of the world, some aspects of it rather than others stand forth as meaningful because of the particular activities and purposes in which one is engaged. Merleau-Ponty calls the function of producing meaning via selective emphasis "summoning," which refers to "the sense in which the medium summons an absent person and causes him to appear."[7] Things are absent in the sense that they are in the background of a person's existence and thus do not have a place in his or her existential field. They are summoned forth and given a place in one's perceptual field, thus becoming a meaningful component of the world. In summoning figures from the background to the foreground, one pulls the absent into the present. As Merleau-Ponty states, one "breath[es] a spirit into them" and thereby assigns life and meaning to the previously lifeless and meaningless.[8]

For Merleau-Ponty, one's ability to summon or project does not mean that a person is the sole creator of meaning. Summoning and projection are bodily, and according to Merleau-Ponty, for that reason the world is objective. Merleau-Ponty describes the objectivity of the world in this way: "the normal subject penetrates into the object by perception, assimilating its structure into his substance, *and* through this body the object directly regulates his movements."[9] While the world has the meaning that a person assigns to it, her contribution to its meaning is only one half of the reciprocal relationship that takes place between subject and object. Subject and object are in a metaphorical dialogue in that each contributes something to the exchange between them that helps constitute what they are. In Merleau-Ponty's account, dialogical exchange primarily takes place in nonreflective ways, although it also can occur by means of conscious intent.

Merleau-Ponty's example of typing illustrates the way in which one's body makes reciprocal dialogue possible. As I type this page, intentional threads run out from my body, reaching out toward the keyboard and incorporating the keyboard into my world in a meaningful way. Incorporation and assimilation occur because my body has knowledge of the keyboard, built through my familiarity with it. The keyboard has a meaningful place within my world because, through my body's familiarity with the keyboard gained through the repeated use of it, a piece of plastic and metal has become an extension of my intentionality. It has become the means by which I take up my world and find in it a place for my goals and aims.

The keyboard is not only an extension of my intentions, however. In turn, the keyboard also regulates my body. As Merleau-Ponty explains, "the subject who learns to type incorporates the key-bank space into his bodily space."[10] The keyboard has a particular shape and a manner of operating that call for a specific bodily comportment in order to use it. Because of my familiarity with the keyboard, my body develops particular habits in using it. My body knows how to manipulate the keys without positing them as objective locations. My fingers learn how and where to stretch to type certain words, and that knowledge becomes sedimented and incorporated as part of my body.

The habits that I develop because of the particular structure of the keyboard compose my body knowledge of the keyboard. Because my habits compose me, to some degree the keyboard thus contributes to my composition. This example is one way of illustrating Merleau-Ponty's point that "[m]y life must have a significance that I do not constitute."[11] Existence is centrifugal, and my body is the means by which I project my world. Because it is my body that appropriates and constitutes my world, however, the constitution of my world is dialogical. Even as I throw out my world, I always find myself already situated within the world, surrounded by a nonreflective fund of experience that is presupposed by my acts. My world is arranged around me such that it speaks to me of myself, but that arrangement happens by means of what Merleau-Ponty calls a "drawing together, by the subject, of the meaning diffused through the object . . . [as well as] by the object, of the subject's intentions."[12]

But what exactly does it mean to refer to the meaning that is diffused through an object? Where or how does the object get the meaning that it contributes to my "dialogue" with it? These are important questions because to engage in a communicative relationship with another, the other's contribution must not be just my words coming from her mouth. Moreover, this is just as true for nonreflective as it is for conscious forms of communication. If the objects that exist in my world merely reflect myself and my meanings back to me, projection would then become the ethically solipsistic way in which a subject, albeit a corporeal one, constructs his or her world. If projection is not to constitute such solipsism, then the question of how others have their meaning apart from me must be answered. How does bodily existence guarantee that the subject encounters another in his or her world?

Merleau-Ponty's response to this question is that an object can confront a person with its own meaning because its meaning is a product of another person's projects. For Merleau-Ponty, it is through projection that things without significance become objects with significance. My intentionality turns a heavy object into a paperweight; it is because of my need to hold papers down that a random stone nearby becomes a cultural object. As Merleau-Ponty explains, human existence "projects itself into the environment in the shape of cultural objects," which is to say that "the spontaneous acts through which man has patterned his life [are] deposited, like some sediment, outside himself and lead an anonymous existence as things."[13] Things in the world are the objectified intentionality of a subject. Things approach me with a meaning that is not mine because their meaning is constituted, at least in part, by a subject who is not me. According to Merleau-Ponty, because "[i]n the cultural object, I feel the close presence of others," a paperweight can enter my world with a meaning diffused throughout it.[14] It is through my perception of another person's possible use of an object that I ran across that the object presents its meaning to me.

For Merleau-Ponty, the question about the possibility of reciprocal dialogue with an object leads to an encounter with another subject. The meaning of an object hinges on the existence of other projecting subjects, and therefore the way in which the body ensures the existence of other subjects must be made clear. Merleau-Ponty acknowledges that one risks solipsism when one turns an objectifying gaze onto another and see another person as something to observe, rather than as someone with whom to communicate. But this lack of communication is possible only because it takes place against a backdrop of possible communication, a backdrop provided by the body. Another may try to avoid communicating with me, Merleau-Ponty explains, "[b]ut let [another subject] . . . even make a gesture of impatience, and already he ceases to transcend me."[15] With the mere movement of her body, another becomes accessible to and communicates with me.

According to Merleau-Ponty, the body is able to be the backdrop that ensures communication because of its anonymity. He claims that just "as the parts of my body together [comprise] a system, so my body and the other's are one whole, two sides of one and the same phenomenon, and the anonymous existence of which my body is the ever-renewed trace henceforth inhabits both bodies simultaneously."[16] For Merleau-Ponty, anonymous existence is that unnamed and perhaps unnamable level of human existence that is prepersonal. Of course, there is a personal level of bodily existence in which I can distinguish my body from yours; but beneath that personal level is a level of existence in which there is a commonality between and a quasi-indifferentiation from other bodies. The wholeness that accompanies individuation, particularity, and distinctiveness is the link that provides the possibility of communication between you and me.[17]

Complementary to the characterization of anonymous existence as prepersonal is Merleau-Ponty's description of it as impersonal.[18] On a fundamental level, my existence is impersonal because the other's "living body has the same structure as mine."[19] I am like you and you are like me on some fundamental level. As the word "anonymous" indicates, my bodily structure is unnamable in that it cannot completely be claimed as uniquely mine. In some significant sense, it could be that of anyone and thus of everyone. The trace of anonymous existence that appears in both of our bodies referred to by Merleau-Ponty is found in the similarity of those bodies. Once again, this is not to say that my body is not mine, but that I "share" my body with others because of our bodies' similar structure.

In perhaps slightly different ways, both the descriptions "prepersonal" and "impersonal" indicate that there is a fundamental aspect of all human bodies that is the same. This, of course, does not mean that all human bodies are identical. Bodies do differ; but on Merleau-Ponty's account, beneath their differences lies a similarity or common ground that is not yet marked by particularity. And it is this similarity that provides the basic possibility for communication because, thanks to it, a body can grasp the corporeal intentions of another. Recalling Merleau-Ponty's claim that "I experience my own body as the power of adopting certain forms of behaviour and a certain world," one can say that "it is precisely my body which perceives the body of another" because my body "discovers in that other body a miraculous prolongation of my own intentions, a familiar way of dealing with the world."[20]

According to Merleau-Ponty, because my body and your body exist on a level other than that of individuation, we can recognize each other's intentions. Because of the body and the knowledge it provides, we gain an understanding of each other that makes coexistence possible. I am not lost in my own world of meaning because when I see another body in action, the objects around it take on a significance beyond that which I give them. As Merleau-Ponty claims, those objects "are no longer simply what I myself could make of them, they are what this other pattern of behaviour is about to make of them," the meaning of which I can understand thanks to bodily existence.[21] Just as the baby embodies the parent's intentions when the baby pretends to bite as the parent playfully bites the baby's finger, I can recognize another person's manner of dealing with an object because I can perceive her intentions in my body. The ability to recognize the meaning of the intentionality of others as they project themselves into the world is what teaches me the existence of others.

Merleau-Ponty surely is right that human bodies share a similar structure.[22] For example, most humans have hands with extended digits and an opposable thumb, and this structure makes objects graspable to all those with similar hands and similar habits of using them.[23] Likewise, human bodies bleed when cut and must eat if they are to continue existing; bleeding and the need for nourishment are similarities between human bodies. That the structures of human bodies sometimes can provide a shared meaning to the world does not mean, however, that all or even many aspects of the world are had in common. Abstracted from the various contexts in which human bodying takes place, similarities between humans are not significant or "weighty" enough to serve as an automatic or certain foundation for an easy understanding across their differences.[24] Once considered within some particular context, human activities such as grasping, eating, and bleeding are similarities only in a very limited respect and cannot be assumed to be the same. The meanings of food, hunger, and eating, for example, are likely to be very different for anorexic and nonanorexic bodies. It is largely fruitless to try to understand those meanings by trying to focus on an allegedly common, shared body that underlies the gender, race, culture, and personal histories of those bodies. Bodies cannot be appealed to as some sort of foundational "given" that easily solves the problem of communicating across their differences. Neglecting this fact, as Merleau-Ponty's notion of the anonymous or impersonal body tends to do, leads one to overlook the different habits incorporated into bodily structures and thus the different meanings that bodily gestures have as a result.

What Merleau-Ponty fails to realize in his appeal to the common structure of the anonymous human body is that I have not necessarily been taught the existence of others in my easy recognition of the familiar in another. He is wrong that I should depend on the body to provide me with a familiar world in my perception of bodily habits and patterns of behaviors presented to me by another. Instead, I sometimes find such a familiar world because I can see nothing but my own intentions in another's behavior. Rather than making communication possible, conceiving of communication as a prolongation of my intentions is precisely that which tends to impede it.

Suppose that I suggest to a friend an interpretation of some recent political event, and the pattern of behavior with which I am presented is this: a loud voice, a body and face that lean sharply toward me, and vigorous and forceful gestures in the air with his arms and hands. My body nonconsciously "replies" by drawing itself in. My bodying becomes still and quiet and subtly but literally constricts itself by pulling arms and legs in and slightly tucking in the head to take up as little space as possible. If I am to "discover in that other body [in this case, my friends' body] a miraculous prolongation of my own intentions," as Merleau-Ponty's projective intentionality would have me do, then what I discover is an angry and hostile attack of my suggestion.[25] And, if my friend is to discover in my bodily activity a prolongation of his intentions, what he discovers is a haughty dismissal of his comments. But in this case, my friend and I have not really understood what the other's bodying has said. Instead, each of us merely has imposed our intentionality upon the other's bodily activity. It is true that if I manifested my friend's pattern of bodily behavior, I would be angrily attacking another's ideas. As a woman and given my particular upbringing as a child, my bodily habits are such that I would understand the vigor and force of the bodying with which I am confronted as evidence of hostile aggression. But I also know as a result of many painful misunderstandings of him that as a man, my friend's style of engagement in and excitement by an idea includes the very behaviors just described. Moreover, according to my understanding of my own bodily behavior, my apparent withdrawal does not signal an intentional ignoring of my friend but instead means that I am protecting myself because I feel as if I am being attacked. If I omit the particularities of gender and upbringing from my understanding of my friend's bodily gestures and behaviors and of his understanding of mine and instead assume a pre-gender, "pre-upbringing" similarity of the meaning of bodily behavior, then I risk completely misunderstanding what his bodying communicates to me and mine to him.

In this example, I am not claiming that men are essentially aggressive, that women are essentially passive, or that all men are aggressive and all women are passive. This account reflects my life as a woman who experiences herself as avoiding aggression and confrontation. I believe, however, that the example illuminates more than my own experience. Because of the way gender has been historically and socially constituted, in the Western world women often tend to be less and men more aggressive. Because gender is not unreal just because it is not essential, it must be taken into account when constructing a phenomenology of corporeal existence.

A former student of mine from China tended to deferentially tilt her head downward when talking with her professors so that she did not look them in the eye. While this particular bodily habit speaks of respect for authority in her home nation, it tends to speak of disrespect and inattentiveness in the United States. Unless her bodily activity was understood as having a particular culture and nationality, I and her other professors could not understand what her bodying communicated to us. Likewise, she told me that the relatively loose and uncontained way that people in the United States comport their bodies, which I tend to understand as a sign of being relaxed and confident, appeared rude and disrespectful to her. (Mis)finding the familiar in each other's bodies in this case would tell both the student and her professors that the other was disrespectful, producing hostile and disrespectful working relationships between them out of sincere attempts to be friendly and easygoing in the one case and polite and respectful in the other.

Examples of such miscommunication are easy to come by once one begins to search for them. The drooping, slumping body of a student in my class tends to speak to me of negligence and laziness, but it might be a sign of exhaustion and not necessarily indicate boredom or disinterest. A friend's cold, unapproachable body may be a sign of worry over and preoccupation with something at work, not a rebuff of my attentions as I had thought. A former colleague's touching and squeezing my arm might be merely an expression of friendship and not a sexual approach, as it seemed. A neighbor's vigorous snow shoveling might be an instance of exercise and not an expression of pent-up anger or frustration, as I thought. Of course, the meaning of these bodily gestures and behaviors is more likely ambiguous and not dichotomous as my quick summary of them might suggest. The ambiguity of bodily behavior in these instances only strengthens my point, however, that one cannot merely assume that one has understood another's bodily activities and habits correctly by projecting one's own intentionality onto them.

My goal with these examples has not been to give exhaustive accounts of which particularities are relevant or how they are relevant to the meaning of the situation at hand. All of the examples are in need of much greater detail about the bodies involved because the particularities in them affected, in different ways, the way I (mis)understood the behaviors in each of the situations and how the others (mis)understood mine. Providing the examples, however, illuminates the problematic nature of Merleau-Ponty's characterization of the body and its patterns of behavior as anonymous. By appealing to the anonymous body in his explanation of intersubjectivity, Merleau-Ponty adheres to the very philosophical tradition with which he was trying to break. Throughout the history of philosophy, philosophers have claimed that there is an essential "core" in humans that underlies all of their cultural and other differences. Some have called this core "Reason"; others, "the Universal Mind"; and still others, "the Transcendental Ego." Despite his attempts to break away from tradition, Merleau-Ponty differs from these philosophers merely by locating this fundamental core in "the body." On his account, at their foundation, individual bodies have a universally shared commonality that is then overlaid by the differences that their particularities give them. While such an account might eliminate concerns about how community might be possible in the face of differences between people, it does so at the expense of the differences themselves.

Instead of looking for a bodily core or structure unmarked by differences, one could hold that bodies are constituted by means of transactional bodyings of gender, race, class, age, sexuality, nationality, culture, experiences and upbringing, and more. In doing so, however, does one not then affirm people's differences at the expense of the possibility of community? While the question of communicative coexistence does become much more complicated and difficult when one rejects the anonymous body, this does not necessarily mean that communication with and understanding of another is impossible. Nor does it necessarily mean that no common ground between bodies can exist. It does mean, however, that one cannot assume that bodily habits, behaviors, and structures automatically provide a common ground for communication and community that has not yet been inscribed by differences and particularities. There are no shortcuts provided by "the body."[26] To assume that there are, as Merleau-Ponty tends to do with his positing of an anonymous body, is merely to impose one person's way of understanding her world on another and thus to fail to realize that others may transact with their worlds differently. When I impose on another the way that I transact with my world, I dominate her by refusing to recognize all the particularities that constitute her. I dominate her by taking my particular nonreflective habits of understanding as normative and thus overlooking the possibly different contributions of meaning to the world that she might make. Avoiding such domination means that common ground between bodily beings must take their differences into account. A common ground is something for which we must strive, not a starting point from which we depart. As Dewey writes, communication occurs when "[s]omething is literally *made* common in at least two different centres of behavior."[27] Commonality is an active achievement. Similarities among people are something that must be created, cultivated, and nurtured so that a nondomineering form of coexistence is possible, not something to assume as a transcendental condition for the possibility of communication.[28]

Merleau-Ponty rightly states that corporeal existence is not self-transparent. However, his insistence upon the opacity of bodies seems to lapse when he gazes upon the body of another, turning his phenomenology of perception into something like what Elizabeth Spelman has called "boomerang perception," in which "I look at you and come right back to myself."[29] To his credit, Merleau-Ponty occasionally admits that another "may one day shatter the image that I have formed of him." But feminist, pragmatist, and other types of philosophers need to remind themselves not to slip back, as Merleau-Ponty does, into thinking that others' bodily behaviors can be understood in a manner that is not affected by their own particular habits of understanding.[30] I cannot assume that I understand another's bodying correctly, and if I attempt to do so without paying attention to the particularities of others' bodily activities, I am almost sure to misunderstand.[31] Communication does not occur when others are only reflections of me back to myself. To quickly assume that I understand another is, as María Lugones has explained, to attempt to exhaust her by my easy construction of her. Exhausting her in this way is not to really know her, "and without knowing the other, one is really alone in the other's presence because the other is only dimly present to one."[32]

Whether impersonal or prepersonal, Merleau-Ponty's anonymous body imposes a commonality upon different bodies and in doing so, impedes the communication and common ground between corporeal subjects that his account seeks to explain. The anonymity of the body reveals itself to be an assumption of a connection among bodies rather than an explanation of how community and connection might be achieved given the particular ways that various people live their bodies. Only by rejecting Merleau-Ponty's concept of the anonymous body can feminists create a genuine option of breaking out of the ethically solipsistic subjectivity against which Merleau-Ponty tries to argue. Taking seriously the idea of others as different from oneself not only does not make community impossible, it is crucial to the possibility for communication with and understanding of another.[33]

How then might such communication be achieved? The first step toward it has already been taken when we ask whether the communication that is assumed to be occurring actually is happening. This first step is akin to Socratic wisdom, or recognition of one's ignorance: one must realize that communication may not be taking place before one can begin to work toward it. One must realize that the habitual, nonreflective ways in which one understands another person may be contributing to a misunderstanding of her. In attending to bodies that are different from my own, communication with another becomes possible because acknowledging the ways in which a person's bodying, including its gestures, comportment, and style as well as appearance, is different from mine disturbs my assumption that I already understand its meaning. Rather than try to discover the familiar in another, one needs first to make strange that which seems familiar. When I have rid myself of the assumption that I automatically understand another through my habitual ways of engaging with her, a second step becomes possible. This second step is the reconfiguration of my nonreflective habits of engaging with others so that they are open to, rather than close off, the particularities and distinctiveness of others. I call this reconfiguration "hypothetical construction." Hypothetical construction is a process by which one creates meaning with others by offering potential meaning to them as a hypothesis.

An offer of a hypothesis may be a strange metaphor because one usually says that one puts forth—projects—a hypothesis. I use the phrase deliberately, however. A hypothesis is a fallible contribution to the construction of the meaning of an encounter with others. In contrast to the imposition of meaning provided by projection, hypothesis is that protomeaning that requests and is nondogmatically open to suggestions and modifications of others. It includes what Lorraine Code calls a "resourceful" skepticism, which is not the nihilistic belief that no meaning can be found but instead a wariness of hasty conclusions and a readiness to reconsider one's judgments.[34] Resourceful skepticism is important because of the transactional character of the meaning of situations. As transactional, meaning is something to be mutually negotiated and developed by all the parties involved in the situation in question. Hypothetical construction thus suggests a way that my world takes on meaning with and through others because meaning is appreciated as constructive, as a building-together of meaning through debate, conflict, negotiation, disagreement, and agreement that is sometimes but not always consciously performed. That the incipient meaning I initially give an encounter is offered, not projected, means that the preliminary meaning I offer is an invitation presented to others, which they can choose to accept, reject, revise, or supplement as part of our negotiation. A hypothesis is offered as an invitation to others to participate in and thus make possible a mutually configured construction of meaning.

Hypothetical construction is a deliberate activity that works to disrupt the habitual, nonconscious ways by which one approaches and understands others as one transacts with the world. This is not to say that human existence is fundamentally projective, rather than transactional, and for this reason is in need of hypothetical construction; rather it is to acknowledge that the transactions between one person and another can be characterized by attempts of each to impose oneself on another. Hypothetical construction is the attempt to remake one's nonreflective being-in-the-world, when needed, so that it is welcoming rather than domineering. By disrupting one's habitual ways of understanding and transacting with others and bringing conscious reflection to bear upon them, hypothetical construction makes possible their gradual reconfiguration. This allows one to broaden the meanings of the world and, if desired, change the habitual way one bodily transacts with others.

Hypothetical construction does not assume that one can change, merely through a sheer act of disembodied will, one's style of bodily being in the world. Each organism always already finds itself in the world having transacted with it in its own distinctive manner, with its particular bodily practices and habits. Instead, hypothetical construction acknowledges the plasticity of habit as well as the interconstituency of body and mind, the subconscious and conscious, and the automatic and the willed. One can become reflective about one's habits, bringing conscious thought to bear on them such that one is aware of and might change them. The conscious aspects of human bodily being can come to bear on the subconscious, just as the subconscious continually impacts conscious life. Rather than a dualism between mind and body, the transactional relationship between conscious and subconscious habits best explains how bodily engagement with the world slowly can be made to change.

Human beings can, to some degree, restyle their bodily habits. By consciously thinking of my bodily comportment as a hypothesis, I can become consciously aware of the meaning that I offer others. I can come to recognize that my bodily habits and self-understanding are achieved by means of others. I am not transparent to myself, nor is there necessarily only one way to understand my bodily behavior, or that of others' bodies. For these reasons, I cannot claim absolute authority for my particular understanding of my bodily habits.[35] For example, in the case of my seemingly aggressive and hostile friend, I see my shrinking, withdrawing body as a message to my friend that he is overwhelming me and a request that he "back off" a bit. My self-understanding is, however, no more fully "right" or "wrong" than is his understanding of my bodying as haughty and aloof. Bodily activities and habits support a number of possible meanings, which is not to say that there can be no incorrect understandings of them. For that reason, the plurality of meaning and the ambiguity of bodying need to be taken into account by all parties involved when trying to communicate with one another. The meaning of my bodily activity and behavior, as well as that of others, needs to be seen as coming about through the communication that others and I undertake in unspoken as well as spoken ways. The verbal component of communication in hypothetical construction can be particularly important for bringing out the ambiguity of bodily behavior. It often is important for my realization that there are multiple ways to understand my body, that you understand my body differently than I do, and that you tell me how you understand my body. Our initial understandings of the meaning of bodily habits need to be thought as "working truths" about the meaning of bodying, "truths" that are subject to revision based on the contribution of meaning made by one another.

With an awareness of the complexity of the meanings of my bodily behavior, I can deliberately and consciously comport myself differently. When engaging with my aggressive friend, I try to look him in the eye, I lean toward him, actively listening to him, and I speak up, even if only to tell him that he is overwhelming me. At first, this will be difficult and awkward. It will jar with the usual way I transact with my world and will not feel "natural." But, after time and with practice, it will begin to change what counts as "natural" for me. My bodily habits and style will begin to incorporate new practices, gradually changing the way that I habitually transact with the world. As a result of this transformation, when engaging with my friend, I will be less uncomfortable being fully present, both bodily and verbally, in a lively and engaging conversation.

I primarily have described the process of hypothetical construction as if only one party is involved in it, but implicit in my description of it, and indeed crucial to its success, is the participation of the other party(ies) in the process. In hypothetical construction, the other person is also (re)understanding her bodying, learning about the complexity of meaning her bodily behaviors have in her conversation with another, and coming to see her own understanding of her bodily habits as a hypothesis. With that knowledge, she can begin to change her bodily comportment and activities, gradually developing new ways of habitually transacting with the world. In the case of my friend, he realized that his bodying communicated an aggressive attack as well as excitement about the issue at hand. Knowing that, he began to tone down his bodily gestures, tempering them so that they were less likely to be interpreted as strident and intimidating.

My friend's change in bodily comportment is intimately related to my own. My blossoming assertiveness helps bring about my friend's tempering of himself. Because I no longer appear to withdraw from my friend and our encounter, he no longer needs to go to extremes to draw me into conversation. And because he no longer goes to such extremes, I no longer tend to withdraw, which in turn gives me more space in which to approach him, and so on. What hypothetical construction thus involves is a transactional circle. For me to stop withdrawing, my friend must temper what I view as his aggressiveness, but in order for him to temper himself, I must stop withdrawing. How then does the change in our transaction ever begin? As is the case with all transactional circles, there is no proper starting place to prescribe. One must find a way to jump into the circle, making a small change at one point on it; this has the potential to change the entire circle itself, making it nonvicious and similar to a spiral.

The change that hypothetical construction helps make possible is not one in which it is necessary, or even desirable, that the comportment of each party involved becomes identical to one another. The point of hypothetical construction is not that all differences are smoothed out in the process of constructing the communal meaning of bodies and their encounters.

Rather, it is to negotiate meaning in bodily and verbal ways that acknowledges and respects the different protomeanings that individuals bring to one another. *Precisely because* different understandings of bodying can be respected as valid in hypothetical construction, modifications in bodily comportment and habit may be desired to facilitate improved communication. Instead of being a homogenizing disregard of the distinctiveness of others, modifying one's behavior in accord with another's understanding of it can be a respectful acknowledgment of that person's particular way of transacting with the world.

Let me say a bit more about the preservation of differences in communication. Respecting another's differences in and through a dynamic, mutual constitution of meaning requires that meaning no longer be thought of as a product of a single subject's intentionality. As Dewey describes the "essence and import" of communication through an example of A's request that B bring him a flower,

> [t]he characteristic thing about B's understanding of A's movement and sounds is that he responds to the thing [the flower that A has requested by pointing] from the standpoint of A. He perceives the thing as it may function in A's experience, instead of just egocentrically. Similarly, A in making the request conceives the thing not only in its direct relationship to himself, but as a thing capable of being grasped and handled by B. He sees the thing as it may function in B's experience.[36]

Dewey speaks here of something similar to what María Lugones calls "world-traveling," in which one attempts to understand others by understanding, as she says, *"what it is to be them and what it is to be ourselves in their eyes,"* rather than merely in one's own.[37] By world-traveling, one allows for a pluralistic world and a complex picture of how common meaning is forged out of, but does not necessarily eliminate, different perspectives and interests.

Philosophers, including Dewey, sometimes speak of communication and the creation of a common ground in the problematic language of, in Dewey's words, "put[ting] ourselves in the place of others."[38] This understanding of communication is troubling because it can imply a substitutability of you and your interests for me and mine, a substitution that would erase any differences between us. The type of traveling suggested by this understanding is the opposite of world-traveling as explained by Lugones and an anathema to the notion of transactional bodies as I conceive it. It is a traveling that seeks to enter into another's world to colonize it, rather than to understand and appreciate it on its own terms.

The problematic idea of substitutability suggested in some of Dewey's philosophy is mitigated somewhat by the larger quote of which the preceding fragment is a part. Dewey claims that if we are not merely to impose our own interests upon others, what is needed is for us "to put ourselves in the place of others, to see things from the standpoint of their purposes and values."[39] When understood as seeing things from the standpoint of others, putting oneself in the place of another is less likely to constitute an ethically solipsistic projection of one's interests onto another. To put oneself in the place of another might suggest instead, as Dewey says, to "rende[r] vivid the interests of others . . . [and] to give them the same weight as those which touch our own honor, purse, and power."[40] But while this sentiment is consonant with a world-traveling in which a person sees herself and another from the perspective of the other's world, it does not eliminate the substitutability implied by Dewey's description of communication as putting oneself in the place of others. To the extent that his understanding of communication implies a disregard for the particularities of others, Dewey's philosophy diverges from the account of hypothetical construction outlined here.

If world-traveling is to characterize a transactional notion of communication, it not only cannot colonize others, it also cannot be constituted by mere interaction. One way of misunderstanding Lugones's notion of world-traveling is to think of it as involving a person's traveling from one world to another without this movement transforming either the worlds or the people in them. On this conception, the people and the worlds in question are atomistic, like the ingredients of a tossed salad. They are separate and distinct, without having any constitutive impact upon one another. They are spheres from which one can hop back and forth, as it were, without any change to them or the people who inhabit them. In contrast to an atomistic conception of world-traveling, a transactional world-traveling should be thought of as a stew, in which the worlds and people involved blend together in such a way that each impacts and transforms the other. This stewlike blending does not involve a total collapse of one world into the other. Such a melting-pot model characterizes colonizing, not transactional travel. Understanding world-travel as a stew means that coming to see myself and another from her world has a constitutive effect on what and who my world and I are, as has her seeing herself and me from my world for her and her world.

Returning to the specific case of communication between my friend and me, a transactional conception of meaning in which my friend and I travel to each other's worlds to see each of us through the other's eyes means that I realize that I *am* haughty as well as overwhelmed and that he recognizes that he *is* aggressive as well as excited. This is so even though neither of us intends to be haughty or aggressive and even though it is difficult for each of us to identify ourselves in these ways. My understanding of each of us contributes to the meaning of our behavior and situation as much as his understanding does. As Judith Bradford and Crispin Sartwell have put the same point with respect to how one's voice is heard, "voices are relations of articulation and reception in social contexts; what will get understood is not up to me, or my listeners, but is made out of the interactions between them."[41] Because they are transactional, both my literal and figurative voices are not determined solely by my claim to feel overwhelmed. They are just as much determined by the reception of my behavior as haughty.

The situation of miscommunication between my friend and me is ill-construed as a matter of my getting my friend to realize what I intend. Using Merleau-Ponty's notions of intentionality and projection of meaning is precisely the wrong approach to take here. The situation is best seen as a matter of my recognizing that what is it to be me in my friend's eyes is for me to be haughty and that my haughtiness interferes with our communication. As Dewey would say, communication is for my friend and me "to anticipate together, it is to make a cross-reference which, when acted upon, brings about a partaking in a common, inclusive, undertaking."[42] Unless I am unconcerned about improving the communication between my friend and me, I should try to change the comportment of my body so that it is no longer haughty or overwhelmed, or at least no longer haughty or overwhelmed to the degree that it is off-putting to my friend.

This does not mean that my bodily gestures must become as vigorous as those of my friend to convey excitement at and interest in his ideas. My bodying will probably always be more reserved than is his. But it does mean changing the habitual way I transact with my world and enter into conversations with him out of consideration for him and his particularities, which led him to understand my bodying as haughty. Likewise, out of an acknowledgment of and respect for my understanding of him as aggressive, my friend is also led to change his bodily comportment, not so that he becomes as reserved as I am, but so that his gestures are less vigorous than they were. Thus the spiral of change in which my friend and I are involved means that the comportment of our bodies is made more similar. Transforming our bodies such that their habits are more consonant does not mean that the extremes of our bodying must be brought to the same point somewhere in the middle. Instead it means finding, through negotiations, different points for each of us on a continuum between the extremes—via body language as well as via spoken words—that accommodate each of our differences and provide for greater communication between us.

Focusing on the transactional circle involved in hypothetical construction enables the recognition that such a circle was already in play between my friend and me. Hypothetical construction makes explicit the transactional bodily communication that always already occurs between others and me, which I encounter prior to any conscious reflection upon it. Before we had even begun the conscious process of hypothetical construction and thus recognized the meaning circulating between our bodies, the meaning of my encounter with my friend was being constructed nonreflectively by our transactions. My understanding of him as hostile lead to his understanding of me as haughty, which lead to a bodily response on his part that only seemed to confirm my initial understanding of his aggressiveness, and so on. This misunderstanding of and miscommunication between us was a result of easily finding the familiar in the bodying of another through my communication with him. Hypothetical construction, which makes bodily communication explicit, is crucial to prevent the assumption of the familiar in another and thus the misunderstanding of him or her.

Human organisms are always selectively emphasizing aspects of the world as they transactionally work together to construct its meaning, but they need not do so through the manner of projective intentionality. *Contra* Merleau-Ponty, projective intentionality is not the fundamental mode of human being-in-the-world. It is merely one type of transaction with the world, a type that often is domineering and thus in need of change. By basing his account of intersubjectivity on the concept of projective intentionality, Merleau-Ponty undercuts, with a relationship of domination, the reciprocity between beings. When projective, I dominate others in that I eliminate what is particular, unique, or different about them by imposing my own familiar meaning upon him or her. In that case, communication becomes a sort of ventriloquism in which I place my "words" in the other's "mouth," which can happen in both bodily and verbal ways. When communication is only a covert form of ventriloquism, my intersubjective world turns out to be an ethically solipsistic one in which I only encounter my meanings and myself. On Merleau-Ponty's account, I risk eliminating others in my world, as well as the possibility for surprise by and wonder in the face of the world.[43]

To the question of how communication with others might occur, Merleau-Ponty's answers in his later work, like those in *The Phenomenology of Perception*, are promising and yet ultimately problematic because they are not connected to human existence in sufficiently concrete ways. In *The Visible and the Invisible*, Merleau-Ponty offers an account of intersubjectivity that suggests an understanding of bodies as dynamically co-constituted.[44] In the chapter titled "The Intertwining—The Chiasm," Merleau-Ponty has moved from the concretely phenomenological explanations of corporeal communication presented in *The Phenomenology of Perception* to an abstract account of the condition for the possibility of corporeal communication: the presence of the subject and its world for each other. They are present to one another because of what Merleau-Ponty calls "flesh," a type of being of which subject and object are articulations. Flesh is neither matter nor substance, but an "element" or "prototype" of "Being" that is "the formative medium of the object and the subject."[45] As Elizabeth Grosz explains it, flesh is "a single 'thing' folded back on itself," the "folding" of which gives birth to both subject and object and their interpenetration.[46] Thus the notion of flesh speaks of the intertwining of and exchange ("chiasm") between subject and object, which results in a fundamental ambiguity and possible reciprocity between them. As Merleau-Ponty's example of a person's right hand touching her left hand demonstrates, when clasping my hands together, each of my hands is both touching and being touched.[47] They are ambiguously subject and object at the same time, reversing their positions as subject-touching and object-touched. Merleau-Ponty qualifies his claim about reversibility, stating that it is never achieved in fact, but always slips away just as it is about to be realized. He insists this is not a failure, however, because we experience the transition from subject to object even if the "hinge" attaching them is hidden from us.[48]

The ambiguity, reversibility, and intertwining of subject and object described by Merleau-Ponty in *The Visible and the Invisible* appear to be helpful contributions to an account of how communication with another might be possible. These three notions attempt to bridge the gap between subject and object such that contact and communication between them can occur, without eradicating the differences between them by collapsing them into one another. Yet, because the notions of ambiguity, reversibility, and intertwining are not explored apart from an abstract notion of flesh that is never achieved in practice, Merleau-Ponty's later work does not provide an account of how actual communication between human beings can occur. Instead, it takes a transcendental approach, positing the conditions that must exist if communication is to be possible. The hinge about which Merleau-Ponty speaks is the flesh, which is to say that flesh is the common link that makes connection and communication between subject and object possible. Because a hinge is a third thing that joins two other, separate things, calling it hinge is less accurate than calling flesh the common fabric in which subject and object are differentiable threads.[49] Subject and object are ambiguous, reversible, and intertwined *because* they are part of a common being. In his later work, Merleau-Ponty thus answers the concrete question of how two bodily beings are different and yet can understand or commu-

nicate with one another with the abstract claim that behind their differences lies a sameness—the flesh—that they are.

To reply in this way is to answer the question of how one might create
a common point of understanding by asserting that, on some abstract level,
bodies already have one. This answer is no answer at all but a change of
the subject. Changing the subject is not problematic in and of itself, but it
is problematic in that the original subject is more relevant than the new one
to the issue of understanding and improving the lived experiences of human bodily communication. In addition, to the extent that this reply answers the question rather than changes the subject, it only seems to repeat
Merleau-Ponty's claim in *The Phenomenology of Perception* that one need not
strive for common ground with another because one already has a shared
commonality that guarantees communication. In this way and for all their
differences, the concepts of flesh, in Merleau-Ponty's later work, and the
anonymous body, in his earlier work, function in a similar manner.

Admittedly, the question Merleau-Ponty attempts to answer in his later
work is not the one I having been asking throughout this chapter. That
question—the concrete one of how particular beings with particular differences might participate in communication with one another that does not
overlay another's meaning and perspective with one's own—was the one he
addressed in *The Phenomenology of Perception,* albeit unsuccessfully. In his
later work, however, Merleau-Ponty no longer addresses human beings on
a concrete level. He moves to and remains with an abstract discussion about
being as such, as distinct from beings in particular. This means that, as
Gary Brent Madison claims, one should no longer "merely say—along with
intentional analysis—that subject and object do not exist independent of
each other . . . ; for if they exist together and are correlative, this can only
be because they are both derivative expressions of a more profound reality
that binds them together and which guarantees their cohesion as well as
their (relative) opposition."[50] With his abstraction away from lived experience and concrete bodily beings, Merleau-Ponty is no longer concerned
with how cohesion and opposition are managed on a practical level, which
means that it may seem unfair to criticize his later work for not providing
discussions of those matters.[51]

The fact that Merleau-Ponty does not discuss these matters in connection
with lived experience but instead remains at the level of abstract theory is,
however, precisely my concern with and criticism of his later work.[52] By
not returning to the concrete after moving to the abstract, Merleau-Ponty
does not address the possibility of building common ground for individual
beings. Instead he focuses on uncovering the common ground for human
being as such, saying very little about the varied and particular ways in

which actual human beings live and making little contribution to an understanding of how communication among human beings might actually occur. In asserting my preference for the concrete over the merely abstract, I am not claiming that theoretical abstractions are never important. After all, the account of transactional bodies presented in this book is theoretically abstract to the extent that it sketches a hypothesis of human bodily being as a contribution to a communitywide construction of the meaning of bodily existence. But it is important that abstract discussions not *remain* at the level of theory divorced from particular, concrete practices. Abstract theory eventually should be brought to bear upon the concrete specifics of bodily existence. A discussion of theory should not be merely for the sake of theory itself, but for the sake of creating conceptual tools that can be used to produce change in and improvement of people's lives. Merleau-Ponty's account of flesh in *The Visible and the Invisible* does not address the level of the concrete and, to the extent that the concept of the flesh can be used to do so, it assumes rather than explains organisms' common ground. For these reasons, the account offered in that work fails to provide satisfactory answers about how communication without domination might occur.

In spite of this failure, the concept of ambiguity as presented in *The Visible and the Invisible* is promising for an account of how communication might be possible, but only if detached from the concept of the flesh that grounds it. I am less enthusiastic about the concept of reversibility because it seems to entail the substitutability and interchangeability of bodily beings, which risks denying the particularities of corporeal existence. I also am hesitant about the notion of intertwining because of the atomism implied by the idea of two separate things coming to be twisted or woven together. What the ambiguity of human existence might mean apart from the abstractions of flesh has not been shown by Merleau-Ponty. To construct a concrete meaning for it would involve the down-to-earth, practical work of talking about how particular beings transact and how they might change the ways they transact, a project to which the notion of hypothetical construction is meant to contribute.

As a final note on this subject, I revisit the example of Schneider's alleged sexual inertia, redescribing it as an encounter in which the two people were engaged in a nonreflective mode of transaction that is more open to others rather than the mode of encounter allowed by an account of projective intentionality. Doing so demonstrates that it is not necessarily the case that the pattern of behavior presented in the example is an instance of a man's failure to follow through "properly" in a sexual situation. Instead, the situation might be one in which not just a man, but a man *and* his partner were nonreflectively constructing the meaning of the encounter. As an event dynamically co-constituted in a nondomineering way, the encounter could have resulted in orgasm for the man, but it did not have to do so because his partner's desires and needs also were an important component of the encounter. In the encounter, the man's behavior, and perhaps his words, proposed his own orgasm as a possible meaningful outcome of the sexual encounter. The nonverbal hypothesis was then open for revision based on his partner's hypothesis, probably nonverbal but possibly verbal, about what the encounter might become. Because his partner's experience was an important part of the ultimate meaning of the encounter, a vanishing erection did not signal a "half-fulfilled desire," but rather indicated a desire that *had* been satisfied in the mutual pleasure found in the partner's orgasm. In that case, the result of the sexual encounter was not a failure of projection on the part of the man, but a success in constructing a meaningful situation on the part of *both* parties involved.

My redescription of Schneider's sexual encounter is not intended to discuss whether or not Schneider in particular is dysfunctional. I trust that he is. My point is directed instead at Merleau-Ponty's phenomenology, which because of its account of projective human existence, tends to instruct his readers to understand as failures behaviors in which one does not vigorously project one's intentions on the world. Merleau-Ponty understands a body with a once-erect-now-deflating penis that has not experienced orgasm as ontologically inadequate and a sexual encounter between a man and a woman as meaningful only if the man has an orgasm. But encounters of this sort need not count as failures. In some situations, they might be seen as successful in that the two parties involved constructed the meaning of the encounter in a mutually satisfying way. Of course, we have no particular reason to believe that Schneider and his lover were engaged in an encounter like the one I have just portrayed. But we should not accept Merleau-Ponty's claim that projective intentionality is an appropriate or desirable normative standard by which to measure bodily behavior and activity. Projection is instead a manner of transacting with the world that risks making one oblivious to others.[53]

In contrast to projective intentionality, an understanding of human being-in-the-world as transactional allows room for surprise in the world by finding something other than one's own, familiar intentions and interests. Of course, the reverse of surprise is often the disturbing and disorienting. To really listen, both consciously and nonreflectively, to another person in one's transactions with her is to subject oneself to a remaking of the self that cannot always be predicted or guided into familiar channels.[54] By participating in dialogue with another rather than a monologue with myself, I often not only experience surprise and wonder at her differences but also find myself and my understandings of the world disrupted and challenged. Because it upsets the habits with which I am comfortable, such an experience can be painful. Because projective intentionality discourages challenge and disruption, it might make transaction and hypothetical construction seem unattractive alternatives, but only if what I seek is a world solely of my own making, a world in which growth and change are stunted. If what is sought instead is a world that is rich with the plurality and particularities of others and in which others might transform me through their transactions with me, then a transactional phenomenology can be welcomed for the wonder and challenge that it brings.

For all of the strengths of Merleau-Ponty's phenomenology, it cannot overcome the significant problem of its fundamental basis in projection. Even though Merleau-Ponty's intentional subject is bodily and even though Merleau-Ponty's goal is to provide an account of corporeal intersubjectivity, he cannot avoid completely the ethical solipsism and atomism that are the legacy of Descartes's "I" and Husserl's transcendental ego. But the problems with Merleau-Ponty's work do not eliminate the possibility of a fruitful relationship between feminism and phenomenology. Feminists can and should benefit from a phenomenological focus on the situated, habitual, lived experience of human corporeal existence, but such a focus need not and should not include the concepts of an anonymous body or projective intentionality. Instead of starting with an intentional ego and trying to develop an account of intersubjectivity out of it, a phenomenological account of bodily existence needs to begin with the notion of organism and environment as transactionally constituted. Beginning in that way can lead to an account of the situated, habitual, lived experiences of human bodying, including how nondominating communication and meaning-creation might be possible, an account that does not invoke projective intentionality. It also can help people understand how they might transform their habitual ways of transacting with the world when they are disrespectful or destructive of others.

Reconfiguring Gender
Habit, Bodies, and Cultural Change

Because transaction is a dynamic, ongoing process, the issue of transformation is central to the notion of transactional bodies. Transaction does not necessarily entail significant alteration of personal habits or cultural customs. It may result in monotonous change, in which the circle of transaction reinforces and strengthens, rather than undercuts, habit and custom. While transaction thus offers no guarantees regarding change, it includes the possibility of significant transformation and helps explain how such transformation might occur. To explore how the structures of individual habit and cultural meaning, particularly those involving gender, might be changed, I want to draw together Dewey's understanding of habit with Judith Butler's notion of performativity, as presented in *Gender Trouble*.[1] Habit is an organism's constitutive predisposition to transact with the world in particular ways, and performativity is the process of repetitive activity that constitutively stylizes one's being. Together, these ideas provide powerful tools with which to understand the composition and transformation of gender.

The combination of habit and performativity is felicitous because there are hints in Butler's later work that she wants to push her notion of performativity beyond the linguistic toward the social, a development that the notion of habit can greatly assist.[2] I say "hints" only because most of Butler's work after *Gender Trouble* addresses performativity in the relatively narrow terms of language and speech acts. Language did not occupy a place of privilege when Butler introduced the concept of performativity in her earlier work. Her writings subsequent to *Gender Trouble*, however, increasingly connect performativity to and examine it in particular within the exclusive context of linguistic performances. Most recently, Butler's emphasis on the linguistic has taken the form of arguing that performativity is an activity in which the distinction between the linguistic and the social cannot be made.[3] For this reason, my claim that Butler pushes the concept of performativity beyond the linguistic to the social in her later work may appear to posit a dualism between the linguistic and social that Butler rejects.

I agree with Butler that linguistic performances are significant; indeed the concept of habit is not antithetical to the linguistic. I also agree that no essential or absolute distinction should be posited between the linguistic and the social. Something important is lost, however, if one limits the notion of performativity to the linguistic or abolishes all distinction between linguistic and social performatives such that the social cannot be addressed apart from the linguistic. This is not to establish a dualism between the social and the linguistic as if the two were ingredients in a tossed salad. Rather it is to refuse to melt the two together completely such that they are indistinguishable. In particular situations and for specific purposes, making a distinction between the social and the linguistic can be very helpful for understanding and improving the world; being able to distinguish the nonlinguistic from the linguistic often is important for attending to the "had," lived aspects of experience that are ambiguous and thus "overflow" the words one uses to describe them.[4] By conceiving of performativity along the lines of habit, the richness of Butler's concept of performativity can be retained and reworked such that it continues to shed light on the nonlinguistic aspects of corporeal existence.

As feminists have argued, the need to rethink contemporary conceptions of gender, and the notions of sex and sexuality that transact with them, is urgent.[5] One reason for this urgency is that current categories of sex and gender are extremely rigid: each member of the binary pair is defined in sharp opposition to the other. As a biological designation, one's sex is either male or female. Ambiguity of sex is disallowed, even to the point of surgically "correcting" bodies whose physical attributes are indeterminate. Corresponding to and allegedly following from one's sex are one's gender and sexuality: biological males are to be men, who are to sexually desire biological females only. In turn, biological females are to be women who sexually desire only men. Thus, in many contemporary cultures, the binary structures of sex and gender are interdependent with that of (hetero)sexuality: to be a male/man or a female/woman is to sexually desire only a person who is located on the other side of the sex/gender binary. To challenge the rigid confines of one's gender is therefore to commit gender treachery by challenging the hegemony of all three binaries of sex, (hetero)sexuality, and gender. It is to risk all the psychological, physical, emotional, financial, and other punishments that are meted out to gender traitors in society. Of course, many do successfully challenge those confines, demonstrating that, in the lives of at least some individuals, the gender binary as lived is looser than its ideal admits.[6] Yet even so, the ideal of the binary remains rigid and powerful enough to make life very dangerous for those who attempt to blur its boundaries.

The contingency of gender binarism becomes particularly visible when one remembers that other peoples at other times have had very different gender configurations. In *The Use of Pleasure*, volume 2 of *The History of Sexuality*, Michel Foucault demonstrates that masculinity in early Greek society was not dependent upon the gender of one's sexual partner, thus revealing how erotic behavior between males was problematized then in very different ways than it is now.[7] The *berdache* tradition of many pre–twentieth–century Native American tribes was part of a nonbinary gender system in which a third gender category gave anatomical males the option of assuming neither a masculine nor a feminine role in tribal society. And, arguably, a fourth gender category existed for many pre-twentieth–century Native American tribes: the "amazon" or "manly-hearted woman," who was an anatomical female whose social role combined traditionally feminine and masculine characteristics.[8]

Examples such as these help demonstrate that contemporary configurations of gender are not characterized by an ahistorical necessity. The contingency of gender categories should not be taken to imply, however, that these categories are arbitrary or that they can be quickly or easily changed. One cannot simply shed one's current gender and pick up a new one, such as that of the *berdache* or manly-hearted woman, at will. "A construction is, after all, not the same as an artifice," as Butler has reminded feminists.[9] Gender configuration, as well as the configuration of other aspects of identity such as race and sexuality, is constitutive of subjectivity in a way that is crucial to identity. As Butler puts it, a person's gender constitutes a "domain of constraints without which a certain living and desiring being cannot make its way," without which she would not be the being that she is.[10]

Dewey's analysis of the concept of structure can help us understand Butler's claim that gender constitutes a *productive*, rather than merely repressive, "domain of constraints." Using the example of a house, Dewey explains,

> A house has a structure; in comparison with the disintegration and collapse that would occur without its presence, this structure is fixed. Yet it is not something external to which the changes involved in building and using the house have to submit. It is rather an arrangement of changing events such that properties which change slowly, limit and direct a series of quick changes and give

them an order which they do not otherwise possess. . . . Structure is what makes construction possible and cannot be discovered or defined except in some realized construction, construction being, of course, an evident order of changes.[11]

The structure of a house is not something the house submits to; rather it is what allows the house to effectively be what it is. Likewise, the cultural constructs that structure us *are* us. While Dewey might be more inclined to discuss the particular cultural constructs of class or ethnicity in conjunction with his example of a house, his analyses of structure are illuminative of gender as well. As is the case for all cultural constructs on Dewey's terms, gender is not some external, accidental characteristic overlaying the allegedly internal, essential, nongendered core of ourselves. It instead is one of the ways in and through which we arrange and are arranged as the selves that we are. Relatively, but not absolutely fixed, one's gender constitutes one of, but not the only, key arrangements of the changing events that are one's self.

In addition to presenting the general idea that gender is a domain of constraints that structures existence, Dewey's emphasis on habit can help us understand the particular relationship between bodies and gender and thus the ways in which gender configures one's bodying.[12] One's habits constitute one's way of being and knowing the world and, as such, provide one with efficacy and agency in it. To acquire a new habit is a positive accomplishment. It is to grasp a new significance and to establish a new form of power in and through one's bodying. To incorporate a new habit is for one's body to learn a new way of comporting itself, expanding, in new directions, the power and efficacy one has in the world.

To take just one possible example of the way in which habits provide agency and will, when I have acquired the habit of driving a car with a standard transmission, the knowledge provided by that habit composes my bodying. When I downshift the engine from fifth to fourth gear, my hand and arm know where to move the gear shift so that I indeed shift into the fourth, and not the second, gear. Likewise, my feet and legs know how to operate the clutch and the accelerator pedals so that I neither "peel out" nor stall out when starting forth in first gear. I do all of these things when driving *not* by consciously calculating the distance between the fifth and the fourth and second gears, nor by mentally judging the "depth" of the clutch relative to that of the accelerator. I cannot consciously think the proper way of driving a standard transmission automobile, as I have just done, until my bodying knows how to do so. As Dewey claims, "[o]rdinary psychology reverses the actual state of affairs. . . . [*Contra* ordinary psychology,] [t]he act must come before the thought, and a habit before an ability to evoke the thought at will."[13] It is true that driving can occur by means of mental calculation of the manipulation of gears, clutch, and accelerator. This is done, for example, when learning to drive a car, as compensation for a lack of bodily knowledge of driving. In such a case, I do not so much evoke the thought of how to drive the car as I borrow it from the driving instructor who already possesses bodily knowledge of driving. *I* can only evoke the thought of how to drive and can only be said to know how to drive the car when I no longer make such mental calculations, that is, when my driving knowledge has become sedimented within my bodily activities.

A similar analysis can be made of the activity of walking in high heels. I only know how to walk in high heels once I do not have to attempt to calculate how to place my foot on the ground such that it does not wobble and slip off to the side of my shoe. Such conscious attention paid to the position of my shoes and feet in relation to the floor and the rest of my body is a poor substitute for the nonreflective "feel" of how to balance myself squarely and smoothly on a small, pointy platform in an "automatic" way. Once I have this sort of bodily knowledge, conscious focus on being and remaining on high heels is unnecessary to the success of my walking on them.

An example of walking in high heels introduces the gendered quality of some habits, an issue that I will further address subsequently. Before doing so, it is important to note why Dewey's particular illumination of the role of habit is crucial to a feminist understanding of the gendering of human bodies, and thus of human selves. Dewey develops an explicit account not only of the formation but also of the possible transformation of individual habit. The explicit and strong emphasis on improvement, rather than mere description, in Dewey's understanding of habit is one reason why it attends more effectively to the transaction between body and world than does the account of habit provided by Merleau-Ponty's phenomenology. Equally significant to Dewey's emphasis on transformation of habit is his detailed analysis of the constitutive role that one's environments play in the formation and remaking of habit. For Dewey, because individual habits are formed under conditions set by cultural configurations that precede the individual, cultural customs delimit the particular gendered and other options available to individuals and thus tend to reproduce themselves through individuals' habits. Many times and in many different ways, the world, in its response to one's engagement with it, "instructs" one on "proper" habit formation. Through bodily habits, one incorporates the gender and other constructs of one's culture. The constructs that prevail within the culture(s) in which I am anchored will inform the habits that I develop, that is, the person that I become.

Once we acknowledge the connection between cultural constructs and the formation of bodily habits, we can begin to illuminate the ways that gender informs bodily habits and activities. I am not anchored in my world as a generic person; I am anchored in it as a white, middle-class, Southwestern-raised woman. The ways in which I transact with the world are likely to be very different from those of a man. I have learned to comport my bodying—that is, myself—as a woman is "supposed" to do. This comportment is not some sort of act that I put on, nor is it, for the most part, something that I consciously try to do. I know how to be a woman because and to the extent that I can effortlessly, without thinking, do the things that a woman would do in the ways that a woman would do them. That is, I know how to be a woman because of the bodily habits that I am.

My gendered bodily habits can be seen in my gestures, which express my bodily style. My style, which emerges from and appears as the gestures that I make, is not some sort of veneer that is layered over my body. Rather it is a fundamental characterization of bodily comportment and activity itself. For this reason, as Dewey claims, "[a] man may give himself away in a look or gesture."[14] The man who is revealed through his gestures, however, is not a genderless person, as the false neutrality of Dewey's use of "man" suggests. As entailed by Dewey's own position on the connection between cultural constructs and individual bodily habits, the existence of gender constructs means that the gendered bodily gestures and style of an inhabitant of a culture often mark him or her in very gender-particular ways. The man of whom Dewey speaks gives himself away *as a man*. Likewise, my gestures and style are part of my fundamental bodily comportment, which means that they constitute, in large part, my existence *as a woman*.

An example of the gendered aspect of bodily comportment is found in the fact that, as many middle-class women do, I tend to smile often when I converse with others.[15] While not necessarily or always my conscious intent, such a facial gesture has the effect of presenting myself as a non-threatening person and of smoothing over any difficulties between my interlocutor and me. Frequent, nonconscious smiling is a bodily habit that is part of the style of who I am. Because of the constitutive role of habit in the self, to try to stylize my bodily gestures and comportment such that they exclude frequent smiling requires a deliberate, conscious effort that feels uncomfortable and produces results that seem "unnatural." Through the incorporation of the bodily habit of frequent smiling, as well as other habits, developed in and through my cultural lessons on what it is to be a woman, my life achieves gender-sedimentation, and my habits compose a familiar and "natural" part of my bodily comportment.

Understanding that bodily habits are constitutive of gendered selves, we are now prepared to confront the issue of gender binarism and ask how gender categories might be transformed. The constitutive role of habit means that one's response to the problem of rigid gender categories should *not* be a pronouncement that all cultural structure is oppressive and thus in need of elimination so that one can be "free." As Dewey argues,

> [t]here can be no greater mistake . . . than to treat [freedom from restriction] as an end in itself. . . . For freedom from restriction, the negative side [of freedom], is to be prized only as a means to a freedom which is power: power to frame purposes, to judge wisely, to evaluate desires by the consequences which will result from acting upon them; power to select and order means to carry chosen ends into operation.[16]

What Dewey in 1938 called a great mistake is similar to what Foucault attacked roughly forty years later as the repressive hypothesis: the belief or assumption that freedom is found in the absence of all power and limitation.[17] To act according to this belief by seeking the elimination of all structure is to assume that the solution to a culture's problems regarding gender is to be found in the elimination of all power structures and the habits they help produce. But release from all structures of habit, even if such a thing were possible, would not free one then to be whatever one wants. It would dissolve one into a being with no capacity for or agency to effect transformation and change. This would effectively eliminate, not increase, freedom.

Because freedom is freedom *to* as much, if not more than, freedom *from*, one can only find freedom in and through some sort of structure.[18] As Dewey argues, "[t]o view institutions as enemies of freedom, and all conventions as slaveries, is to deny the only means by which positive freedom in action can be secured."[19] The habitual structures of my life are the means by which I transact with my world, not mere obstacles to that process. Put another way, working with the notion of freedom as found in and through structure, we can say that precisely in order to free ourselves from the current ways in which we are gendered, we should try to change *how* we are gendered. In turn, changing how we are gendered means *replacing*, rather than attempting to jettison entirely, as if we could, our current gendered constructs and habits. As Foucault states, the goal is to "open up the space of freedom understood as a space of concrete freedom, i.e., of possible transformation."[20]

To acknowledge the corporeality of the self is to recognize that there *is no* elimination of habit, per se, only the replacement of some habits with others.[21] Because there is no self apart from the habits that structure it, to eliminate old habits without creating new ones is to ensure that the old habits return. The same can be said on a larger scale for cultures and their particular styles. To effectively tackle problems of gender, one must realize that one is never in some sort of place "outside" of all habit and structure. In the case of habit, there is no such thing as a vacuum. To fail to realize this is to risk reinforcing old habits and customs because to eliminate them without creating new ones is to ensure that only the old habits and customs are available to fill their own place.[22]

How then might one replace current gendered habits with new ones, especially given the force of sedimentation, which seems to make change improbable? And, in addition, how might it be possible to alter gendered habits given the vicious circle that an account of transaction apparently establishes between habit and cultural constructs? If habits form and are formed by a culture's gender constructs, habit and custom might seem to work only to maintain the legitimacy of each other. Each can appear merely to reflect the other on a more general or individual scale and allow for no variation.

Dewey's notion of the plasticity of the self begins to answer the question concerning the circle between individual habit and cultural construct. What is frequently emphasized in the relationship between self and society is solely the society's ability to mold the self. What often is overlooked is the reciprocal ability of the self to transform its environment. As Dewey argues, "[the self] seems putty to be molded according to current designs. That plasticity also means power to change prevailing custom is [too often] ignored."[23] While one's culture does indeed contribute to the formation of one's habits and thus oneself, this process does not transform the once-malleable self into a completely fixed and hardened being. Such a model of the relationship between self and its culture assumes that prevailing custom molds one once and then never influences one again, as if the self's store of plasticity were somehow exhausted by its initial formation. As an organism susceptible to the influence of its cultural and other environments, the self as well as its habits are continually—if slightly, slowly, and sometimes monotonously—being made and remade in their transactions with their surroundings. In the disruption and remaking of the current self by its environment lies the self's power to remake its culture. The self's ongoing plasticity means the ongoing transformation of the self and thus of the culture of which it is a part.

Because of the plasticity of the self, shifts can occur in the transactions between self and world, making it possible for their relationship to be more like a changing spiral than a repetitive circle. In a similar way, as analyzed by Judith Butler in *Gender Trouble*, the performative nature of the self disrupts the circularity of gender between individual and environment.[24] For Butler, gender is not a stable identity that produces gendered effects. Rather "a *stylized repetition of acts*" produces the effects of gender, which is then hypostatized as the acts' causal origin.[25] One's gendered attributes do not express an interior essence, nor do they map onto a given biological sex. Instead, gendered attributes and sexed bodies are the performances of gender that constitute gender and sex themselves. The performativity of gender does not mean that gender can be taken up and discarded at will. As Butler makes explicit in *Bodies That Matter*, "[s]uch a willful and instrumental subject, one who decides *on* its gender, is clearly not its gender from the start and fails to realize that its existence is already decided *by* gender."[26] Performativity is not a decision that one makes, nor is it a discrete or singular act. In Butler's words, it is "neither free play nor theatrical self-presentation; nor can it be simply equated with performance [as commonly conceived]."[27] Rather it is the repetition of cultural norms, a repetition that is made possible by plasticity and that constitutes the very being that one is. It is a reiteration that is *not* chosen or performed by a subject that pre-exists the performance; instead, it is the constraint and regularization that forms one as subject.[28]

Reading performativity as an instance of habit illuminates Butler's claim that performances constitute bodily selves in a thoroughgoing way. Understanding performativity in terms of habit illustrates why gender is not something to be donned and discarded at will, a point on which Butler's *Gender Trouble* was sometimes misunderstood and which *Bodies That Matter* seeks to make clear.[29] Like habit, the performativity of gender means that one is constituted through the regular patterns of activity that stylize one's being in accord with cultural normative standards. In the everyday ways in which one transacts with the world, one repeats and performs gender norms. Our performances are familiar and comfortable to us because they *are* us. Dewey's earlier analogy with the structure of the house is instructive once again. Just as the structure of a house makes it the particular house that it is, one's gendered performances constrain one to be the particular self that one is. In addition, as Dewey does in the case of habit, Butler makes clear that the performativity of gender not only constrains one to be the subject that one is. Performativity is also what provides one agency as a subject. Or, in Butler's words, the ritualized repetition that constitutes gender is "the matrix through which all willing first becomes possible, its enabling cultural condition."[30] While the structure of a house constrains it to be the particular house that it is, it also is the condition for the possibility of its effectiveness as a house. It is what allows it to provide shelter, be aesthetically pleasing, and so on. Likewise, while cultural norms constrain one's performances of gender, producing the particular gendered subject that one is, these constraints are simultaneously the very tools by which effective resistance to hegemonic norms is made possible.

Understanding habit as will also illuminates Butler's often misunderstood claims about agency and change via the performative body. Butler's notion of gender performativity transforms agency from a voluntaristic willing to a reiterative practice, one that is embedded in, not external to, the cultural situations and conditions in which it finds itself.[31] As she tells us, "construction [of our subjectivity] is not opposed to agency; it is the necessary scene of agency, the very terms in which agency is articulated and becomes culturally intelligible."[32] Agency is found in variations of the gender performances that one is constrained to repeat. It is only within the field of cultural norms that subversion of them becomes possible.[33] Change of the prevailing cultural norms that inform bodily habits and gender performativity can come only through the transformation of those norms that takes place through their reiteration. Agency and the change that it can provide are located in subversive repetition, which does not mean deciding *whether* to engage in gender performativity but rather deciding *how* to perform one's gender. In Butler's words,

> [t]o enter into the repetitive practices of this terrain of signification is not a choice, for the 'I' that might enter is always already inside. . . . [Thus,] the task is not whether to repeat, but how to repeat or, indeed to repeat and, through a radical proliferation of gender, *to displace* the very gender norms that enable the repetition itself.[34]

The gendered performances that a culture constrains one to be are not mere constraints. As Butler explains with a very pragmatist-sounding metaphor, they are also the tools with which one might tinker with the culture that has enabled one's use of these tools.[35] By varying the stylization of one's performances and habits, one often subverts, many times unintentionally, the cultural norms that are materialized in them. Butler's analyses of drag demonstrate an extreme version of the subversive variation found in miming, but the main point of them is that we all are in drag, in some metaphorical but significant sense, as we mime the gender ideals that exist only in our appropriation of them. Butler calls this subversive process of reiteration "*working the weakness in the norm*," the weakness of all norms being located precisely in their need for reiteration to exist.[36]

This work has the goal, not of increasing the number of genders—as if one's gender trouble would be over if one only had three or four gender categories as did early Native American societies—but of exposing the failure of gender norms' ability to ever fully uphold their own ideals.[37]

Understood as habit, Butler's concept of gender as performativity explains why the circle between culture and habit is not necessarily vicious. The iterability of gender, as well as of other bodily habits, made possible by one's corporeal plasticity, holds open the possibility of bodying and performing those habits differently. The incorporation of cultural gender constructs means that one can reconfigure one's culture in and through the ways one transactionally bodies it. Each of us alters, however slightly, the grooves engrained in our selves when we retrace them through our habitual actions. Thus, to acknowledge the importance of habit and the role of performativity as that which structures one's gender and sexuality is *not* to claim that one cannot change the ways in and by which one is structured. One can and should see gender binarism as powerfully real in one's life *and* as refashionable because it is not an essential given.

Because of the sedimentation of habit and the comfortable familiarity that accompanies it, however, we might wonder how likely it is that a meaningfully different performance be enacted or a significantly different regrooving be produced.[38] Granted, as Butler believes and I would agree, no performance can ever fully embody the normative ideal to which it aspires. But given the powerful ability that even imperfect or inadequate performances have to lock people into fairly rigid gender roles, more explanation is needed of how the transformation of gender via performativity might occur. We must explore how we might loosen the sedimentation of our habits and performances and combat what Dewey has called the "social arterial sclerosis" that endangers both societal and individual "health."[39]

Both Butler and Dewey ultimately suggest ways of doing so, although Butler wavers at points on whether she believes that sedimentation of habits and performances actually occurs. In *Excitable Speech*, Butler discusses performativity and sedimentation in conjunction with Pierre Bourdieu's concept of *habitus*.[40] While *habitus* is not identical to Dewey's notion of habit, the two concepts bear enough similarities for Butler's comments about *habitus* to be helpful in understanding the problem of the sedimentation of habit. Butler's critique of Bourdieu's *habitus* blends together two somewhat contradictory accounts of how the transformation of sedimented habits might occur. The first denies, in effect, that sedimented habits can change, arguing that the reason that some habits can be transformed is that they never fully "take" in the first place. The second addresses the concern about sedimentation more directly, claiming that sedimented performances can be transformed by being enacted in different contexts than the ones in which they were formed. This second suggestion, which is only briefly sketched by Butler, although it is the more fruitful of the two, complements the more thorough account of the possibility for change provided by Dewey's work.

At the close of *Excitable Speech*, Butler explicitly states her goal of "think[ing] through the logic of iterability as a *social* logic" in particular.[41] Discussing Bourdieu's account "of how norms become embodied, suggesting that they craft and cultivate the *habitus* of the body, the cultural style of gesture and bearing," Butler makes clear that she appreciates Bourdieu's work because its theory of bodily knowingness is social.[42] But she criticizes Bourdieu for not relating his theory of the body to performativity. Because he allegedly does not recognize the iterability of *habitus*, his account emphasizes the formation of *habitus* at the expense of its possible transformation. The result, according to Butler, is a conservative account of embodied norms in which bodies' gestures, practices, and utterances are fixed in advance by those norms in such a way that they cannot effect their transformation.[43]

Butler's concern in her discussion of Bourdieu is not with the notion of *habitus*, per se. She does not object to understanding the formation of bodily habits and practices (namely speech acts, which are the focus of *Excitable Speech*) in conjunction with cultural norms. Rather, Butler worries that Bourdieu's particular account of *habitus* casts social institutions as static and thus fails to recognize how nonconventional utterances might cause social institutions to undergo transformation. As understood by Butler, Bourdieu claims that unconventional utterances, which are instances of habit and performativity, merely highlight the social conditions that determine which utterances are conventional and which are not. They bring to light the power of social norms that usually remains "invisible," but they do not serve as occasions in which what counts as legitimate or conventional might be refigured.

In opposition to Bourdieu, Butler asserts that the *habitus* is not fully sedimented. She agrees with Bourdieu that "[i]nterpellations that 'hail' a subject into being, that is, social performatives that are ritualized and sedimented through time, are central to the very process of subject-formation as well as the embodied, participatory *habitus*."[44] Butler insists, however, that not all interpellations succeed. Some fail, which is to say that some of the social performances that constitute people via their habits fail to do so fully. In that failure, resistance to and transformation of social norms is possible. By misunderstanding the meaning of and the possibilities generated by the failure of unconventional utterances, Bourdieu allegedly misses or suppresses the excess to the process of subject formation described by the notion of *habitus*. *Contra* Bourdieu, Butler claims that the excess of the speaking body to interpellation "remains uncontained by any of its acts of speech."[45]

Here is the first way in which Butler can be read as responding to the concern about sedimentation, a way that complements her position on materiality in *Bodies That Matter*. In that work, Butler claims, "[t]hat this re-iteration [of norms] is necessary is a sign that materialization is never quite complete, that bodies never quite comply with the norms by which their materialization is impelled."[46] Likewise, in *Excitable Speech* and in her more recent "Performativity's Social Magic," Butler argues that social transformation is possible because at least some habits are not fully fixed by social performatives, which are equated to interpellation by Butler and which are equivalent to cultural constructs in my terms.[47] There is a bodily excess or remainder to social performatives that is the site for the possibility of transformation. Put another way, there is an excess to bodily habit that remains uncontained by those habits and thus that can break up the sedimentation of habit, derailing habits from their familiar grooves. Bourdieu's account is seen as problematic by Butler because it allegedly ignores or overlooks this excess and thus casts bodily gestures and activities as effectively determined by the social *habitus*.

Whether or not Butler is right about Bourdieu's notion of *habitus* is not my concern here. In either case, Butler's charge that *habitus* is nothing but a force and effect of social determinism does not apply to habit understood as an aspect of transactional bodies. I will demonstrate why this is so after discussing Butler's solutions to the problem of the sedimentation of habit. Her first solution is troubling for several reasons. To begin, the notion of a bodily excess that escapes habituation raises more questions than it answers. Explaining what bodily excess is and how it performs the work of disruption of social performatives, Butler claims that "[n]o act of speech can fully control or determine the rhetorical effects of the body which speaks."[48] This suggests that the rhetorical effects of the tone of voice, facial expressions, and bodily posture used when speaking are not determined by and thus can challenge what one says, a claim with which I would agree. But this claim, if indeed one that Butler would endorse, does not yet explain how a body exceeds the *social norms* that form it, including its tones, gestures, and postures, even though it may explain how a body exceeds its literal acts of speaking. Literal acts of speaking should not be simply equated with the broader category of social norms even though social norms may be an important way in which particular ways of speaking are enforced. To explain how bodies exceed their literal acts of speaking is not yet to explain how bodies exceed the standards imposed by their social environments.

Because Butler says little about what the "rhetorical effects" of bodies are, I cannot be certain that my reading of this phrase as tone of voice, facial expressions, and bodily posture captures what she intends by the term "bodily excess." Without some sort of explanation of what bodily excess is, Butler's appeal to it is rather vague and empty. Instead of clarifying how the body escapes the effective formation by social norms, the claim of the existence of bodily excess merely insists that such escape does and must occur. Or, if not a bald insistence of this sort, the notion of bodily excess appears to work as a transcendental, rather than as a concrete, explanation of how resistance can happen. As a transcendental notion, bodily excess would be a necessary condition for the possibility of resistance to social norms, but not itself part of the social order, a condition that must be posited for such resistance to take place. In that case, the idea of bodily excess would not be very different from the notion of a pre- or nondiscursive body to which Butler usually and rightly refuses to appeal.[49]

A different way of reading bodily excess would be to understand it as what Dewey calls impulses. Impulses are the "raw" bodily energies that are organized by habit. As loose and undirected, impulses can provide the impetus for change by disrupting established habits. For these reasons, impulses might be seen as instances of the bodily excess of which Butler speaks, the bodily energies that are excessive to habits and thus can serve as agencies of deviation and transformation. However, because impulses are chaotic and ineffectual apart from their organization in habits, the concept of impulse cannot be used to support Butler's appeal to bodily excess. Impulse and habit are not set apart from one another such that impulse effectively functions separately from habit. Habit does not organize impulses understood as distinct from habit. That is, habit is not an agent doing something to something separate from it called impulse. Habit, instead, *is* the organization of impulses themselves. For that reason, even though one legitimately may make a functional distinction between impulse and habit in some contexts, impulse cannot be appealed to as excessive of bodily habits in any substantive way. The disruption of sedimented habits must occur in some other way than by mere appeal to bodily excess in the form of impulse.

Butler's first solution to the problem of sedimentation effectively denies that transformation of sedimented habits can occur. On this first account, bodily excess ensures that habits and social performatives never fully sediment, which is why they can be disrupted. The implication of this claim is that if and once fully sedimented, habits and social performatives cannot be transformed. Of course, many individual habits and cultural constructs *are* fairly well sedimented. On Butler's first answer, one would have no alternative but to give up on the possibility of ever changing them. Butler is right that not all habits are deeply grooved in the way that she fears Bourdieu makes them out to be and that transformation can take place because some habits are still fairly plastic. But we also need a way of understanding how we might transform habits that are no longer fluid. Must we declare these kinds of habits hopelessly stuck and incapable of change?

Butler's second solution to the problem of sedimentation suggests not. I distinguish her second answer from the first although Butler blends the two together. Butler's second solution emerges as she explains that, when objecting to the allegedly static account of *habitus* provided by Bourdieu, she does not make the opposite claim that that all unconventional utterances necessarily break with social norms. This extreme claim, which is what Butler takes Jacques Derrida to be putting forth with his account of iterability, holds that the risk of failure is an inherent structural feature of any and all linguistic marks.[50] As Butler reads him, Derrida holds that failure is a condition of the possibility of utterances' iterability. Butler acknowledges that this position might be seen as attractive because, unlike that of Bourdieu, it allows one to think of performativity and the failure of speech acts in connection with transformation. And, indeed, the accounts of performativity and materialization provided in *Gender Trouble* and *Bodies That Matter* at times suggest that such failure is an intrinsic feature of iterability. Again in *Bodies That Matter*, Butler writes: "[t]hat this reiteration [of norms] is necessary is a sign that materialization is never quite complete, that bodies never quite comply with the norms by which their materialization is impelled."[51] But Butler rightly claims in *Excitable Speech*, perhaps against her own earlier work, that it is not the case "that the speech act, by virtue of its internal powers, breaks with every context from which it emerges."[52] Because a position such as Derrida's allegedly abstracts away from social operations of speech acts when it declares that all utterances fail to fully constitute their subjects, it cannot explain how some utterances have constitutive force. Nor can it enable one to analyze and understand which ones fail and why. Although for different reasons, Butler thus charges Derrida with the same failure to provide an account of iterability as social as she charges Bourdieu.

In contrast to Derrida's alleged abstraction of iterability from the social, Butler's own position in *Excitable Speech* locates the transformative power of performativity in its ability to function in contexts different from that in which it originated. It is not that all speech acts fail as a condition of their possibility, but rather that they can fail in productive, transformative ways when uttered in contexts in which they do not "properly" belong. In the performance of some habits in different contexts, those contexts and the social norms that govern them can begin to shift such that they start to take on new forms and new meanings. This is Butler's second way, and the way that Bourdieu allegedly misses, of understanding how performativity is excessive. Habits need not fix one into sedimented social positions governed by fixed social norms because "the efforts of performative discourse exceed and confound the authorizing contexts from which they emerge."[53] As Butler goes on to claim, "the speech act, as a rite of institution, is one whose contexts are never fully determined in advance, and . . . the possibility for the speech act to take on a nonordinary meaning, to function in contexts where it has not belonged, is precisely the political promise of the performative."[54]

Butler's second solution to the problem of sedimentation, which focuses on habits in connection with their context or environment, is the more fruitful of the two she provides. She does not expand on this solution, however, beyond the few quotes given previously, making this second response merely a tantalizing suggestion.[55] This is perhaps because she intends her second solution to be an extension of, rather than an alternative to, her first. In that case, the bodily "excess" of which Butler speaks occurs in, or perhaps precisely *is*, the confounding of social norms that can occur when habits are performed in different contexts. The confounding is "excessive" in that it exceeds the normal expectations of what bodily habits might mean.

To call this confounding an "excess" is more misleading than helpful; it suggests a static, separate thing that stands apart from social performatives and habits and attempts to disrupt them from without, rather than suggesting the transactional process of actively remaking itself. As Dewey might say, this is another one of those cases when philosophers would be better off using verbs and adverbs rather than nouns because of their respective dynamic and static connotations.[56] Because appeal to and use of the language of "excess" is problematic and because Butler says so little about the confounding of contexts, I turn to Dewey's account of how the efficacy of imperfect performances and habits might be combated through the interplay of habit and environment. Understood as an aspect of transactional bodies, habit neither posits a deterministic view of human patterns of activity, which Bourdieu's notion of *habitus* allegedly does, nor abstractly implies that human bodying necessarily breaks with social norms, as Derrida's remarks on iterability allegedly do. An account of performativity that recognizes the social and contextual nature of its logic can be found in the notion of habit as constitutive of transaction.

Dewey's comments on youth, a term that is often but not always meant chronologically, are a good starting place for this account. According to Dewey, it is the young in a society, understood literally, who tend to have relatively fluid habits. Thus it is they who are the best sites of possible cultural transformation because they can be educated to change existing cultural constructs.[57] In contrast to adults, the young have more flexible habits. They often are able to make changes that adults cannot and are willing to disrupt current cultural patterns that adults will not. Educating the young does not mean teaching them particular things about gender that they must or must not body. To cast the issue this way is to fail to acknowledge habit as the mechanism by which change occurs. Educating instead means helping the young to form the habit of questioning, rethinking, and rebodying their own and their cultures' gender habits.

By helping the young keep their habits fluid, education does not dissolve all habit into a formless, mushy flux. Education is as much about developing particular kinds of structures in one's life as it is about making possible future growth and change, especially since growth and change require structure. What education should do, paradoxical though it might sound, is to enable people to develop firm habits that support flexible modes of being, because flexible modes of being are only possible by means of particular kinds of habit. One's habits make up who one is. In that way, they are structures of stability and identity. Ideally, their stability should be dynamic, capable of growth and change, rather than fixed. As Dewey puts it, "[w]hat is necessary is that habits be formed which are more intelligent, more sensitively percipient, more informed with foresight, more aware of what they are about, more direct and sincere, more flexibly responsive than those now current."[58]

So much of Dewey's hope about the prospect for change is reserved for the young in a literal sense that at one point Dewey suggests that it will take the death of older generations for real change to occur. As he claims, "[a] nation is always renewed by the death of its old constituents and the birth of those who are . . . young and fresh."[59] Acknowledging that individual habits in adults tend to be more deeply engrained and thus more rigid, inflexible, and difficult to change, Dewey nonetheless holds out hope for adults as well. The relative rigidity of adult habits, combined with the complexity of culture, means that adults too can be youthful sites of resistance and transformation.

Because adults transact with many different sorts of social and cultural institutions, their habits constitute a variety of different and potentially conflicting dispositions. In isolation, each of an adult's particular habits may be inflexible because of the rigidity of the institution that helped form it, but precisely this rigidity can help create the impetus for change when it causes a particular habit to conflict with others. Taken individually, an adult's rigid habits bode ill for her potential to change the gender structures in society. Taken as a whole, however, her habits make up a complex web of overlapping habits in which individual habits began to wear upon and challenge and influence each other. When they do so, the resulting friction between and weakening of some habits disrupts the usual ways adults habitually transact with the world, opening up possibilities for reconfigurations of habit and thus of culture as well.[60] And eventually, with an increased number and variety of habits that are interrelated, one's habit-forming itself may become subject, as Dewey says, "to the habit of recognizing that new modes of association will exact a new use of it. Thus habit is formed in view of possible future changes and does not harden so readily."[61] With these kinds of habits, even the chronologically old can remain young.

The sedimentation of habit does not necessarily preclude the reconfiguration of them. Adults can be sites of transformation and resistance even when their habits and the cultures in which they are formed are extremely rigid. The complexity of one's habits, joined with and due in part to the complexity of the world in which one transacts, means that the sedimentation of gender will never be completely final because of the potentially dislodging disruptions that such complexity provides. The complexity of habit means that one's habits can never fully congeal into what Butler has called "gender coherence."[62] The lack of agreement between the various habits that one is undercuts any final, stable, unified identity that habit, as constitutive of the self, might provide.

A brief example of how the intersection of habits related to gender can lead to conflict, and thus to the reconfiguration of the self via transformation of habit, will help demonstrate this point. The illustration is a simple one that is perhaps all too familiar to women who are academic philosophers but one that I hope to illuminate in a fresh way by considering it anew with the notion of habit. The case in question is "simply" that of being a woman and an academic philosopher. To be a "real" woman in Western culture has meant and, to a considerable extent, still means to comport oneself in a generally deferential, nonconfrontational, and passive manner: smiling, "containing" one's bodying so that it occupies minimal physical space, and so on. But to be a "real" philosopher is to be more like a man: to comport oneself in a relatively confrontational, aggressive, and active manner, with a bodily style that declares the right to occupy physical space and that does not seek to minimize conflict. For many women philosophers, to be a woman philosopher is to have developed the conflicting habits of both a "good" woman that politely defers to others by means of her bodily and verbal gestures and a "good" philosopher whose bodily and verbal gestures are part of his aggressive argumentation and defense of his claims.

In subtle and often unconscious ways, friction between these conflicting habits occurs virtually any time a woman philosopher transacts with others, whether inside or outside the academy. The different, rigid habits that she has, in combination with the different and often rigid contexts in which she is situated, can all combine and recombine at various times and in a variety of ways to produce a tangled clash of habits that is her self. The product of this complexity and friction is a bodying in conflict, at times more and less aggressive in its gestures, depending a great deal on its environment. Talking to one's mother likely will produce different tensions and thus different responses to one's environment than will responding to questions while giving a scholarly paper. Such constant conflict wears on the rigidity of both habits and demands a reconfiguration of them that can alter, to a degree, what it means for a woman philosopher both to be a woman and to be a philosopher. Such a reconfiguration might result in an aggressive daughter or a polite scholar who genuinely listens to others or both. It could also produce a woman who is both daughter and scholar and who is alternatively gentle and forceful, depending on the specific situation. Combinations of some or all of these are probable, and the list of possibilities could go on. In particular, the list should include the likely adverse affects on the quality of a woman's lived experience caused by the conflict of habits, but such adversity should not count against the notion of transaction because it offers no promises that the reconfiguration of habit and culture will be pleasant. Enjoyable or not, a woman philosopher's bodying can generate ways of being gendered that slightly shake sedimented masculine and feminine habits.

The remaking of a woman philosopher's habits such that she is gendered in less inflexible ways has ramifications not only for her own habits; it also has implications for the various institutions with which she transacts, such as family and academy, and thus for other people developing their habits through transaction with those institutions. Both inside and outside the academy, her newly reconfigured habits will impact on the cultural level what others take to be being a woman and being a philosopher. Admittedly, this impact will be a small and gradual one that is always at risk of being co-opted by existing power structures. A single reconfiguration of habit does not carry enough weight to effect the massive change needed to radically transform gender binaries and the implications for sex and sexuality that follow from them. Through the effects of many such local and minor alterations of the habits that produce a culture's gender constructs, however, the reconfiguration of a culture's gender categories can begin. And in that beginning, we might get a glimpse of what lies beyond the binary gendered options available today.

Of course, there no easy answers, quick fixes, or automatic guarantees concerning the type and amount of transformation, institutional or individual, that will occur as a result of the friction between particular habits of an individual. Institutions, such as family and the academy, can play a large role in promoting the rigid tensions that can help bring about the transformation of a person's habits and, thus, also of the institutions themselves. But institutions also can, and often do, resist change and thus undermine the new directions that they themselves enabled a person's habits to take. Like habits, cultural structures can tend to be sedimented and fixed. This does not mean that institutions should be viewed unequivocally as the enemies of individual freedom because institutional support for individual habits is crucial to the ongoing life of those habits. The issue instead is what kinds of institutions exist and what kinds of individual habits do they help make possible. Cultural structures need to be formed and transformed in ways that make them more dynamic and flexible. Without such a dynamic quality, cultural institutions can tend to smother the change in individual habits—and, thus, also any resulting change in the institutions themselves—to which they contributed by means of the friction between habits they helped generate.

Because many cultural structures presently are not dynamically formed, how might they be transformed such that they support rather than undermine desired changes in individuals' habits? And how can an individual's habits result in effective change in the institutions in which she is engaged if the sedimentation of institutions tends to undermine transformation? Addressing the first question, the preceding account of how to loosen sedimented habits at the level of the individual can be applied to sedimented cultural constructs at the level of the institution. Just as an individual constitutes a complex web of habits that individually may be rigid but that can generate friction when they come into contact with one another, so too is a society made up of institutions and customs that may be rigid but that can challenge each other when they come into conflict.

One instance of this conflict can be found in the recent decisions of some businesses in the United States, including some universities, to provide health care and other benefits to the same-sex partners of their employees.

I doubt that these decisions often are the result of a business's alleged concern for the well being and fair treatment of its gay and lesbian employees. More likely is that a business's custom of attempting to recruit and retain employees to increase its reputation and pad its pocketbook came into conflict with its heterosexist custom of recognizing only married, heterosexual partners of employees as legitimate recipients of such benefits. Considered individually, each of these customs may tend to be fairly rigid and thus resistant to change. But when their environment leads them to clash with one another, as it does when the economy is such that a business is having difficulty retaining and recruiting qualified heterosexual or at least seemingly heterosexual employees, the resulting friction can lead to transformation. In the case of same-sex partner benefits, the friction has led to a modification of the custom of denying benefits to nonheterosexual employees. And because this custom transacts with the heterosexist definition of the family in Western culture, its transformation contributes to a slight modification of customs involving the institution of the family.

The economy is an important environmental aspect of the transformation of business and familial customs in the United States. Another key factor is the feminist, gay, and lesbian political movements of the past thirty to forty years. Although not yet mainstream or dominant, these movements constitute a cultural custom in their own right that clashes with other customs, helping create the friction that can bring about change. In the case of same-sex partner benefits, it was not merely the custom of making money and the custom of only acknowledging the partners of married, heterosexual people that came into conflict. The feminist custom of demanding the abolishment of compulsory heterosexuality, including the discrimination against nonheterosexuals that results from it, was also part of the web of transacting customs that helped create the friction that led to the transformation of the business world. Put another way, I think it is no coincidence that the custom of acknowledging only the partners of married, heterosexual people began to change at the end of the twentieth century. This custom and the custom of making money have been in existence in the business world for a long time. It was only with an established pattern of feminist, gay, and lesbian visibility and activism that enough friction was generated for heterosexist business and familial practices slowly to begin to change.

I do not wish to oversimplify the situation of same-sex partner benefits for employees. Certainly many complicated factors have played a part in producing whatever feminist-friendly transformations have come about in the corporate and academic worlds, and, indeed, many more such transformations are needed still. Granting this complicated web of factors, I want to highlight the importance for the possibility of changing misogynist and heterosexist cultural structures of the existence in a society of feminist customs. More than just a change in the habits of an individual *qua* individual is needed for feminist changes to be effected in society or culture. What also are needed are what I am broadly calling feminist cultural structures, that is, a variety of forms of feminist connections across and between individuals that extend beyond the habits of any single individual.

The point about feminist cultural structures leads back to the second question, the one of how changes in an individual can result in changes to the institutions in which the individual is engaged. Put another way, the question is one of how making changes to one's individual habits can constitute more than a limited working on oneself, so to speak. The beginning of an answer to this question is that it is rare that changes to one person's habits can change entire institutions. A person's habits are always in transaction with and thus have an impact on the institutions in which she is engaged. The impact of one person, however, many times does not carry enough force to counter the inertia of cultural custom, and, thus, an individual's impact often is absorbed within or co-opted by cultural institutions. The impact on cultural customs of many people's habits, on the other hand, can be strong enough to effect change at a cultural level when the impact of one person's habits is not. While one person's development of the habit of speaking out against heterosexist discrimination often does not suffice to modify an institution's practices, many people's development of similar habits can create enough pressure on an institution to initiate change. For changes in an individual to result also in changes to an institution, an individual needs the efforts of other individuals attempting to make the same sorts of changes.

Herein lies the importance of feminist cultural structures, including but not limited to political activism, for they help create and bring together people who are attempting to make similar feminist transformations to their individual habits. Recalling Dewey's somewhat paradoxical sounding advice that people need to form the habit of not forming fixed habits, we could say that a person who is concerned about social and political change needs to cultivate the individual habit of not focusing solely on her or her own individual habits. For feminist changes to an individual's habits to have a better chance of constituting change beyond the individual, one of the habits needed of individuals is that of actively connecting work on one's habits with that of others. This can happen through informal associations, alliances, friendships, and conversations as well as through more formally organized social and political activism.

My claim that current gender structures can be changed only by adopting new habits or cultural constructs is not a claim that the current "bad" configuration of gender categories should be exchanged for a new-and-improved "good" set that is free from all the problems of its predecessor. Such a move would change gender categories by switching out old gender ideals for new ones, but would not displace the notion of gender as a seamless and coherent identity that rigidly fixes who one is. Rather, my claim is that feminists, pragmatists, and others should seek out the reconfiguration of habit and the configurations of gender, sex, and sexuality that structure human existence. Only by doing so can we free ourselves of the rigidity and stagnation of the self that accompany gender binarism.

Transactional Somaesthetics
Nietzsche, Women, and the Transformation of Bodily Experience

"Through the long succession of millennia, man has not known himself
physiologically: he does not know himself even today."
—Friedrich Nietzsche, 1888[1]

Friedrich Nietzsche was one of the first Western philosophers to make the
body central to his work in a positive way. He even went so far as to suggest
that the entirety of philosophy has been "an interpretation of the body and
a *misunderstanding* of the body."[2] For Nietzsche, the self is corporeal, and
thus the self-overcoming of humanity will happen or not depending upon
the degree of humans' bodily health. Bodily health requires turning from
the otherworldly, whether that of the religious or secular, to the here and
now of human existence. According to Nietzsche, philosophy can encourage such health by paying attention to bodily matters in a literal way. By
doing so, the discipline of philosophy might begin to correct its centuries-
old misunderstanding of bodies and to help humans transform their relationship to their corporeality.

The concrete way in which Nietzsche addresses bodily matters brings
his philosophy into an interesting intersection with Dewey's pragmatism
and the notion of transactional bodies. Affirming a nonfoundational, body-
oriented, transactional philosophy can be seen as one way of carrying on
after the death of God, as Nietzsche hopes some are strong enough to do.
To many, associating Nietzsche's philosophy with Dewey and transactional
bodies may seem odd, if not downright misguided. To take just one of
many possible points of conflict, both Dewey's pragmatism and the notion
of transactional bodies embrace an inclusive democracy, whereas Nietzsche
scorned democracy as the politics of the levelers who would eliminate all

possibility for greatness in humankind. But the differences between Nietzsche and Dewey—some superficial, some not—should not obscure the deep affinities that Dewey's pragmatism has with Nietzsche's project of self-overcoming.[3] Nor should they prevent us from seeing that the pragmatist and the pragmatist-feminist are much closer to Nietzsche's "free spirit" than they are to Nietzsche's "last man." Reading Nietzsche's philosophy of corporeal existence in the context of transactional bodies can be a fruitful way of exploring the value for feminism and pragmatism had by Nietzsche's emphasis on bodies. It also will provide an opportunity to explore guidelines for the improvement of bodily experience.

Nietzsche's philosophy contributes to the development of bodily practices that operate with an understanding of bodies as transactional and that attempt to improve lived experience in concrete ways. Borrowing from Richard Shusterman, I call the development of such bodily practices "somaesthetics."[4] Somaesthetics involves integrating bodily practices into the discipline of philosophy itself such that truth and wisdom are pursued through somatic experience.[5] This is a radical task, one that involves a change in philosophy that deeply threatens its tidy distinctions between mind and body, as well as its sense of what counts as "real" philosophy. Nietzsche's work pursues this task in that, while it sometimes treats the body as a metaphor, it literally addresses the body as a source of philosophical truth and wisdom. Because Nietzsche directs his readers to the concrete details of somatic experience, his philosophy is a fruitful resource for thinking about somaesthetic philosophy. However, because of the fatalism and the sexism that mar his emphasis on the body, Nietzsche's work is problematic and thus must be departed from in crucial ways. Whereas Nietzsche appears to have believed, at least in his work of 1888, that improvement of our somatic experience was impossible, somaesthetics as I conceive it includes the transformation of bodily experience and lived existence. It also attempts to avoid the sexism that is present in Nietzsche's corpus.

While the body clearly plays a central role in Nietzsche's work, he never presents a fully developed account of its meaning. He tells us that "the awakened, the enlightened man says: I am body entirely . . . and soul is only a word for something in the body" and that the self "is your body."[6] Aside from a few brief remarks such as these, Nietzsche does not flesh out in a full way what exactly corporeality means for his notion of self. Perhaps as a result, scholars have produced many different accounts of what the body means in Nietzsche's texts: the body as crudely materialistic,[7] as phenomenological,[8] as individualistic,[9] as voluntaristic,[10] as a metaphor for interpretation,[11] and as evidence of a "thin" metaphysical commitment on

Nietzsche's part.[12] I suggest here that Nietzsche emphasizes bodies in the context of somaesthetics in an attempt to cure humans of their guilt and bad conscience.

In a series of five sections in *Twilight of the Idols,* Nietzsche develops an account of the "error of causality" as it applies to the will and other "spiritual" phenomena.[13] In their desperation for explanations that will provide order and meaning to the world, humans soothe their existential anxiety with metaphysics and attribute definitive causes to the world rather than simply accept the sheer happening of events. Nietzsche argues that rather than explain the necessary linkages between events, causality is a creative designation of events attributed to them by humans. The notion of causality is both a useful and dangerous fiction, but it is a fiction *only,* and thus one errs when one understands it metaphysically as a force that necessarily links events together.

According to Nietzsche, the error of causality is pervasive, and one of the more important places in which it surfaces is in the account of human psychic life and agency as willful. When humans attribute free will to themselves, they believe themselves to be "causal agents in the act of willing" such that all the antecedents of an act performed are present in their consciousness.[14] As alleged causal agents, humans are free when performing an act and thus are responsible for it. The connection between free will and responsibility is crucial, according to Nietzsche, because it is the reason that humans can be made guilty and punished for their acts. In fact, Nietzsche claims that the need to see oneself as guilty is precisely the purpose of the notion of free will: "[m]en were thought of as 'free' so that they could become *guilty:* consequently, every action *had* to be thought of as willed, the origin of every action lying in the consciousness."[15]

Nietzsche claims that guilt and the accompanying structures of bad conscience are evidence of sickliness and decadence. Ashamed of their animal instincts, humans no longer allow themselves to direct their cruelty and joy in destruction outward. Docile and tamed, they turn their instincts for attack inward, persecuting and torturing themselves rather than their enemies. With this internalization, the soul and its guilt and bad conscience are created.[16] According to Nietzsche, these structures of subjectivity, made possible by and dependent upon the notion of free will, are crucial to the moralization of humans and to the hold had by theology over the sickly herd animals that human beings have become. As he explains, "[t]he whole of the old-style psychology, the psychology of the will, has as its precondition the desire of its authors, the priests at the head of the ancient communities, to create for themselves a *right* to ordain punishments —or their desire to create for God a right to do so. . . . "[17]

If it is the case that human existence continues to be sickly as long as humans believe in the fiction of free will, then the elimination of the metaphysical idea of free will is crucial to the possibility of improved health. Eliminating the notion of free will requires recognizing that psychological phenomena are the effects and accompaniments of physiological conditions —the "judgments of our muscles," as Nietzsche says—that have been misunderstood as disembodied ideas or states.[18] The "good conscience" is not a psychological state produced by virtuous actions. Rather, as Nietzsche claims, it is "a physiological condition sometimes so like a sound digestion to be mistaken for it."[19] The will is the feeling of power that accompanies expressions of bodily strength, not a metaphysical agency that causes the body to act. The same holds true for unpleasant feelings: "[t]he maltreatment of the body prepares the ground for the sequence of 'feelings of guilt,' i.e., a general state of suffering that demands an explanation."[20] Nietzsche construes physiological states of discomfort or distress as "spiritual" states of suffering, e.g., sinfulness. Further evidence of the misunderstanding of physiology and its relationship to psychology is that even when humans do acknowledge their feelings, emotions, and general affect as physiological, they tend to explain them by positing spiritual causes for them. For example, they often claim that the Christian God bestows upon them feelings of calm when instead it is that their physiological strength and plenitude make them calm and thus allow them to believe in the fiction of a trusting god.[21]

As these examples suggest, Nietzsche's cure for the belief in the metaphysics of free will operates by focusing on physiology in a very concrete and literal way. Of course, the body sometimes functions as a metaphor in Nietzsche's work; but Nietzsche's references to corporeality should not be considered merely as metaphorical.[22] To do so is to continue the mistake of philosophy's traditional avoidance of the materiality of human bodies. Treating bodily life as mere metaphor avoids confronting the concrete ways in which humans live their corporeality, as well as the transformation in philosophy that must occur if it is to embrace human existence as bodily.

Reading the body as functioning in Nietzsche's work as nonmetaphorical means acknowledging Nietzsche's claim that what one often takes as the cause of decadence—for example, Christian morality and the alleged vice and sin that it combats—is merely the effect of physiological distress.[23] And focusing on physiological distress means attending to physiological conditions and functions. What is needed, as Nietzsche says, is "to know the size of one's stomach" because meals that are too small and meals that are long and drawn-out are bad for the digestion and, hence, bad for the spirit. Likewise, Nietzsche believes that coffee should be avoided because it "spreads darkness," and one's tea should not be weak because that can make one sickly.[24]

For Nietzsche, physiological details correlate with a person's greatness, or lack thereof. One's digestive habits speak volumes about one's spirit: sluggishness of the intestines is an indication of mediocrity for the tempo of one's metabolism is directly related to the "mobility of lameness of the spirit's *feet*."[25] Similarly, Nietzsche suggests that consumption of alcohol is the sign of a person's lesser nature because alcohol does not exhilarate, but rather dulls the spirit. As he says, "I . . . cannot advise all *more spiritual* natures earnestly enough to abstain entirely from alcohol."[26] Lest we misunderstand Nietzsche on the importance of bodily matters considered in such concrete, detailed ways, he explains:

> One will ask me why on earth I've been relating all these small things which are generally considered matters of complete indifference: I only harm myself, the more so if I am destined to represent great tasks. Answer: these small things—nutrition, place, climate, recreation, the whole casuistry of selfishness—are inconceivably more important than everything one has taken to be important so far. Precisely here one must begin to *relearn*. . . . All the problems of politics, of social organization, and of education have been falsified through and through . . . because one learned to despise "little" things, which means the basic concerns of life itself.[27]

The correlation between the "little things" of the body and the condition of the spirit often seems to be important to Nietzsche merely because bodily details reveal the health of the spirit. Nietzsche often suggests that bodily matters fix one's spiritual condition in such a way that neither can be changed. Bodily matters thus cannot serve as a means by which we might transform, and not just reveal, the spirit. Nietzsche's fatalism with respect to human existence is suggested when he claims in *The Will to Power* that "there is no 'improvement.' . . . Decadence itself is nothing *to be* fought."[28] And at the close of his discussion of bodily "little things" in *Ecce Homo*, Nietzsche declares, "[m]y formula for greatness in a human being is *amor fati:* that one wants nothing to be different, not forward, not backward, not in all eternity. Not merely to bear what is necessary, still less conceal it—all idealism is mendaciousness in the face of what is necessary—but *love* it."[29] Nietzsche thus suggests that one's bodily condition is a product of necessity and therefore is incapable of change. In that case, attention to the body in order to improve it would be an example of idealistic mendaciousness that demonstrates that a person is not strong enough to love what she is.

Yet, at other times, the tone of *Ecce Homo* suggests that Nietzsche can be read precisely as counseling his readers on how to improve their physiological condition. As Nietzsche speaks descriptively about the particularities of his body, he appears to be using his own physiological experiences as the basis for advice to his readers. After noting his preference for water over wine, Nietzsche advises more spiritual natures to abstain from alcohol as he does.[30] Speaking in the imperative, Nietzsche writes, "*sit* as little as possible; give no credence to any thought that was not born outdoors while one moved about freely—in which the muscles are not celebrating a feast, too," suggesting not only that moving about when thinking is Nietzsche's practice, but also that Nietzsche's readers should experiment with such a practice as well.[31] Nietzsche's advice is not for everyone to do exactly has he does. As Nietzsche says in the context of the issue of the strength of one's tea, "[e]verybody has his own measure, often between the narrowest and most delicate limits."[32] But precisely in his recognition of differing physiological measures, Nietzsche hints nonfatalistically that all of us should attend to our bodily conditions so that we might improve them.

At moments such as these, even Nietzsche's later work cannot be read as consistently fatalistic. Having problematized Nietzsche's fatalism, however, let me make clear that my primary goal is not to settle the question of Nietzsche's real intent when speaking of bodies. Nor is it to attempt to eliminate tensions between Nietzsche's fatalistic remarks about bodies and his suggestions concerning the possibility of somatic transformation. I want instead to use Nietzsche's claim about the import of the "little things" of the body to suggest, perhaps *contra* Nietzsche, that a person might transform her lived existence by paying attention to her body and its nonverbal messages. One can heighten somatic awareness so that how one feels and functions is changed. Whether fatalistic or not, Nietzsche's work is valuable because it recognizes the importance of corporeality to the felt quality of lived existence. As Nietzsche himself puts it in a different context, "Essential; to start from the *body* and employ it as a guide. [Compared to the spirit], [i]t is the much richer phenomenon, which allows of clearer observations."[33]

Reading Nietzsche in the context of developing a somaesthetics means that we should hesitate to read Nietzsche's detailed attentions to his own and others' bodily functions as the ramblings of a madman. We also should hesitate to read them as having autobiographical value only.[34] While many of the sections in Nietzsche's works about his body are autobiographical, they also can been seen as constituting a somaesthetics particular to his physiology. Nietzsche's various accounts of his diet and daily schedule can be taken as examples of a transformative practice of bodying in which his readers should participate by developing their own, individualized somaesthetics.[35] When Nietzsche explains his digestive idiosyncrasies—his aversion to wine and coffee, his preference for tea but only in the morning, and his love of water—he can be read as someone who is attuned to the nuances and reactions of his bodying and the effect they have on his well-being. To understand "the size of one's stomach" is to understand how one might transform one's physiological, and thus also one's psychological, affect. To be able to fine tune one's bodying by attending to what are usually considered unimportant trivialities is to have within one's power the best tool for the promotion of the flourishing, free-spirited "great health" that Nietzsche promotes.

The value of Nietzsche's emphasis on the "little things" of the body notwithstanding, a somaesthetics developed with the aid of Nietzsche's work presents significant dangers, particularly for women. In the abstract, Nietzsche's example of paying attention to the lived experience of one's bodying seems to be something for women to follow and for feminists, pragmatists, and other philosophers to endorse. Not only could the quality of women's somatic experience improve with such an attunement, but a greater awareness of one's bodily feelings and experiences also could provide the knowledge and motivation needed to initiate social and political changes that would transform women's lives. However, attending to bodies has been and continues to be the work of women, and relegating this work to the sphere of women has been a crucial factor in their oppression. Given this, for women to participate in somaesthetics risks strengthening the negative and virtually exclusive connection between women and bodywork.

Women of all races and classes have long been associated with bodies and their perceived irrationality, sexuality, and deceptiveness, whereas white, property-owning men have been associated with the mind and its alleged rationality, neutrality, and clarity.[36] The Western tradition's hierarchy of mind over body has helped sustain the hierarchy of men over women, as well as the hierarchy of some men over other men. The devaluing of bodies has been particularly damaging to women of color, whose race and gender have historically connected them to bodily matters in negative ways even more tightly than they have connected white women. As a result of their association with bodies, women have nearly always been the ones to attend to the "little things" of which Nietzsche speaks. The concrete trivialities of bodies, in particular those of others' bodies, that come with caring for the home and family have long been women's domain. Women have had to concern themselves with which food is most nutritious for bodies and which clothes will best keep bodies warm and comfortable. In particular, as the primary caregivers for infants and young children, women have had to focus on the somatic experience of babies as evidenced through their cries, gurgles, facial expressions, and body language.

Given women's historical and current connection with bodies, using Nietzsche as a starting point for the development of a somaesthetics can be problematic in four related ways. The first two are not necessarily unique to Nietzsche's philosophy but are troubling nonetheless. First, for women to participate in somaesthetics could be dangerous because their somaesthetic practices might not contribute to a revaluation of bodies; they might only further sediment the connections between women and bodily matters in stereotypical ways, as trivialities and "women's work." As Elizabeth Spelman has demonstrated, Western philosophy has long argued for the importance of the soul or mind over bodies by holding up "for our inspection the silly and sordid lives of those [women] who pay too much attention to their bodies" and arguing, as Plato explicitly does, that "[t]o have more concern for your body than your soul is to act just like a woman."[37] Thus, strengthening the connection between women and bodies thus risks only increasing problems of sexism and racism.

Second, drawing from Nietzsche to develop a somaesthetics is potentially problematic because of the way he largely overlooks the work that women do, and have done, as bodily practitioners. Nietzsche may be right that man has not and does not know himself physiologically, but women tend to know men's physiological concerns well since they have been and largely continue to be the ones who attend to them.[38] Although Nietzsche rarely acknowledges their existence, many cultures already have, and have had for some time, somaestheticians in their midst. While a discipline of the body has at times been practiced and valued by some men, it is largely women who have cared for and tried to improve bodily experience.[39] Granted, women are not the same type of somaesthetician of which Nietzsche serves as an example, a type that I call an autosomaesthetician, because their bodywork has not focused on their own bodies and bodily experience. Women have been heterosomaestheticians: those who attend to the bodily matters of others. Nonetheless, because historically most bodywork has been heterosomaesthetic, to the extent that any kind of somaesthetics has existed to this point, women largely have been the practitioners of it. Nietzsche's virtual silence about the attention that women have paid to others' bodies makes their heterosomaesthetic work invisible and thus contributes to making invisible women themselves.

Third, by overlooking the heterosomaesthetic work of women, Nietzsche trivializes the capabilities of women vis-à-vis their bodies, even as he draws upon them in his ideal of the strong individual. Nietzsche describes the strong individual with feminine metaphors of pregnancy and maternal instinct but does not think that women can ever become the healthy free spirit that he describes.[40] Admittedly, Nietzsche's reason for excluding women from the project of becoming a free spirit is that he thinks that by virtue of their "feminine instincts," women already possess the sort of traits for which some men should strive. Thus, any transformation of what woman is would be retrogressive. On Nietzsche's terms, women are wily, deceptive, and concerned with finery and appearance, rather than truth, and for them to change would be for them to dull the femininity that gives them their vitality and power. This explains why Nietzsche charges that feminists are "abortive": they allegedly seek to eliminate, rather than enhance, women's strengths.[41] Nietzsche therefore denies women the chance to participate in self-overcoming because he appears to have high esteem for them, even if accompanied by envy of their duplicity and maternal creativity.

But Nietzsche's valorization of women's feminine instincts does not eliminate the problems of his exclusion of actual women from participation in his ideal of the strong individual. Nietzsche's "positive" comments on women are not so much a recognition of their strengths, as they are a trivialization and romanticization of women's lives. Nietzsche's treatment of women serves not to preserve or encourage women's alleged creative abundance, as he claims it does, but to stifle women's potential for growth by insisting upon their subordination to men. For Nietzsche, women are something to be "maintained, taken care of, protected, and indulged [by men] like a more delicate, strangely wild, and often pleasant domestic animal."[42] This is because women are creatures who have "an instinct for a *secondary* role," which Nietzsche claims explains their genius for lying and deception.[43] By caging women in their secondary role of domestic animal, Nietzsche champions women's subordination even as he praises, or rather precisely by means of his praise for, women's mendacious qualities. By linking his praise for women with their subordination, Nietzsche helps secure the domination of women through the romanticization of their feminine "virtues," rendering women's lives stagnant and fixed. For these reasons, Nietzsche's praise of women should be seen as detrimental to, not supportive of, them.

Nietzsche stifles and trivializes women not only by claiming that they have no need to transform themselves. He also demeans women by denying that they are capable of participation in projects of self-transformation in the first place. Ironically, the reason Nietzsche gives for women's incapability of becoming strong individuals is that they do not adequately understand bodily matters. In one of the few places Nietzsche acknowledges women's heterosomaesthetic work, he writes:

> Stupidity in the kitchen; woman as cook: the gruesome thoughtlessness to which the feeding of the family and of the master of the house is abandoned! Woman does not understand what food *means*—and wants to cook. If woman were a thinking creature, she, as cook for a millennia, would surely have had to discover the greatest physiological facts. . . . Bad cooks—and the utter lack of reason in the kitchen—have delayed human development longest and impaired it most: nor have things improved much even today.[44]

Here, in the case of food and nutrition, Nietzsche excludes women from participating in the ideal of the strong individual not because of his alleged "esteem" for them, as in the case of pregnancy and maternity, but because of his outright contempt. Women allegedly lack a proper understanding of the profound impact that food has on bodies, and therefore they also lack a proper understanding of matters of the spirit. According to Nietzsche, as bad cooks, women have demonstrated their physiological stupidity, and thus they have shown that they are incapable of contributing to the self-overcoming of humanity.

Whether out of contempt or esteem for women, Nietzsche continually establishes his ideal for men by drawing upon bodily domains traditionally associated with women's lives while excluding women's participation in that ideal. Notwithstanding his so-called positive comments about women's feminine instincts, Nietzsche's overall view of women is one that trivializes and belittles them.

When Nietzsche excludes women from participation in the very ideals of which they are the models, such exclusion functions not to preserve women's creative vitality, as Nietzsche claims, but to eliminate the possibility of women becoming something greater than they currently are. The dismissal of women on Nietzsche's part leads to the fourth, and perhaps most significant, way in which involving Nietzsche in the development of somaesthetics can be problematic. Somewhat paradoxically, Nietzsche's exclusion of women from the category of the strong individual can function to oppress women through their very inclusion in it. More specifically, women's exclusion from autosomaesthetic practices can function to ensure that women continue to be oppressed by the expectation that they perform heterosomaesthetic work. Because of women's exclusion from participation in the Nietzschean ideal, to draw from his work to develop a somaesthetics is to risk suggesting that the body in question in somaesthetics is implicitly male. This would mean that for a woman to engage in somaesthetics is for her to engage in the care of and attunement toward his body, not her own. If only men are seen as capable or worthy of or as needing autosomaesthetic work, for women to become somaestheticians is for them to become exclusively heterosomaestheticians. And to become exclusively heterosomaestheticians is for women to continue the attunement toward others' bodies that helps maintain their status as second-class citizens. Nietzsche's complex exclusion-through-inclusion of women in his philosophy thus perpetuates an oppressive relationship among women, men, and their bodies.

Even though Nietzsche is a misogynist, his turn to concrete bodily matters is extremely important for philosophy, and his work can be an important resource for the development of a somaesthetics that is friendly to women. Nietzsche is right that a crucial change needed in philosophy is a greater focus on corporeal existence. He is also right that paying attention to the concrete "little things" of bodily life is much more important for people's lives than often is thought. A feminist response to the risks of male domination and gender inequality that Nietzsche's work presents for somaesthetics should not be to reject the notion of somaesthetics per se. Rather than return to the neglect of bodies in an attempt to evade their gender, race, sexuality, class, ethnicity, and more, feminists need to find ways to develop somaesthetics that do not perpetuate oppressive social, political, and cultural structures.

Nietzsche's work has the potential to aid in such a project by suggesting some fruitful guidelines for somaesthetic practice that undercut his own sexism. These guidelines are not meant to deny Nietzsche's insistence that each individual should practice a somaesthetics tailored uniquely to her or his body. Somaesthetic work must indeed be relative to the individual. Even so, Nietzsche's analyses of decadence have implications for the way in which all effective somaesthetics might be developed; therefore some generalizations about somaesthetic work are possible. I offer here three such general guidelines for somaesthetics: first, the critical approach to one's feelings and sensations that is needed if somaesthetic work is to be successful; second, the reconceptualization of the will and, thus, also of how one might be effective in one's attempts to change one's lived experience; and third, the need for help from others to establish an improved attunement to one's bodying.

Beginning with the first guideline and perhaps *contra* some of Nietzsche's own claims, the claim that a person should attend to her body should be not taken to suggest that bodies are simply or transparently accessible. The habits and feelings of bodies are complex and often opaque and, thus, must be approached with a critical, interpretative eye. As Nietzsche claims, psychological feelings of guilt and sinfulness are not signs that a person is sinful; instead they can be seen as signs of physiological distress. An implication of this claim is that, as a part of encouraging one's health, a person must learn to distrust her psychological feelings, even though—or, precisely because—they feel so natural and right. As Nietzsche says, "[l]et us above all mistrust our first impulses . . . *they are almost always good.*"[45] If a recovery from a guilty, bad conscience is possible, a person must become suspicious of the psychological feelings that are most immediate and comfortable to her.

When it comes to physical feelings or somatic sensations, on the other hand, Nietzsche apparently says little about what sort of approach one should take. He advises that the body should be one's guide because it "allows of clearer observations."[46] On his own terms, however, assuming clarity of bodies will not produce a satisfactory somaesthetics. For Nietzsche, the psychological and physiological cannot be sharply separated from one another, and thus his advice that a person distrust her psychological feelings must be read at the same time as advice that she be suspicious of her physiological affect as well. As does Dewey, Nietzsche rejects pronounced divisions between the psyche and the soma, viewing the human organism as a psycho-physical creature whose consciousness developed as an outgrowth and extension of its physicality.[47] As Nietzsche claims, "[t]he creative body created spirit for itself, as a hand of its will," and thus what we call "spirit" or "soul" is merely the "social structure of the drives and affects," that is, of the multiplicity of the body.[48] Understanding bodies as multiple and not unified, as Nietzsche does, one must understand consciousness as an instrument by which some bodies organize their multiplicity and plurality.[49] Bodies have unity, but not a unity that eliminates their multiplicity or the complex behaviors of and relations among various bodily impulses and functions. The psyche helps effect bodily unity, but not in a way that posits the psyche as an entity separate from the body.

The psychosomatic nature of human existence undercuts any appeal to clear observations of bodily feelings in two related ways. First, the particular type of relationship had by the psyche and soma means that consciousness does not render bodies easily readable. Because the functional unity of bodies achieved through consciousness does not eliminate their multiplicity, bodily experience is rarely, if ever, the simple, transparent phenomenon that it can seem to be. For this reason, corporeal sensations cannot and should not be uncritically appealed to as immediate revelations of the truth of bodily experience. Furthermore, because the soma cannot be sharply separated from the psyche, the fact that a culture has impacted one's psyche means that it also has impacted one's body. One cannot appeal to the body, as distinct from the psyche, as a pure location untouched by decadence. The (mal)formation of the psyche effected by a decadent culture effects the (mal)formation of physiology and vice versa, which means that any unhealthiness of one spills over to the other. Nietzsche's suspicions of psychological feelings cannot be contained to the realm of the psychical. They too must spill over to the realm of the corporeal and produce a critical attitude toward bodily sensations.

As does that of Dewey, Nietzsche's rejection of a dualist conception of the body and mind, which is not an adoption of a monism of the body, means that somatic feelings should not automatically or necessarily be trusted as indicators of healthy bodily existence.[50] The very act or movement that feels right may be the primary obstacle to improved somatic experience. Bodying is in need of critical interpretation; for that reason, we cannot understand, in an overly simple, straightforward way, Nietzsche's command that a person start with the body as an injunction to listen to one's bodying. Because of the complexity and opacity of bodies, the things that a person's body tells her through its sensations, pains, and pleasures must be interrogated for their implications and meanings.

The second guideline for somaesthetics, which is the need to reconceptualize the will to make changes to lived experience, also follows from Nietzsche's declaration that the self is the body. To practice somaesthetics on Nietzschean terms, a person must rethink the means by which she might improve or adjust her bodily practices and activities. Considered as some sort of noncorporeal power that can effectively direct or transform bodying, the will has no part to play in a somaesthetics. Or, rather, somaesthetics forces the rethinking of will as bodily efficacy. To claim, as Nietzsche does, that the will is a harmful fiction that needs to be eliminated for the sake of improved health is not to claim that one cannot speak of agency and change. Nor is it to claim that consciousness has no role to play in the changing of bodily practices. Indeed, bodily change comes in part through an attainment of conscious awareness of the ways in which a person comports herself and of the buried bodily sensations that most people are too physiologically obtuse to notice. Consciousness must now be thought of as an instrument of bodying, as an extension of bodily activity that is an aide to bodily reeducation, however, not as the taskmaster that will, apart from a body's habits, coerce a body into a new comportment. Likewise, agency must be rethought in terms of bodily effects, practices, and habits, rather than in terms of noncorporeal forces.

If a person cannot automatically or immediately trust her bodily sensations and if the will is wrongly conceived as the noncorporeal master of somatic experience, she needs the help of others to determine whether particular changes to her somatic experience are desirable. This is the third guideline for somaesthetic practice, one that is especially consonant with an understanding of bodies as transactional. For somaesthetics, the interpretation of bodily experience must be a dynamic, communal process that, if it is to be successful, recognizes the constitutive impact of others on oneself. A person often needs the guidance and input of others to reeducate her bodily sensations so that they are more reliable indicators of psychophysical health.

Because of Nietzsche's reputation for promoting a stark individualism, a somaesthetic guideline developed out of his work that invokes a person's interdependence with others may appear wrongheaded. Nietzsche's endorsements of an atomistic individualism that dualistically divides the individual from society are too numerous and well known to repeat here. In contrast to those numerous remarks are the scant number of ones in which he comments about "the false autonomy of the 'individual' as atom."[51] There is little of substance in Nietzsche's corpus that explicitly encourages his readers to conceive of his individualism as transactional, that is, as an individualism in which the boundaries between the individual and society are permeable and fluid. Nietzsche's disdain for the herd and praise for the strong individual would appear to make unlikely a guideline that encouraged dependence upon others in a somaesthetics developed with the aid of his work.

But the moments in which Nietzsche appears to promote a nontransactional individualism do not discredit the inclusion of a guideline requiring assistance from others when attending to one's somatic experience. On Nietzsche's own terms, the individual cannot be atomistic. For Nietzsche, the individual self is bodily in a concrete, literal way, and "real" bodies do not survive, much less flourish, if not in transaction with the world, including the people in it. Whether or not Nietzsche endorsed an atomistic individualism as a result of his elitism, his concrete emphasis on bodies implies a nonatomistic self that is necessarily in transaction with its surroundings. Setting aside the issue of whether Nietzsche *did* promote an atomistic individualism, he and a somaesthetics developed with the help of his work cannot consistently do so. While my claim that a person's understanding of her bodying occurs through a transactional process may conflict with many of Nietzsche's explicit pronouncements about the self, it agrees with Nietzsche's own emphasis on bodies. As bodily, a person needs the help of others if she is to understand and change her bodily sensations, experience, and comportment.

To help make this claim clearer, as well as to suggest how all three of the guidelines might function in somaesthetic practice, I turn to an example of a bodily technique that illustrates the notion of a transactional somaesthetics. Called the Alexander Technique and practiced by Dewey, this bodily practice was developed by F. Matthias Alexander in the early part of the twentieth century.[52] Briefly put, the Alexander Technique is a method for retraining a person's habitual use of her body to improve her lived experience, both psychological and physical. The technique is not about curing specific physical ailments, nor is it about obtaining correct posture, although one's posture will change with use of the technique, and Alexander and others have reported that bodily pain and malfunction were eliminated by use of it. Rather, the technique is a consciously constructive reeducation of bodying. By becoming reflectively aware of the way in which one usually (mis)comports one's body, a person can begin to inhibit the usual ways in which she does so, which opens up the possibility of doing so differently. For example, Alexander held that many people hold their heads too far down and back in relationship to their neck and spine, forcing the weight of their heads to be supported by the muscles in their upper backs rather than by their skeletal structures. Among other things, the work that these muscles must do to support the head produces tension and stress in the neck, shoulders, and back, contributing to an overall exhaustion by the end of the day. The Alexander Technique teaches people to adjust the position of the head so that it is forward and up with respect to the neck and torso, centering the weight of the head on the spinal column.

Such readjustment sounds simple enough but proves enormously difficult for most people to perform. This is because changing bodily habits is not a matter of will power, or at least not in the usual sense of that word. Here we can appreciate Nietzsche's insistence that human beings are not the consciously "causal agents in the act of willing" that they often think they are. Merely mentally ordering oneself to hold one's head differently and then trying to do so is not effective in making changes to habitual activities and behaviors. Most people do not have sufficient bodily awareness to conceptualize accurately in what way the head is too far down and back and what moving the head up and forward to the recommended position would feel or be like. ("Conceptualize" here should be taken in a psycho-physical sense of bodily imagining what a given position feels or looks like.) Most people do not have enough of a felt sense of their bodies to even register the way in which they are currently comported, much less to try to comport them differently. This is why the help of someone who is trained in the technique is crucial to reeducating one's bodying. By using slight pressure of her hands on the neck and head, an Alexander technician can move a person's head into the recommended position, giving her the felt experience of "forward and up."

Having a felt experience is not the same thing as altering bodily habits. When a person, after having her head and neck repositioned, tries to move from a standing to sitting position, she immediately, "without thinking," tends to resort to her usual bodily comportment, shifting the head back and down. It is as if bodies do not know how to do the things they do if they do not comport themselves in their usual, comfortable, "natural" ways. Telling oneself to move or perform some task differently tends to result either in moving in usual ways regardless of efforts to do otherwise, or in an inability to move at all because of the inhibition of one's usual way of moving.

In the traditional sense of will, a person's merely willing herself to change her bodily habits will not work because it does not take into account the constitution of bodily habits by physical and social environments.[53] For example, many chairs contribute to the body-damaging habit of curving the spine into a C-shape because they "cup" around the body with fluffy, unsupportive cushions, causing the human body to collapse forward upon itself. They do not encourage the muscles of the back and torso to support an S-shaped curve in the spine by means of firm, planar surfaces and adequate "butt space" (a technical term in chair design) between the seat and back of the chair. To stop leaning back into a C-shaped curve when in a chair means not merely for a person to will herself to sit differently, but also for her to change her bodily habits. To change her bodily habits entails changing the chairs available for her to sit on because her transactions with chairs help constitute her bodily habits when sitting.

In addition to changing a person's physical environment, changes in the social environment are also needed to change a person's bodily habits. Alternatively sitting and lying on the floor often can be a better bodily alternative to sitting on a chair, especially when a situation, such as an academic conference, requires long periods of sitting. But sitting on the floor is considered unprofessional in the Western world. The floor is the "proper" space for infants, not adults, and thus adults rarely comport themselves on floors. The social hierarchies that are built around where people sit help keep damaging bodily habits in place. In the case of chairs, both the physical pieces of furniture available to sit on and the social and cultural meanings of what is sat on need to be changed to encourage beneficial changes to bodily habits.

This brief explanation of the Alexander Technique clarifies how the three guidelines for somaesthetics I have suggested could function in practice. Regarding the first guideline, which calls for a critical attitude towards one's bodily sensations, in the use of the Alexander Technique, bodily feelings are not always or immediately to be trusted as natural "givens" that faithfully guide a person to an optimal experience. As Alexander explains, "the prevalence of sensory untrustworthiness is of the utmost significance in relation to the problem of the control of human reaction."[54] We can see this in the example of the head and neck: to trust what feels normal or natural in the positioning of the head is virtually to guarantee a reversion to the old form of bodily comportment. What happens in this case is that, in Alexander's words, "the lure of the familiar proves too strong for him and keeps him tied down to the habitual use of himself which *feels right*."[55] The familiar and comfortable are often precisely what is to be fought in somaesthetic work because they are what trap one, at least initially, in problematic uses of oneself.[56] Nietzsche's insistence in *Beyond Good and Evil* that we not remain stuck to people, nations, and virtues should be understood to apply to bodily feelings and activities as well.[57] For the sake of improved somatic experience, one often must fight the lure of the familiar that bodily feelings contain. We might say with Nietzsche that "[c]onvictions"—those contained in our muscles, as well as in our minds— "are more dangerous enemies of truth than lies."[58] Somaesthetics should not just instruct a person to start with the body, but should problematize the body as a starting point itself. Those engaged in somaesthetic work must interrogate and reeducate their bodies' affective and sensory abilities if they are to provide standards for improved somatic experiences and practices.

As the example of, and my own limited experience with, the Alexander Technique shows, however, reeducating one's affective and sensory abilities is nearly impossible to do on one's own. Here we see the third guideline put into practice, that of depending on others to help improve one's bodily experience. Until my bodily habits have changed so that the new comportment of my head and neck is what feels "natural," I cannot use my bodily feelings to judge whether or not I have correctly positioned my head in the forward and up position. This is why practicing a new bodily comportment on one's own immediately after being shown it is potentially counterproductive. While one may indeed be changing one's bodily habits, the change might be for the worse instead of the better. I need the guidance of another, through both her verbal instructions and her repositioning of my body with her hands in order to slowly learn what an improved bodily comportment feels like and, thus, to be able to achieve it on my own.

I not only need the direction of another because of the untrustworthiness of my own somatic feelings; in line with the second guideline, which calls for a reconceptualization of the will, I also need the direction of another because of the inefficacy of my mental "will power." In using the Alexander Technique, the physical repositioning of a person's body by another is crucial to the transformation of her bodily agency. The traditional, noncorporeal notion of will not only is not efficacious in such transformation, but it can actively interfere with effective bodily change. As Alexander explains, until one's bodying is reeducated, "any 'will power' exerted by a pupil whose use of himself was misdirected would be exerted in the wrong direction, so that the harder he tried to carry out such an instruction and the more he 'willed' himself to succeed, the more his use would be misdirected." [59] As part of a successful somaesthetics, one must learn how *not* to try to will bodily changes, understanding "will" here in its traditional sense. One gains the will to effect a positive change in bodying when, and only when, that change has been incorporated into bodily movements. To begin the process of that change, rather than relying on her "will power," a person must rely on a critical, interpretative attunement to her sense and feelings that is facilitated by the voice and touch of another.

At this point, I return to the problems of sexism that are dangers for a transactional somaesthetics developed in conjunction with Nietzsche's philosophy. The guidelines I have developed for somaesthetics with the aid of Nietzsche's work address his own sexist treatment of women. That is, Nietzsche's philosophy itself includes resources that counter the misogyny in his thought. First, by rejecting mind-body dualism, the guideline calling for a reconceptualization of the will eliminates a key piece of conceptual support for the rigid association of men and minds, and of women and bodies. Because mind and body transact as a psychosomatic whole, women cannot be consistently or exclusively identified "merely" with bodies, nor men identified "merely" with minds. Identification with the bodily must also include identification with the mental, psychological, and spiritual, and vice versa. Additionally, because somaesthetics demands the rethinking of the will as corporeal, association with bodies can no longer be linked coherently with the negative notions of the passive and inert. An association with bodies must be linked instead with the source of agency, efficacy, and activity.

The guideline recognizing the need for the interrogation of one's bodily feelings and practices provides an opportunity for a somaesthetician to draw upon feminist work that has already begun questioning the meaning of psycho-physical feelings, such as emotions, and on the value of some autosomaesthetic practices of women. In her examination of the "micropolitics" of the innocent pleasures of many women's everyday duties, Sandra Bartky argues that while a women's caregiving can be the source of great pleasure in her life, it can often disempower women by continually directing their energies and desires toward the projects and lives of others.[60] A woman cannot simply take the joy she feels when doing her husband's laundry, for example, as an indication that her experience is a positive one. This is because women's subordination is often located "in the duties [they] are happy to perform and in what [they] thought were the innocent pleasures of everyday life."[61] By examining the heterosomaesthetic work of women's caregiving, Bartky encourages women to engage in the autosomaesthetic practice of critiquing the pleasures provided by many of their everyday experiences.

Sandra Bartky and Susan Bordo, among other feminists, have problematized the few types of autosomaesthetic work that women have been permitted and even expected to perform.[62] Autosomaesthetic practices such as wearing makeup, removing body hair, and restricting food intake often function to discipline women into ideals of femininity that serve to limit, rather than expand, women's strength by requiring that their time, energy, and money be spent on such practices rather than on more empowering activities. What Bartky and Bordo demonstrate is that the fact that a somaesthetic practice is *auto*somaesthetic does not necessarily make it beneficial, nor does it place it beyond the need of critical examination. In somaesthetic work, there is no final certainty, no guarantee that a particular bodily practice or feeling is always or necessarily unproblematic. The critical work of questioning one's bodily feelings and practices, as well as questioning one's beliefs about what counts as beneficial to bodying, needs to be ongoing work that responds to psychosomatic and environmental changes. In the case of beautifying and slimming her body, as with all bodily practices, a woman must challenge prevalent assumptions about the value of the particular somaesthetic work that she does.

With the guideline that recognizes the need for assistance from others for successful autosomaesthetic work, somaesthetics undercuts the Western tradition's ideal of the lone individual who relies on no one but himself to accomplish his achievements. This ideal has been harmful to women in particular because it makes invisible the supportive work for such accomplishments that women have often performed. By acknowledging that interdependence with others is required for improved somatic experience, somaesthetics combats the making-invisible of others and the exclusion-through-inclusion, including that in which Nietzsche himself engaged, that can occur when one fails to recognize the constitutive role that others play in one's somatic experiences. Affirming the positive role that others can play in the examination and formation of one's bodying, somaesthetics operates with a transactional notion of the self, which undercuts the dualism of dependence and independence.

Because of its emphasis on interdependence, the guideline acknowledging the need for help from others to improve somatic experience might evoke concern. By endorsing transaction with others, the guideline might seem opposed to feminist aims in particular because it appears to give other people in a woman's life too much power to establish the meaning, veracity, and even sheer existence of her felt experiences. The sort of situation in which women have little or no epistemic authority in their lives and over their experiences has been and continues to be a crucial factor in women's oppression and thus is something that feminism seeks to combat. If a somaesthetic guideline undermines the voice of those, like women, who usually are not in a position of epistemic privilege, that guideline would seem to reinforce, rather than combat, oppression. The danger expressed in this concern is real and, moreover, cannot be eliminated completely. It does not mean, however, that the guideline acknowledging the need for help from others is antifeminist. The relations of power between people mean that there will always be a risk that in the mutually transactional process of understanding, evaluating, and changing a person's somatic experience, another's voice will override and silence that of a woman whose bodily experience is in question. But feminism's response to this danger should not be a naïve experientialism, in which what women immediately feel is necessarily and automatically granted unconditional validity. Such an uncritical approach to women's experience casts women as self-transparent and thus infallible with respect to themselves; this, in addition to or, rather, as an effect of idealizing women, discourages women from exploring and understanding additional or different meanings that their experiences might have.

Put another way, the concern expressed about the guideline acknowledging the need for help from others is a concern about the openness to others entailed by a transactional notion of the self. This openness includes not just the opportunity to benefit from others, but also the danger of being vulnerable to them. If the self is not sealed off in an atomistic way, then the possibility exists not only for women to learn about their somatic experiences from others, but also for them to have their somatic experiences changed in harmful ways. And the possibility for harm and, thus, the danger in somaesthetic work are much greater for those who are awarded relatively little authority over their own lives and experiences.

Rather than lead to a rejection of a transactional notion of the self, this concern demonstrates that it is important to recognize imbalances in power and authority so that one's transactions are not characterized by pseudodemocracy.[63] Pseudodemocracy occurs when those with a greater voice in a particular situation pretend that everyone has an equal say, making the operations of authority and power within the situation invisible.

When rendered invisible, oppressive inequalities of power and authority are unlikely to be mitigated or changed. The concern also points to the related need to discriminate in some situations with whom one transacts and to what degree one does so. The transactional character of human existence cannot be abolished, but sometimes and in some situations one can and should attempt to avoid the influence of particular people. Because of the crucial effect that others can have on one's somatic experience, somaesthetic work is best done with the help of a person or persons whose judgment one trusts. Of course, the presence of trust offers no absolute guarantees of safety in somaesthetic work, but absolute guarantees are not what pragmatist feminism seeks. By pursuing relationships of trust in somaesthetic work, a person can mitigate some of the dangers of transaction by regulating who will play a key role in constituting her. Even in trusting relationships, however, the need to be critically aware of and responsive to relations of power in transactions with others is important. For example, when working with an Alexander Technique instructor who is a woman, a woman participant still must address the imbalances of authority that might occur because of the race, class, sexuality, and nationality of both women, as well as because of the medical authority of the instructor.

Finally, operating with a transactional notion of corporeality means that somaesthetics undercuts attempts to understand the distinction between auto- and heterosomaesthetic work as a dualism. Auto- and heterosomaesthetic work cannot be taken to be utterly different and opposed to one another. In the sense that all somaesthetic work requires the input and perspective of others, all somaesthetics is heterosomaesthetic to a degree, and thus there is no absolute difference between the two types of practices. For that reason, they are not like the ingredients of a tossed salad. The lines drawn between auto- and heterosomaesthetics must be thought of as permeable and fluid. This does not mean, however, that the distinction between auto- and heterosomaesthetics should be dropped altogether. Maintaining a distinction between them preserves important differences between somaesthetic work that focuses primarily on one's own bodying and that which focuses primarily on the bodying of another. While both types of work involve another person, the two types are not identical and should not be treated as such.

Melting auto- and heterosomaesthetic work completely together is dangerous particularly for women. It can contribute to situations in which a woman is expected to devote herself to the care of another in such a way that she understands and experiences self-denial not as care of another at the expense of care of herself, but precisely *as* care of herself.[64] Not being allowed to distinguish one's own desires and needs from those of another is damaging to the person whose needs and desires are neglected. And self-neglect not only prevents one from caring for oneself, it also prevents one from effectively caring for others. Women must be allowed to "selfishly" heap up riches in her own soul to be able to give to others, which is to say that effective heterosomaesthetic work presupposes autosomaesthetic work.[65] For the sake of care of self and for care of another, it is important to retain the distinction between auto- and heterosomaesthetic work, even as one should reject dualistic understandings of it. Auto- and heterosomaesthetic work should be seen as ingredients of a stew, rather than of a melting pot. That the two types of somaesthetics are not substantially different does not warrant collapsing their differences into a complete identity.

My claim that a transactional somaesthetics contains resources to combat the sexism in Nietzsche's work should not be understood as a claim to have eliminated all the risks for women that somaesthetic work possibly entails, nor as a claim that we should dismiss Nietzsche's own sexism. In particular, I think that the first problematic aspect of somaesthetic work, regarding the negative association between women and bodies, is one that will not quickly be eliminated. Habits, both individual and cultural, concerning conceptions of women and bodies are not easy to change when they are deeply engrained. As a woman engaging in somaesthetic practices, in both philosophy and "real" life, I cannot be certain my work does not contribute to the strengthening of the negative connection between women and bodily matters. But this danger should not stop feminists, pragmatists, and other philosophers from exploring what a somaesthetics might be and asking how somaesthetic theory and practice might be made more supportive of women. This unavoidable risk suggests a fourth and final guideline to be made explicit for somaestheticians: that of developing one's somaesthetics in and through an awareness of social, political, and cultural environments. Nietzsche is right that every bodying has its own measure, and thus somaesthetic practices should be designed for the specific needs of particular individuals. But focus on the individual should not be accomplished at the expense of an understanding of the gendered, sexed, raced, classed, and other meanings that are potentially attributed to bodies through somatic practices. Attunement to bodily life must be individualized in such a way that the individual is transactionally situated in a wider social setting. Only with such an attunement can somaesthetics be a practice to endorse.

Transactional Knowing

Toward a Pragmatist-Feminist Standpoint Theory

As Nietzsche once claimed, "[t]he unconscious disguise of physiological needs under the cloa[k] of the objective . . . goes to frightening lengths" in philosophy.[1] Because of human corporeality, the objectivist claim that objectivity is attained when humans know the world as impartial, neutral observers is extremely problematic. *Contra* objectivism, humans cannot see from a "God's eye" point of view untouched by human interests and perspectives. Gender, race, class, sexuality, personal history, national origin, and other corporeal particularities constitute human beings in such a way that they are always already shaped by their interests, needs, and desires. Selective emphasis is unavoidable: humans necessarily focus on some aspects of the world rather than on others. Because knowledge is the product of a personal and engaged, rather than impersonal and detached, subject, even objectivism is the product of an interested rather than disinterested perspective.[2]

But the rejection of objectivism need not and should not result in a judgmental relativism in which no distinction can be made between better and worse perspectives.[3] While objectivism has failed to provide acceptable epistemological standards, its failure does not mean that human beings can do without some sort of epistemological criteria. The activities of human life constantly require making distinctions and choices, and thus all humans operate with and require standards by which they can make such judgments and decisions. Liberatory projects, such as those pursued by feminists and pragmatists, are in particular need of such standards because they aim to change cultural and political structures so that the lives of the oppressed are improved.

Because the perspectival nature of human beings does not eliminate the need for epistemological standards, the rejection of objectivism must be followed up with a reconstruction of a new ideal of "objectivity." To think objectivity in terms other than those provided by objectivism, one needs a notion of objectivity that is based on the transactional relationship between organisms and world. Responding to the feminist standpoint theory of Sandra Harding, I contribute here to the task of reconstructing objectivity by developing what I call a pragmatist-feminist standpoint theory. Harding's version of feminist standpoint theory is valuable because it attempts to reconstruct objectivity as perspectival. According to Harding, the particular perspectives of women constitute a starting point for objective research. By implicitly retaining a model of truth as achieved by those with the clearest vision of the world, however, Harding's theory assumes that some people can attain a measure of infallibility similar to that allegedly provided by a "God's eye" point of view. A pragmatist-feminist account of truth as that which promotes the flourishing of transactional bodies can furnish Harding with an understanding of epistemology that is not cast in the terms of objectivism. By doing so, pragmatist feminism can help feminist standpoint theory achieve its goal of reconstructing objectivity.

Harding's account of feminist standpoint theory claims that knowledge can be conceived as objective without assuming a disinterested, impersonal "God's eye" point of view only if philosophical, scientific, and other kinds of research start from the perspective of women's lives. Unlike men, whose view of the social relations of patriarchal society is distorted by their position as "master," women have a privileged perspective on reality because they are marginalized. Because of their marginalization, they have less interest in ignoring or remaining oblivious to society's gender inequalities; thus, their perspective can provide the starting point for accounts of knowledge that are undistorted by gender loyalties.[4]

Harding makes a distinction between a standpoint, in which experience is socially mediated through politics and critical inquiry, and a mere perspective, which is provided by unmediated experience.[5] Women's experiences and stories are valuable for what they reveal about a patriarchal social order, but, like all human beings, women are shaped by patriarchy and thus can espouse sexist views. For that reason, Harding does not merely use the stories and experiences that constitute women's perspectives to ground her position; the critical standpoint developed out of them anchors it instead. As a critical standpoint, feminist standpoint theory includes standards for judgment and discrimination, which a simple injunction to listen to women does not.[6]

Central to Harding's feminist standpoint theory is her concept of "strong objectivity." Harding chooses this term to distinguish her conception from traditional notions of objectivity, which, she claims, by drawing from a masculine perspective only, are not objective enough.[7] The contrast Harding draws between her position and objectivism's narrowness of perspective implies that her notion of objectivity is a type of pluralism: a broadening of perspectives so that those other than white, heterosexual, middle-class males are included in the starting point for scientific and other research. Harding often suggests that such a pluralism of perspectives is what she means by strong objectivity:

> The goal of maximizing the objectivity of research should require overcoming *excessive* reliance on distinctively masculine lives and making use *also* of women's lives as origins for scientific problematics, sources of scientific evidence, and checks against the validity of knowledge claims.[8]

> Listening carefully to different voices and attending thoughtfully to others' values and interests can enlarge our vision and begin to correct for inevitable enthnocentrisms.[9]

> For men, the view from women's lives can illuminate their own lives by creating a broader context and contrasting perspective from which to examine critically the institutions and practices within which occur their own beliefs and behaviors, social relations and institutions.[10]

"Pluralist objectivity," as I will call it, increases objectivity by maximizing the number of different perspectives allowed to contribute to knowledge claims. Its pluralism is what makes Harding's formulation of objectivity stronger than that of objectivism.

Distinct from, but related to, pluralist objectivity is the second sense of objectivity implied by Harding: objectivity as "background-revealing." According to Harding, to operate under the directive of strong objectivity means also to examine critically one's own position from the viewpoint of another.[11] Becoming objective requires the ability to see the background beliefs that inform one's position, beliefs that are usually so familiar to, and thus hidden from, oneself that it takes another to help one identify them. Harding's account of strong objectivity recognizes that people—and men, in particular—are not self-transparent; thus, they need the perspectives of others to root out the biases that exist in their world views. Harding's position "starts thought in the perspective from the life of the Other, allowing the Other to gaze back 'shamelessly' at the self who had reserved for himself the right to gaze 'anonymously' at whomever he chooses."[12] In that way, feminist standpoint theory "makes strange what had appeared familiar," that is, makes the very familiarity of a man's perspective seem strange to him.[13]

Background-revealing objectivity is similar to pluralist objectivity in that both require multiple perspectives to maximize objectivity. As developed by Harding, however, background-revealing objectivity goes further than pluralist objectivity in specifying which background assumptions need examination and, therefore, which perspectives are to be listened to so that objectivity is increased. To the extent that pluralism might suggest a judgmental or epistemological relativism in which all perspectives are equally valid, Harding distances herself from pluralism with her definition of objectivity as background-revealing. According to Harding, while "listening carefully to different voices can enlarge our vision," we must note that "the dominant values, interests, and voices are not among these 'different' ones."[14] The "Other" is not just anyone who occupies a different perspective from one's own. It is the person in a position marginalized by society. Because Western culture is patriarchal, it is the hidden beliefs of patriarchy that have been exempt from critical examination and are in need of exposure. Because we all, Western men and women alike, have been shaped by the dominant masculine perspective in our culture, for each of us, the perspective of the "Other" is the perspective from women's lives. For these reasons, both women and men need to listen to and start their research from the particular perspective of women.

That women, like men, need to begin with the perspective of women means that Harding's mature standpoint theory does not assume that the oppressed are somehow more "innocent" than their oppressors.[15] Like their oppressors, the oppressed are impacted by the oppressive society in which they live. If the dominant masculine perspective in Western culture has shaped all members of it, women as well as men have been constituted by patriarchy. That Harding is not guilty of romanticizing the perspectives of women in her later work is an important strength of her position. But, at the same time, the rejection of the innocence of the oppressed produces a serious problem for feminist standpoint theory. If the perspective of the oppressed is distorted by oppression, it can no better provide a valid starting point for knowledge claims than can that of the oppressor.[16] This problem occurs for Harding's position because of the foundational ideal of truth that continues to function in it. I will return to this issue after discussing the third form of objectivity that operates in Harding's standpoint theory. For now, I note that a consequence of Harding's notion of objectivity as background-revealing is that the perspective of the oppressed may be just as clouded as that of the oppressor.

In addition to revealing hidden background beliefs, starting from the particular perspective of women maximizes objectivity in another distinct, but related, way. Harding implies a third definition of objectivity, one in which the perspective of marginalized women produces less partial and distorted knowledge than does the view from a dominant, masculine perspective. The definition of objectivity as "less partial and distorted" is distinct from pluralist objectivity because "distorted" is *not* meant by Harding as a synonym for "partial." This point is crucial to Harding's claim that her conception of objectivity is strong. It is not the case that a masculine perspective is distorted *because* it is partial, as pluralist objectivity could claim. Rather, *apart from* or *in addition to* its partiality, it is also distorted. As Harding states, "the unselfconscious [masculine] perspective claiming universality is in fact not only partial but also distorting in ways that go beyond its partiality."[17] According to Harding, knowledge generated by starting from women's lives is less partial and distorted than that generated from the dominant perspective because research based on women's experiences furnishes "less false" claims to knowledge than does research based on experiences of men.[18]

This last claim distinguishes Harding's less partial and distorted objectivity from not only pluralist, but also from background-revealing objectivity. Less partial and distorted objectivity does not merely claim that the perspective from women's lives allows one to highlight background assumptions in one's cultural belief system; it also claims that this perspective provides truer accounts of the world than does the dominant perspective. This does not mean that the perspective from women's lives is completely impartial or undistorted. On Harding's account, all perspectives are partial and distorted by relations of domination. Thus, for Harding, there is no Archimedian point of absolute infallibility from which to begin one's account of the world.[19] Harding argues, however, that just because there is no one true account of the world, one is not forced to give up attempts to distinguish between more and less false accounts of the world.[20] According to Harding, one can still judge some accounts to be less false than others even if no account is absolutely true.[21]

Harding's argument regarding the "less false" is a result of her effort to combine the postmodern claim that there is no one true story about the world with the feminist need to distinguish between better and worse, sexist and nonsexist accounts of the world. Harding's self-described "semi-rapprochement between standpoint and postmodernist tendencies" is motivated by criticisms of earlier versions of feminist standpoint theory made by those such as Jane Flax and Donna Haraway.[22] Flax charges feminist standpoint theory with assuming the existence of "a reality that is out there waiting for our representation" and that "the oppressed have a privileged (and not just different) relation and ability to comprehend" it.[23] Likewise, Haraway criticizes feminist standpoint theory for relying on the dual notion of a reality capable of accurate reflection and a feminist standpoint that is pure and innocent enough to produce such reflection.[24] And, indeed, early versions of feminist standpoint theory, such as that of Nancy Hartsock, made these very assumptions, if not explicit claims, when arguing that a metaphysical hierarchy of activity explains women's privileged location. Adopting Marx's distinctions between dual levels of reality, Hartsock claims that "reality itself consists of 'sensuous human activity, practice.' "[25] Unlike men's work, the work of women is immersed in concrete, sensuous, material processes, and so knowledge developed from women's activity is more closely linked to reality and able "to go beneath the surface of appearances to reveal the real but concealed social relations."[26] Because of the emphasis it gives to the particular material activity of maternity, Hartsock's account suggests that men could never inhabit a privileged perspective as well as women, if they could inhabit it at all, because they could never be as fully embedded in material activity as women.

By rejecting the claim that "our 'best' representations of the world are transparent to the world—that is, are true," Harding attempts to distance herself from notions of truth as faithful mirrors of the world that are available to women only.[27] Harding claims that her position does not need to maintain that claims made from women's perspectives are true, that is, that they faithfully mirror or transparently represent the world independently of human beings. All her position needs, she claims, is a criterion of less falsity in which all claims are admittedly distorted and thus not true representations of the world, but in which some claims can be shown to represent the world in a less false manner. Along these lines, Harding rhetorically asks, "[b]ut once the idea of absolute falsity also [in addition to absolute truth] becomes indefensible, what could be the use of the concept of truth? The notion [of truth] is inextricably linked to objectivism and its absolutist standards. . . . Who needs truth in science? Only those who are still wedded to the neutrality ideal."[28]

Harding's move from a criterion of absolute truth to one of less falsity does not distance her, as she had hoped it would, from foundational notions of truth as faithful mirroring. Just as the question "What makes something true?" needs explanation, so does the question "What makes something less false?" The shift from absolute truth or falsity to degrees of truth or falsity does not eliminate Harding's dependence upon an account of what truth is.[29] Because Harding does not explicitly develop a notion of truth as something other than mirroring reality, she implicitly relies on the very same notion to justify why women's perspectives are less false than those of men. Her claim that some perspectives (such as those of women) mirror reality better than do others (such as those of men) and, thus, are less false is able to function only by means of the standard of transparency supplied by an account of truth as faithful mirroring. Because, for Harding, "distorted" is not simply a synonym for "partial," describing claims as more or less distorted implies that her position judges various perspectives on their greater or lesser ability to clearly represent the world. Harding's claim that no perspective can represent the world completely and accurately does not diminish the fact that the standard by which greater and lesser degrees of representation are measured remains that of truth as mirroring reality.

Continued reliance in Harding's work on a foundational ideal of truth as mirroring is evident in much of the language she uses to describe the advantages of feminist standpoint theory. Sounding much like Hartsock, Harding claims that research starting from women's lives will provide us with "clearer and more nearly complete visions of social reality" and that feminist struggles can allow us to "begin to see beneath the appearances created by an unjust social order to the reality of how this social order is in fact constructed and maintained."[30] The problematic distinction between dual levels of reality and the troubling dependence upon a material hierarchy that functioned in early versions of feminist standpoint theory continues to operate in Harding's mature development of her position. Rather than disrupt the dichotomy between absolute truth and falsity, Harding's appeal to a criterion of "less false" merely locates her claims between them.[31]

The problem with Harding's continued reliance on foundational hierarchies of truth and falsity is not only its dependence on a foundational metaphysics and epistemology, per se; more importantly, such reliance merely reverses the traditional, unjustified metaphysical privileging of a male perspective over a female one. As Daniel Conway has suggested, such a reversal risks being "an inverted, matriarchal version of patriarchal objectivity" that merely replaces the patriarchal "god-trick" with a "goddess-trick" of Harding's own design.[32] Without an alternate account of what truth is, an appeal to women's perspectives as "less false" is just as arbitrary and problematic as is a sexist culture's assumption that a masculine perspective should be privileged over a feminine one. Even when made with the good intention of pointing out what the world is "really" like for women, such appeals do not eliminate the oppressive effects of the claim to have a truer view of reality than does another.[33] Harding resists providing an alternative account of truth because she erroneously assumes that truth can only mean what traditional philosophy has said it does. But truth is not necessarily tied to objectivism and absolutism; thus, it is not the case that only those who are wed to the neutrality ideal need truth. Feminist standpoint theory needs an alternative account of truth precisely so that it can divorce itself from the neutrality ideal and the type of epistemic justification that it allegedly provides.

My suggestion that Harding's work needs an alternative account of truth does not misconstrue the aims and purposes of feminist standpoint theory as epistemological, as opposed to the political. Harding has expressed this concern when summing up the aims of her standpoint theory in response to her critics. Replying to criticism of her reliance on a concept of "true reality," Harding has insisted that feminist standpoint theory concerns "relations of power and knowledge" and is distorted when it is characterized as a project "of figuring out how to justify the truth of feminist claims to more accurate accounts of reality."[34] Precisely because politics and epistemology are inseparable, however, feminist standpoint theory must not flinch from the fact that it is and should be in the business of providing epistemic justification.[35] However, epistemic justification need not be conceived traditionally. Exactly what sort of business epistemic justification might or should be is precisely what is at issue here. Epistemic justification is crucial to Harding's position because only with it can feminist standpoint theory avoid "preaching to the choir" and inadvertently supporting the relativism Harding wants to avoid.[36] Without epistemic justification, Harding's account has no response to the unpersuaded who might ask, "why start with women's lives if I have sexist rather than feminist sympathies?" And, without a response, Harding cannot avoid playing into a judgmental relativism that claims, "you have your political commitments and thus your starting point for research, I have mine, and there is no basis on which you can claim yours is better than mine."

Harding seems to recognize this problem and the corresponding need for justification in her discussion of conflicting First and Third world perspectives on the role and effects of modern science and technology in *Whose Science? Whose Knowledge?* As she claims in that context, "[g]iven the different frameworks of the two stories" about Western science, "defenders of each [story] can claim that the other is partial and distorted."[37] But, while Harding acknowledges that "what is needed [are] . . . standards competent to distinguish between" the stories, she is only able to respond to that need with the admission that "at present, it is difficult to locate such standards."[38] The inability to provide such standards is an effect of Harding's continued reliance on foundational notions of truth. This inability severely jeopardizes, if not completely undermines, feminist standpoint theory, including its attempt to provide an account of knowledge that is both objective and situated in women's lives. Feminist standpoint theory must pay further attention to the epistemic justification for starting with women's lives it offers through its criterion of the "less false." Only by explicitly providing an account of truth that is not based on mirroring reality can it provide justification for its starting point of women's lives that does not implicitly appeal to representational accounts of reality. Precisely so that feminist standpoint theory can avoid being a project of justification by means of implicit appeal to objectivism, it must focus on the issue of truth.

Harding's standpoint theory is not alone in its continued reliance on a definition of truth as perfectly mirroring a reality divorced from experience. Even some philosophers who explicitly claim to eschew epistemology, such as Richard Rorty, indirectly rely on it, making a concept of truth as mirroring seem unavoidable. By rejecting epistemology for conversations that have no epistemological basis or function, Rorty implicitly accepts a definition of truth as mirroring nature by offering no alternative to it.[39] The problem with a definition of truth as that which corresponds to reality is that it fails to grasp that truth claims are not used merely to describe states of affairs, nor are they very useful for mere description of existing facts. Knowledge and truth have the purpose of putting existing facts and events to use in the transformation of the world. What is needed in philosophy is the recognition of the connection of knowledge and truth to life. This will extract them from what Dewey called "that species of intellectual lock-jaw called [traditional] epistemology"[40] and put them to work in service of existence so they might produce the richest and fullest experience possible.

The nonfoundational standards for justification and the alternative accounts of truth and objectivity needed by feminist standpoint theory can be developed out of an understanding of bodies as transactional. On that understanding, the study of how organisms know things takes the form of investigating and devising means for reorganizing one's transactions with the world, not of cataloguing data or constructing systems of abstract knowledge. Knowing is not an activity organisms do simply for its own sake. Organisms seek to know for the sake of securing the changes that they wish to effect in their lives, experiences, and selves. Knowledge should not be conceived as the result of perfectly mirroring a static world that stands beyond organic life. Rather, it should be conceived as a transactional method of experimental inquiry in which one investigates the problematic situations with which one is confronted in order to develop possible solutions to them, solutions which are then tested in lived experience to see if the desired results occur.[41] Defining knowledge in this way transforms knowing from being a passive recording of the features of the world to being a dynamic activity by which organisms guide and are guided by their transactions with the world.

Like knowledge, the concept of truth needs reconceptualization so that it is seen as a judgment of the degree of success of attempts to reorganize experience. A judgment or belief is true not if it matches the state of affairs it attempts to report, but if, when acted on, it produces the desired transformation of organisms and environments. In that way, truth refers to the future career of a judgment and, in particular, the ability of that judgment to effect an improved transaction between living beings and the world. Truth must pass the test of experience. When considering the truth of a claim, one is not asking whether it mirrors reality, but whether it satisfies various desires and needs. While the specifics of what those needs are will vary based on the particular situation in question, the fundamental value guiding the ends-in-view in the situation is that of satisfaction. Only those ends that have passed the test of the satisfying the needs and desires of those in question count as true. While the notion of transaction is instrumental in that it focuses on the means by which one might achieve one's desired ends, it is not viciously instrumental because it also includes a critique of ends. Not just any end is satisfactory on a pragmatist-feminist account.

In addition to serving as the broad end that shapes the specific ends to be attained in specific problematic situations, satisfaction in experience plays an important role in the initial identification of a situation as problematic. Lack of satisfaction indicates why a situation is troubling and, thus, in need of inquiry so that it might be transformed. Admittedly, the specifics of why a situation is unsatisfactory will vary depending on the particular situation, but the lack of satisfaction, broadly speaking, is what spurs one to experimentally inquire into a situation in the first place. Relating the need for knowledge to the concept of satisfaction thus connects epistemology to the concrete problems experienced in everyday life. It explains how felt difficulties in life, and not the problems of academic epistemology, should generate the problems of knowledge into which philosophers and other researchers inquire.

Given the importance of satisfaction to a transactional account of truth, it is crucial to recognize that satisfaction here means a rich sense of flourishing that is not reducible to a utilitarian definition of happiness as the maximization of pleasure. Happiness or satisfaction in a quasi-utilitarian or crudely instrumental sense is inadequate because, borrowing Dewey's words, "to 'make others happy' except through liberating their power and engaging them in activities that enlarge the meaning of life is to harm them."[42] The quality of experience is composed not by its agreeableness, but more importantly by its promotion of continuing growth and further expansion of experience, which often involves unpleasantness and pain.[43] Something becomes true when it encourages flourishing, not necessarily when it makes one feel good. Something becomes true when it promotes the liberation of powers, the enlargement of life's meaning, and the growth of experience through enriched transactions with the world.

A word or two is in order about the concept of experience as used here. The term does not refer only to human experience because the test of experience that truth must pass involves more than just human life. Dewey often makes statements of the sort that claims to truth should not be considered true until "tested in the satisfaction of the most intimate and comprehensive of human needs."[44] In that his claim is that truth is a matter of satisfaction in the here and now of this world, rather than the otherworldly, Dewey's point is well taken. In his attempts to steer his readers away from an objectivist notion of truth, however, Dewey risks overemphasizing human organisms at the expense of nonhuman ones. While Dewey's emphasis on human needs should be heard in the context in which it was intended, it remains too strong.[45] A pragmatist-feminist account of truth requires more explicit inclusion of the needs of nonhuman needs and interests than Dewey provides.

Because bodies are transactional, human experience always already involves more than humans considered as isolated from their environments and the other living organisms that populate them. Truth can be achieved only through transaction with one's physical, cultural, political, and other environments because there is no self apart from the world in which it exists. Humans are not set apart from an independent reality as detached spectators, but are always already participants in a world that is in part shaped by them. All human activity, as well as any satisfaction found in it, is a matter of mutual transformation of the self and its world, human and nonhuman, organic and inorganic alike. The transactional relationship between humans and their various environments means that the definition of truth as transactions that produce flourishing experiences necessarily includes the flourishing of animals, plants, soil, and other components of the nonhuman environment.[46]

In particular, when human needs are at issue, a pragmatist-feminist account of truth also requires focus on the question of who counts as human that is more explicit than what Dewey tends to provide. Women of all races, men of color, lesbians and gay men, and people with physical and mental disabilities are just some of the human beings who historically have been and currently often are discounted as not being fully human. The reconceptualization of truth as transactional flourishing must include not only the ideal of maximum inclusion of various organisms' needs, interests, and desires but also a historical awareness of who is likely to be left out of the attempt to produce richer experiences. It also must include a contemporary awareness of who actually is being left out in the particular situation in question. Awareness of exclusion should be funded with historically based general guidelines that help one identify likely habits of exclusion and oppression. At the same time, it should gear those guidelines to specific situations because patterns of inclusion and exclusion can be particular to, and vary in, specific situations.

The co-constitution and co-transformation of humans and their environments means that a transactional account of truth is not a correspondence theory. Although Dewey does, on the occasion, use the word "correspondence" in connection with his account of truth, he does so not in the sense of mirroring reality, as does the correspondence theory of truth; instead he uses the word transactionally "in the sense in which two friends correspond, that is, interact as checks, as stimuli, as mutual aids and mutual correctors."[47] Truth occurs when humans and their environments respond to and transact with one another in such a way that flourishing is achieved for both.[48] Truth is not a matter of humans "fitting" their beliefs to the world. Nor is it a matter of matching internal representations to external reality. It is a mutual negotiation and transformation of a relationship between humans and their environments, including the nonhuman, which promotes the thriving of both. For that reason, feminists working to redefine objectivity should be wary of retaining a notion of correspondence understood as a "fit with the world."[49] At minimum, redefinitions of objectivity that speak of correspondence must be accompanied by an account of correspondence alternative to what the philosophical tradition in the West has provided. Otherwise, the existing definition of correspondence is left in place, and attempts to transform objectivity are undermined with the return to a definition of truth as mirroring reality.

Although rejecting the concept of mirroring, a transactional account of truth does not deny a reality that at times objects to organisms' purposes or requires them to modify their beliefs and plans. Tying truth to interests, needs, satisfactions, and purposes does not turn truth into a hollow standard in which anything goes because everything is merely subjective. Such concerns reflect the operation of a dualism of objective and subjective that pragmatist feminism avoids with its account of transaction. Personal, subjective interests are formed through transaction with the objective world, not in isolation from it. These transactions and the world involved in them must be taken into account if one's interests are to have any chance of being satisfied. The world delimits one's desires just as one's desires delimit the world. Each serves as a limitation of the other that keeps it in check.

Because they are intimately connected to needs, desires, and interests through transaction with an ever-changing world, truths are neither timeless nor unchanging. They are historically and temporally constituted, capable of revision based on the changing needs of the particular organisms and nonorganic bodies involved. Further, the fact that situations change means that truths are not just capable of, but often in need of, transformation. To view truth as transactional not only supports the idea of change in truth; it also obliges one to reexamine and update current truths if they no longer serve interests and needs. This obligation does not imply a Cartesian razing of all established beliefs. It is not possible to reject all currently accepted truths at once.[50] As a lived rather than as an academic problem, doubt is not universal; it is specific to particular problematic situations. The need to critically examine and revise various truths arises from them, producing context-dependent inquiry that transforms accepted truth piece by piece, situation by situation.

Just as truths are not timeless or unchanging, neither are the selves whose interests, desires, and needs truth involves. In the attempt to transform a problematic situation, one transforms not just the situation, but also the selves formed through transaction in it. Desires and interests are constitutive of the self in that when one attempts to change a situation to provide greater satisfaction, one not only changes the situation but also changes oneself through its transformation. Dewey puts the relationship of self and desire well when he says that "[a] self changes its structure and its value according to the kind of object which it desires and seeks; according, that is, to the different kinds of objects in which active interest is taken."[51] As a result, to pursue a particular desire through the transformation of experience is to pursue a particular self. The self is always in the process of remaking itself, and in doing so, it becomes what it desires.[52] Both the self and its desires and interests change as a result of inquiry, which means that the truths one pursues, that is, the satisfaction of desires and enriching of experiences that one attempts to achieve, also must continually change.

A transactional notion of truth allows for distinctions between better and worse claims or theories without appeal to a foundationalist notion of truth as faithful mirroring of a reality hidden beneath appearances. Claims can be judged to be true or false based on the degree to which they promote flourishing in and through transactions with the world, rather than on the degree of their transparency to reality. The appeal to mirroring made by Western philosophical tradition needs to be replaced with a method of experimental inquiry because such a method allows for historical, socially constituted, fallible, *and* warranted truths that have been tested in experience for their ability to promote flourishing. In this way, truth understood as flourishing transactions leads beyond the dualism of objectivism and relativism. One can reject the false dilemma of having either absolute truth or a complete inability to make epistemological judgments, as well as the false dilemma of having either the rigor of "objective," impersonal standards or the "anything goes" of mere "subjective," biased pseudo-standards.[53] The emphasis on transactional flourishing provides standards for objectivity that are constituted through the exigencies of corporeal existence, rather than located in an extrahistorical or presocial realm.

These standards are not of a sort that can be abstractly listed or itemized. In general, they share the common structure of being based on the needs of those in a particular situation, varying in their specifics based on the differences of each situation. In this way, they may not seem "iron-clad" enough to count as objective standards if one's ideal of an objective standard is that which exists apart from concrete situations to be applied to them in a "top-down" fashion. If, instead, one's notion of objective standards is based on recognition of the perspectival nature of corporeal existence, a notion of standards that are generated out of, rather than apart from, situations is preferable. A specific situation involving particular individuals with their particular needs and desires puts forth particular issues that must be addressed if the situation is to be positively transformed. Situations generate nonarbitrary benchmarks by which to judge changes made to them, benchmarks that involve something other than just one person getting her way and that are responsive to, rather than dismissive of, the various subjective needs and desires involved in them.

Complementing feminist standpoint theory with an epistemology based on transactional bodies creates what we might call a pragmatist-feminist standpoint theory. Such a theory helps feminists move away from questions about which standpoint describes reality in less distorting ways, to questions about which standpoints can help promote flourishing transactions. The shift away from foundational justifications for beginning with women's rather than men's lives does not sacrifice the ability to make judgments about better and worse starting points. A pragmatist-feminist standpoint theory allows one to make those judgments on contextual instead of absolute grounds. This shift is important because it allows standpoint theory to avoid merely endorsing the reverse side of the same sexist coin that claimed privilege for a masculine perspective.

The move away from a foundational metaphysics is important also because it allows standpoint theory to better focus on the otherwise hidden questions: who is the "we" deciding upon "our" goals and, more to the point, what if "we" do not agree? Harding's account of feminist standpoint theory can provide answers as long as the questions are understood to be those of conflict between relatively homogenous feminine and masculine perspectives. Harding apparently resolves oppositions between conflicting standpoints and their goals by assigning metaphysical priority to women's description of reality and to the goals generated from it. Aside from the problematic implications of priority, Harding's position becomes even more difficult once she no longer essentializes women (or men) and instead acknowledges the complexity of all subject positions. Once multiple marginalized standpoints and, thus, multiple liberatory projects are involved, it is not clear how feminist standpoint theory can handle conflicting claims of liberatory epistemologies. As critics of Harding have pointed out, her position never resolves the problem of conflict and has no answer to this question other than the thin suggestion that one welcome this tension as a source of creativity.[54]

An epistemology based on transactional bodies is better equipped to handle such tension and to use it as a source of creativity. There is no need to appeal to true(r) descriptions of reality to resolve opposition between conflicting claims. Indeed, such an appeal tends to shut out of the conversations and communities needed to resolve conflict those people with perceived "less true" perspectives. Instead of declaring at the outset that some people have "less false" perspectives, all parties in a problematic situation should have a voice in the project of creating perhaps as-yet-unforeseen solutions that accommodate the needs and encourage the flourishing of the parties involved. The answer to who gets to resolve conflicting claims about what counts as flourishing and the conflicting answers to the question "flourishing for whom?" is, in a significant sense, everyone. Those in both the so-called "center" and "margins" need to be involved in the process of resolving opposition. This process must take into account the needs of all "locations," not just the needs of the marginalized groups at the expense of the dominating ones, or vice versa.[55]

This is not to claim that including all relevant parties, or even determining who the various parties in an issue are, will be an easy or, ultimately, successful project. Nor is it to claim that all parties have the same sort of access to or power within the rhetorical and physical spaces that delimit whose voices are heard.[56] It *is* to claim that radical inclusion should be the ideal toward which feminists, pragmatists, and others work, even if they fall short of it. Indeed, it should be a working ideal even if one necessarily falls short of it because of the exclusions that seem inevitable in the process of securing space for greater inclusion.[57] I have in mind here the example of the seeming necessity to exclude members of violent white supremacist groups from public space for the purpose of broadening it to include black, Latino, Native, and other people of color. As with all cultural spaces, spaces of radical democratic inclusion are constituted by vectors of power and, paradoxically, might require exclusion as a condition for the possibility of their existence. Yet the possibility of the practical necessity of such types of exclusion does not invalidate the ideal of always seeking to be as inclusive in one's dealings as possible. Nor does it warrant an *a priori* declaration that exclusion of those who themselves exclude is necessary. In some problematic situations, this may be so, in others not. Each situation must be examined for what it requires to maximize inclusion.

The possibility and power of radical inclusion is well illustrated by the life of Daryl Davis, a black man who has spent years seeking to understand and combat racism by pursuing conversations with, attending rallies and marches of, and even developing friendships with members of the Ku Klux Klan.[58] Many people in general, and probably most black people in particular, see the Klan as a group that must be excluded from the *polis* to secure the inclusion of black people. Rather than dismiss, avoid, or attempt to silence Klan members, however, Davis listened to their views on the world even though they often angered him. He did not attack or badger them with his own different views, but ventured his opinions only after a level of trust and common ground between him and the Klan members had been established. The result of Davis's transactions with the Klan was not just an improved understanding of the Klan's racism. Nor was it merely the unexpected discovery of some similar beliefs and commitments between Klan members and him, nor the development of friendships, one of which resulted in Davis's becoming the godfather of the daughter of the Imperial Wizard of the Ku Klux Klan. It was a change in opinion about black people on the part of some Klan members, occasionally accompanied by their quitting the Klan altogether.

This transformation occurred because, even though he vehemently disagreed with them, Davis was willing to treat Klan members as people who are potentially worthy of respect, honesty, and fair treatment. He included those who seemed most deserving of exclusion, and his gesture of goodwill transformed the lives of some members of the Klan. Of course, Davis's example does not mean that the ideal of radical inclusion can be put into practice in every situation. Davis did not get along with every Klan member he met, and his book is not intended as a how-to manual for fighting racism. What Davis's life demonstrates is the importance of the ideal of radical inclusion as a guide for practice. It also shows how inclusion can sometimes be extended in beneficial ways beyond that which currently seems conceivable. The ideal of inclusion needs to be one in which as many people as possible struggle over what counts as a satisfactory resolution of a problematic situation, such as that of racial conflict, even if that ideal cannot always be put into practice.

Because bodies are not atomistic, everyone must be involved in such struggles, both ideally and as far as can be accomplished practically. A society or community is not a tossed salad, in which its different ingredients exist side by side without any constitutive effect upon one another. Because the self is transactional, and more like a stew in which ingredients co-constitute each other even as they remain distinct from one another, everyone's capacity to flourish affects and is affected by every other one in the society. To switch from culinary to agricultural metaphors, because others share the societal soil in which each of us grows, ultimately the more everyone in a society thrives, the more any individual self is able to thrive. Because bodies are transactional, to neglect the needs of any group is to deprive all groups of a crucial condition for the possibility of their flourishing.[59]

Acknowledging the transactional nature of bodies and their environments, one must relinquish what Lorraine Code has called the "autonomy obsession" that has plagued much of Western philosophy.[60] This obsession manifests itself in the demand for a sharp distinction between knower and known and between subject and object. In my view, the autonomy obsession also can manifest itself in the tendency to divide off an "us" that can and should decide what a satisfactory resolution to the struggle in question might be without the participation of the "them." Giving up the autonomy obsession means not only that dominant groups are not autonomous in the ways they often have been posited as being, but also that dominated groups are not autonomous. Giving up the autonomy obsession means that *everyone* needs to recognize her or his heteronomy. Ways are needed to work with interdependent and conflicting needs and desires without considering the needs and desires of one group at the exclusion of those of another.

To emphasize the needs of the dominating group(s) is not to claim that solutions to women's oppression must include sexist as well as nonsexist components. Conceiving of the dialogue between perspectives in this way is to base one's conception on an atomistic notion of the perspectives involved. That bodies are transactional means that the claims put forward, as well as the solutions that are generated from them, are not the private property of their originators, but are jointly constructed with others.[61] The notion of transactional bodies entails a resourceful skepticism, which is not a denial of all claims but a wariness of hasty conclusions and a readiness to reconsider one's own proposals.[62] On this account, communication with another occurs through a process of mutual transformation brought about by transactional, experimental inquiry, a process in which claims are offered to another as hypotheses that are open to modification by her.[63]

The concept of transactional bodies further implies that everyone not only *should* be, but *is* involved to some degree in the mutual process of creating solutions, even if that involvement takes the form of ignoring or refusing to listen to another. The needs of dominating and of dominated are at issue in and are part of any solution any time there is conflict. Recognizing this fact shifts the focus of one's epistemological projects in a positive way. The question is never one of whether everyone is to be involved or not, but whether everyone will be involved in ways that either promote or limit their flourishing. The choice is not whether to include certain people and their perspectives; it is whether to include them by conceiving of their various needs in a static, isolated, atomistic way that demands rejecting one person's needs for those of another, or by means of a creative solution that attempts to incorporate all needs through their mutual transformation.

On a pragmatist feminist account, such mutual transformation is welcome, rather than troublesome, because no party is self-transparent; all parties need each other to help them see themselves. The insistence on mutual transformation suggests that a pragmatist-feminist standpoint theory differs from Harding's position by emphasizing more strongly the self-opacity of *all* people. Harding's account of feminist standpoint theory rightly stresses the lack of self-transparency on the part of the dominant when it claims that marginalized perspectives are needed to uncover hidden assumptions that the dominant cannot see. But Harding implies that self-opacity is relatively one-sided, that it is much more characteristic of dominant than of marginalized perspectives. In its claim that the projects developed from women's lives are less partial and distorted, Harding's standpoint theory suggests that someone speaking from a feminist standpoint has relatively little need for the help of others in seeing the hidden assumptions and background beliefs of her own position. While it does not promise absolute infallibility, feminist standpoint theory claims to provide the most certain foundation available and thus discourages context-sensitive questions about the benefits of beginning with women's lives. A pragmatist-feminist standpoint theory, on the other hand, holds open the possibility that all perspectives and standpoints may be in need of transformation through transactional dialogue with another. Operating with a thoroughgoing fallibility, a pragmatist-feminist standpoint theory assumes that no perspective or standpoint is self-transparent. Even someone speaking from a feminist standpoint—as well as a pragmatist-feminist standpoint—may have problematic, hidden assumptions that she cannot see on her own and needs others to help her uncover.

Because pragmatism's appeal to experience does not treat experience as a transparent, self-evident ground for epistemological claims, a pragmatist-feminist standpoint that draws on an epistemology of transactional bodies does not treat the category of experience foundationally.[64] The rejection of the privatization of experience entails that no one person can claim absolute authority for her experience and the perspective generated from it. This does not mean that a woman's perspective necessarily is false; it means that, like men's perspectives, women's perspectives are finite and capable of, and often in need of, revision based on reflective interpretations provided by women and men alike.[65] One can and should affirm the distinctiveness of women's perspectives from those of men at the same time that one acknowledges the need for the transaction of many different perspectives to counter the limitation of each of them.[66]

There admittedly are dangers inherent in a position that holds open marginalized perspectives, such as those of women, to modification by dominant members of society, such as men. These dangers cannot be made to go away completely because, in a transactional world, no final guarantees or securities are possible. If bodies are transactional, others will have deeply constitutive effects on who one is and what one becomes, and there is no way to ultimately seal oneself off from these effects. Nor would sealing oneself off completely in this way be beneficial. Even if it could be done, not only would the dangers posed by others be eliminated, but one's ability to grow and learn also would be lost. The security of a guaranteed, safe world entails a static world populated by unchanging organisms—that is, a dead world with dead organisms. Growth and risk go hand in hand, which means that one cannot grow without risking oneself. And without growth, there is no dynamic life, only stagnation and fixity.

The response to the dangers of transaction should not be to eliminate them, but to attempt to mitigate them when appropriate. For example, as the work of various women's groups throughout history attests, spaces in which members of marginalized groups can gather without the presence of dominant groups often can help nurture voices that are at risk of being silenced in broader groups. But for these groups to try to enact an atomism by separating completely from the society around them in an attempt to protect their members from oppression would not be to eliminate all danger. Rather it would be to risk stifling and constraining their voices in an attempt to manage the rigid boundaries between "inside" and "outside" the group. The epistemological and moral dangers are just too great for communities to attempt to close themselves off permanently. Those dangers include, as Alison Jaggar has argued, "repression and denial of autonomy, dogmatism, intellectual dishonesty and self-deception, elitism, and partialism."[67] Although temporarily closed communities can be important places for the development of voices that challenge the status quo, those communities need to open themselves up at some point to a richer transaction with other communities.

By addressing some of the dangers of transaction, I do not want to suggest that imbalances within transaction are always problematic and in need of elimination. The possible dangers of transaction and the need to mitigate them are important matters, but imbalances within transaction should not always or necessarily be seen in a negative light. Each particular situation of transaction must be examined in the context in which it occurs. In some contexts, an imbalance in the way in which organisms constitute each other through their transactions can be beneficial and desirable. For example, in the classroom, because of their greater experience and familiarity with their field, professors usually do and should have more authority than do their students. Consequently, a professor's contribution to the transactions of the classroom tends to be greater than that of students. For this reason, as feminists working on pedagogy have discovered, the guiding ideal for a feminist classroom should not be one of the professor's mere letting go of authority.[68] It needs, instead, to be one of configuring her authority and power such that she enables students to have greater voice and agency within it. The question in this particular situation should not be whether an imbalance of power and authority should exist, but rather what form should power and authority take.[69]

Transactional understanding of experience is also not foundational because the process of experimental inquiry transforms the initial experience that presented itself as problematic. The experience with which one begins inquiry is not the same one with which inquiry concludes. The experience that is modified by inquiry and action, and not the initial experience itself, serves as a testing ground for the truthfulness of attempted changes to the problematic experience. For pragmatist feminism, experience is not a static, infallible foundation on which to base knowledge. By distinguishing between the experiences that initiate inquiry and the transformed experiences that are the result of it, a person can both acknowledge the importance of her experiences and critique her initial understandings and conceptions of them.[70] In this way, women's experiences can be recognized, validated, and used as starting points for inquiry without relativizing or uncritically accepting them. On this approach, women's experiences do not have to be used as starting points only. Their experiences as transformed by inquiry also can be used as testing points for the value of the changes made to a situation.

Precisely because experience is transformed through transaction, it may seem problematic to define truth as that which satisfies desires, needs, and interests. There appears to be no initial desire that necessarily endures the change effected by inquiry against which to check whether the transformation was indeed desirable. How can one determine if the desired results of inquiry came about if there is no atomistic self that endures the transformations brought about by inquiry? And whose desires are being satisfied if the self and its desire change as a result of the altered transaction?

That the self changes through its transactions with the world does not mean that transforming a problematic situation and the person that is formed by it entails the inability to check the results of change with that person's experience. The constitutive role of habit in the self explains how the self remains coherent enough throughout transaction for it to be possible to make this check. Selves are not a formless flux, completely dissolved and remade through each transaction with the world. Habit is too stubbornly thoroughgoing for it to be modified through the transformation of one situation. The changes that the self undergoes in transaction are piecemeal and partial, which is not to deny that the self is remade through transaction but only to deny that it is remade "from scratch," as it were. Both continuity and difference, with regard to the self, are the results of the process of transaction. The constitutive power of habit ensures enough continuity to identify the self across transaction at the same time that it makes possible changes in the self. The results of an attempt to improve a situation can be checked against the lived experience of the self because, even though it changes when the situation around it does, the self maintains continuity with itself across its transformation due to the staying force of habit.

Habit also explains why it is likely that significant change will be effected by means of the gradual transformation of self and environment through transaction, rather than by a sudden, one-time revolution. The notion of habit does not entail social conservatism, nor does it deny the importance of social struggle. Rather, it recognizes the force of lag in life produced by sedimented predispositions.[71] By itself, sudden revolution tends to be an ineffective shortcut that cannot make deep changes. It works against, rather than with, the constitutive role that habit plays in life. In Dewey's words, it "fails to realize the full force of . . . institutions as embodied habits," and, thus, fails to address the old "habits of thought and feeling" that "persist and insensibly assimilate to themselves the outer innovation" brought about by revolution.[72] Attempts at sudden and drastic change when one is frustrated by the slow pace of transformation often are understandable psychologically, but they tend to be a relatively futile last resort at change when a society has failed to perpetually renew and transform itself. As Dewey explains, "[i]f conditions do not permit renewal to take place continuously it will take place explosively," but this means that they take place only destructively rather than also constructively.[73] Even worse, the nondemocratic methods frequently involved in sudden change mean that often the only change made is that the dominated are transformed into the dominating, leaving intact, through a mere reversal of it, the very hierarchy being fought.[74] To effect significant change, the transformation of personal and institutional habits must occur.

While feminist standpoint theory needs help from pragmatism, it also has important contributions to make to a pragmatist-feminist standpoint theory. Although everyone may need to be involved in creating solutions to conflict through mutual transformation, Harding suggests that such creativity is more likely to come from a marginalized than from a dominant point of view because the former offers a fresh perspective. If one is genuinely concerned about the flourishing of all, one should tend to start one's projects from the view of women's, rather than men's, lives. Feminist standpoint theory provides a compelling further reason to do so: Western culture has a long history of dominant perspectives' silencing marginal perspectives by attempting to speak for them or claiming to know what is best for them. To help ensure not only that they are allowed to speak but also that they are heard, marginalized rather than dominant perspectives should tend to be the first place to which a pragmatist-feminist standpoint theory turns and on which it focuses in its search for solutions to problematic situations.

By including the words "tend to" in a pragmatist-feminist injunction to start from women's lives, this injunction, as all pragmatist-feminist injunctions, is a working hypothesis, a general guideline with which to direct inquiry. It is not an inviolable rule or a directive that can never admit of exception. Its appropriateness will vary in different situations. The fruitfulness of working with this guideline will be tested and retested in every experience and situation to which it is applied, and it is always open to modification based on future experience. The past flourishing produced by use of this guideline has established its truth, but that truth is historical, contextual, and flexible and may change if experience shows the need for its revision. In this way, a pragmatist-feminist standpoint theory urges philosophers and others to begin from women's lives because doing so currently is the best working hypothesis for producing the flourishing of all. But it also cautions them not to treat that hypothesis as an unquestionable rule. They—we—should remain open to the changes in and improvements of the injunction to start with women's lives that future experience may suggest.

Implicit in the preceding sketch of a pragmatist-feminist standpoint theory is the suggestion that we tease out the pragmatist elements of Harding's position.[75] While Harding's account of feminist standpoint theory, and its definition of objectivity as less partial and distorted in particular, suffers from dependence on a problematic definition of truth as mirroring reality, other aspects of her position complement a pragmatist-feminist standpoint theory. Harding's notion of objectivity as pluralistic is a valuable resource. Although Harding attempts to distance herself from pluralism, worried that it necessarily entails judgmental relativism, the broadening of perspectives is an important goal recognized by both Harding and pragmatist feminism. And, because pluralism need not entail a lack of criteria with which to make distinctions between better and worse reconfigurations of sexist culture, pluralism is a key component in an improved notion of objectivity.

Additional pragmatist-feminist strains in Harding's work make her position even more amenable to an account of bodies as transactional. While the tone of Harding's work often suggests that the injunction to start from the lives of the oppressed need not be questioned by feminists, she says at one point that one needs "to determine which social situations tend to generate the most objective knowledge claims" and that "some [social values and interests] have systematically generated less partial and distorted beliefs than others."[76] When she does so, she indicates that her injunction is a flexible, not rigid, guideline that is to be relied upon not because of an unquestionable faith in it, but because of the fruitful results to this point of doing so. In addition, Harding's description of the type of claims provided by science—and, by extension, by feminist standpoint theory— agrees with a transactional account of truth as flexible, nondogmatic, and ever changing. When Harding claims that "scientific claims are supposed to be held not as true but, only provisionally, as 'least false' until counter-evidence or a new conceptual framework no longer provides them with the status of 'less false' than those against which they have been tested," she describes science in a way that complements a notion of truth as hypothetical.[77] Because she continues to operate with a notion of truth as mirroring reality, Harding insists that "science never gets us truth"; but with a redefinition of truth as transactional, we might say that Harding's description of science demonstrates precisely how truth is always a matter of working hypotheses.[78]

Intersecting Harding's feminist standpoint theory with pragmatist feminism helps Harding better achieve her goal of producing a reconfigured objectivity that acknowledges the perspectival nature of corporeal existence. But a pragmatist-feminist standpoint theory will not provide easy answers to questions about dealing with the complex problems that erupt in a post-Enlightenment world. Broadening the number of viewpoints that are to be included in the processes of negotiating flourishing transactions makes these processes more complicated than does Harding's feminist standpoint theory. But the ability to make theories messy is an asset, not a liability, of pragmatist feminism. Tempting though they may be, overly tidy answers usually only gloss over the difficulties that must be dealt with if any meaningful improvements to lived experience are to be made. By enabling feminist standpoint theory to shift away from a criterion of distortion to a criterion of flourishing through transaction, pragmatist feminism eliminates the comfortable security offered by a claim to a clearer vision of reality. Rather than provide comfort, it demands the hard work of negotiating a satisfactory solution to problems had with others, including those who are responsible for those very problems.

Transaction and the Dynamic Distinctiveness of Races

To change that which is "outside" a body is to change that body as well, which is why Dewey writes "[o]ne might as well study an organism in complete detachment from its environment as try to study an electric clock on the wall in disregard of the wire leading to it."[1] Just as an electric clock cannot tell time if electricity does not flow into it, an organism cannot function apart from the environments that "flow" through it. Unlike the relationship between an electric clock and electricity, however, the relationships between organisms and their various environments are reciprocal. Not only do organisms exist by means of their environments, but their environments also exist by means of the impact that organisms have on them.

While Dewey's metaphor of an electric clock and wire fails to capture fully the live circuit between organic bodies and environments, it does emphasize successfully the importance of including environments in one's understanding of bodies. Just as one cannot adequately understand the electric clock separated from its power source, one cannot best understand bodies sharply detached from their environments because, as Dewey claims,

> life goes on in an environment; not merely *in* it but because of it, through interaction with it. No creature lives merely under its skin; its subcutaneous organs are means of connection with what lies beyond its bodily frame, and to which, in order to live, it must adjust itself. . . . The career and destiny of a living being are bound up with its interchanges with its environment, not externally but in the most intimate way.[2]

In some situations and for some purposes, the skin marks a limit between the body's inside and outside. As a boundary, skin constitutes a functional, rather than substantive, essential, or fixed, delimitation. In many cases, to understand and attempt to improve bodily experience means to turn one's attention to a multitude of physical, social, political, and cultural environments, rather than to "the body" per se. Or better, to focus attention on these various environments can be precisely to attend to the bodily beings that transact with them. As an organ, on the other hand, skin is more than mere boundary. It functions as the site of transaction between inside and outside a body. In addition to looking outside a body to grasp its inside, in many situations, one also must look at the skin itself, that is, at the event of transaction between inside and outside.

Much of this book has focused on the way in which the concept of transaction undercuts an understanding of bodies and environments as related like the ingredients of a tossed salad. This emphasis is meant to counter the concept of atomism, with regard to bodies, that is prevalent in philosophy. It should not be taken as an indication that distinctiveness is less important to transaction than is continuity. These seemingly opposed characteristics are both vitally important to the concept of transaction. This should be clear from the metaphor of stew: in their transaction with each other, the vegetables of a stew dynamically constitute each other as the vegetables that they are or that they become in the stew. The vegetables are changed in texture, color, and flavor by the process of stewing, but they do not thereby become one indistinguishable lump. In a stew, rather than undermine the distinctiveness of one another, the vegetables' contribution to each other's constitution helps compose their distinctiveness. In turn, their distinctiveness gives each of them something particular to contribute to the others.

The idea of the preservation of dynamic distinctiveness through transaction has a number of significant implications. I want here to consider it in connection with critical race theory.[3] Addressing concerns about the concept of transaction that critical race theory implicitly raises will produce richer understandings of race and of transaction. Using transaction to understand race means conceiving of races as dynamically co-constituting each other in such a way that their distinctiveness is preserved.[4] Taking white and black people as an example, the concept of transaction means that in and through their transactions, white and black people "stew" together in such a way that what constitutes whiteness is effected by what counts as blackness, and vice versa. This does not mean that white and black people necessarily melt together into one race of identical, khaki-colored people. The distinctiveness of white and of black people is preserved, not eliminated, but it is preserved in a relationship of dynamic connection. The larger story is more complex than this oversimplification indicates. An understanding of race as transactional recognizes that not just two, but many different races transact with each other, which means that white, black, red, brown, yellow, and mixed-race people co-constitute each other's racial existence at the same time that their racial distinctiveness is dynamically preserved. An even more thorough application of the concept of transaction would include the way in which a person's nationality, gender, sexuality, and class status transact with his or her race, making the "stew" of various races a mixture that includes much more than just race.

The concept of transaction suggests the preservation of the white as well as the nonwhite races, which is potentially problematic from an antiracist perspective. Although the event of transaction has negative effects in some situations and positive effects in others, in the case of white people's transactions with people of color, the effects historically have been overwhelmingly harmful. If the existence of whiteness necessarily results in the domination of people of color by white people, understanding race as transactional would seem to support white supremacy by carving out conceptual space for the preservation of whiteness. In response to this possibility, I examine here the particular consequence of understanding race as transactional: the preservation of whiteness. If race is understood as transactional, must the effect of conceiving of whiteness as preserved necessarily be negative? Or is there a way in which it can be beneficial from an antiracist point of view?

The journal *Race Traitor* answers an emphatic "no" to whether making conceptual room for the preservation of whiteness can be positive. The journal implicitly discourages using the concept of transaction to understand race. Arguing against the new field of "white studies," editor Noel Ignatiev denies that whiteness can signify anything other than the oppression of people designated as not white.[5] Whiteness—as distinct from ethnic and national identities such as being Irish, Polish, Jewish, Italian, German, Anglo-Saxon, and so on—has no positive content or meaning to draw upon, according to Ignatiev. It has no distinctive history or culture other than that of dominating and exploiting others. While some scholars have tried to argue that elements of popular culture such as gun shows, the Elvis cult, and ice hockey are white but nonracist, Ignatiev denies that any cultural element can contribute to the formation of a nonoppressive white identity because, as he claims, "[l]ike everything else about whiteness, [an alleged element of white culture] has nothing to do with culture. It has to do with exclusion."[6]

For this reason, Ignatiev holds that for white people to preserve their whiteness, even if with the intent of expressing racial pride rather than that of deprecating other races, is for them to feed directly into the hands of white supremacy. Without criteria by which to distinguish racist from nonracist white pride, the preservation of whiteness and indeed the entire field of white studies can be used to lend theoretical legitimization to white supremacists' racist claims. Because whiteness historically has functioned, and continues to function, to oppress darker skinned groups of people, Ignatiev claims such criteria will be hard, even impossible, to come by. In Ignatiev's view, if "[w]hiteness is one pole of an unequal relationship, which can no more exist without oppression than slavery could exist without slaves," the concept of whiteness cannot be transformed into something nonracist.[7] It can only further white supremacy, which is why it must be abolished, not preserved.

Put another way, the issue pressed by Ignatiev is whether pro-whiteness is necessarily anti-blackness, as well as anti-brownness, anti-yellowness, and so on. Must the preservation of whiteness entail a deprecation of other racial groups? Or can it take the form of white people's self-affirmation such that racially egalitarian values and pro-whiteness can coexist? Recent empirical work on aversive racism and pro-whiteness demonstrates the similarity of the effects of anti-blackness and "egalitarian" pro-whiteness, lending support to Ignatiev's concerns about conceiving of whiteness as preserved in the transaction between races.[8] Traditional psychological racism is direct and overt; it characterizes members of white supremacist groups such as the Ku Klux Klan. In contrast, aversive racism is indirect and subtle, characterizing the attitudes of many well-intentioned white people who embrace racially egalitarian values and consider themselves unprejudiced.[9] Aversive racism tends to manifest itself in ambiguous situations in which the distinction between appropriate and inappropriate behavior vis-à-vis race is unclear or in which the context of a situation allows racial bias to be attributed to nonracial factors.[10]

For example, in a controlled experiment using a fictional court transcript of a criminal case involving murder, white participants in one condition of the experiment were presented with prosecution evidence that was very weak. In addition to being presented with this evidence, white participants in a second condition also received an admission of the defendant's guilt that was confessed to a third party and ruled as inadmissible evidence because the third party could not be located to appear in court. In their ratings of the defendant's guilt when the defendant was black, traditional racists in the second condition were much more certain of the defendant's guilt; when the defendant was white, however, they followed the judge's instructions perfectly and were equally certain or uncertain of the defendant's guilt. In contrast, when the defendant was black, egalitarian "nonracists" followed the judge's instructions and disregarded the incriminating evidence; they were equally certain or uncertain of the black defendant's guilt whether or not they were exposed to the confession. When the defendant was white, however, egalitarian nonracists were less certain of the defendant's guilt when the confession was presented than when it was omitted.[11]

The traditional racists were anti-black, and the egalitarian nonracists were pro-white. Unlike the traditional racists, the egalitarian nonracists were very careful not to discriminate *against* the black defendant when inadmissible evidence against him was presented. What they did instead was discriminate *in favor of* the white defendant when exposed to the incriminating evidence. In the case of the white defendant, the confession was taken by the egalitarian nonracists as an unfair attempt by the prosecution to wrongly bias the jurors against the defendant. For the white defendant *only*, the prosecution's introduction of the confession was seen as a "cheap shot" that angered participants. The participants expressed no such anger in the case of the black defendant.[12] Thus, the egalitarian nonracists were not anti-black because they did not let the inadmissible confession influence the degree to which they thought the black defendant was guilty. Rather, they were pro-white in that they let the inadmissible confession influence the degree to which they thought the white defendant was guilty. While the damaging confession did not hurt the case of the black defendant, it actually helped that of the white defendant.

This experiment demonstrates that pro-whiteness and anti-blackness can be distinguished psychologically. The different ways in which the egalitarian nonracist participants responded to the inadmissible confession in the case of white and black defendants shows that those participants were not biased against blackness, but *were* biased in favor of whiteness. However, in support of Ignatiev's position against thinking of whiteness as preserved, the experiment also demonstrates that the effects of pro-whiteness and anti-blackness disadvantage black people in equivalent ways. Even though the distinction between anti-blackness and pro-whiteness can be useful for distinguishing different types of psychological reactions to situations involving race, it does not mean that pro-whiteness does not have adverse effects on people of color. This is significant because the effects, not the mere psychology, of pro-whiteness are most relevant to racism and its elimination. As compared to a black defendant who made no incriminating confession, a black defendant who did make such a confession was treated fairly by the egalitarian white participants. Compared to a white defendant who made such a confession, the black defendant who confessed was not treated fairly by the white egalitarians. The white defendant received beneficial treatment that the black defendant did not, disadvantaging the black defendant in a significant way—solely because of the defendant's race. Even if one claims that the black defendant received justice while the white defendant received mercy, the verdicts are racist because they awarded special treatment to the white defendant because he or she was white. While the anti-outgroup bias of traditional racists and the pro-ingroup bias of egalitarian nonracists do so in different ways, both unfairly discriminate based on race. Both pro-whiteness and anti-blackness attitudes are racist because they have racist effects.

The results of the experiment suggest that if a person is antiracist, the concepts with which she theorizes race should speak of the elimination, rather than the preservation, of whiteness. In that case, understanding race as transactional would seem to promote racism by making room for the retention of the distinctiveness of whiteness in the "stew" of various races. Once we recognize the constitutive role of habit in the self, however, we can see how being antiracist does not conflict with an understanding of race in which whiteness is preserved. Race is not a veneer laid over a racially neutral core of a person. It is not something that can be eliminated by the conscious decision not to have a race or the rational understanding that biologistic conceptions of race have no scientific validity, as Ignatiev seems to hold.[13] In a world where races exist, race forms the very habits of bodying that make up who a person is.[14] While these racial habits can be, and often are, altered through a person's transactions with her environments, they will not quickly disappear. Whiteness will be preserved for quite a while into the future because of white people's racial bodying as they transact with the world. This does not mean that steps cannot be taken to eliminate racism; it means that strategies are needed for the elimination of racism that acknowledge the ongoing existence of whiteness.

The reality of whiteness as bodied in individual and cultural racial habits explains why I address the white race in general instead of particular ethnicities currently taken to be white.[15] It is important not to neglect the differences among ethnic groups considered to be white, including the different relationships they have to whiteness, as use of the clumsy phrase "the white race" tends to do. For that reason, the concept of ethnicity should not be wholly assimilated into that of race. Yet it is equally important that race not be wholly assimilated into ethnicity, for to do so is to render ourselves incapable of recognizing white privilege so that we may dismantle it.[16] Whatever their historical and current differences and relationships to oppression, Irish, Italian, German, Jewish, Polish, and other ethnic groups that currently count as white benefit from their classification as white and, thus, have something in common that the term "race" captures but "ethnicity" does not. To discuss transaction in terms of whiteness rather than Irishness, Polishness, and other ethnicities need not be a failure of political nerve, as Ignatiev asserts.[17] It instead can be an important strategy for maintaining a theoretical space in which white supremacy can be confronted.

That the distinctiveness of whiteness is preserved through transaction does not mean that it can or should remain unchanged. Whiteness undergoes transformation, even as it is preserved, because white people are not atomistically sealed off from people of other races. The notion of transaction reworks the idea of preservation such that it is dynamic rather than static. This type of preservation could be called an "evolving preservation" to capture its sense of continuity *and* change. Or, we could say that thinking of whiteness as transactional undercuts the dualism, with which Ignatiev's position operates, of eliminating or preserving whiteness. In the foreseeable future, whiteness will neither immediately disappear nor simply remain the same. At this point in history, whiteness will be preserved in transaction with other races, but not in such a way that rules out its transformation and even possible future elimination. This type of preservation is exemplified by a stew, rather than by a tossed salad. It entails the alteration of whiteness and that of other races through transaction, even as it retains the distinctiveness of racial groups.

Our original question remains, however. Using the concept of transaction to understand race has demonstrated why whiteness will be preserved, but it has not yet shown how thinking of whiteness as preserved can be beneficial rather than harmful. Most of the transactions between white and nonwhite races have been disastrous for people of color, as the enslavement of Africans and the colonizing of the Americas attest. Can conceiving of whiteness as preserved work against racism, and, if so, how?

Lucius Outlaw's answer to this question is distinctive because, in addition to making the claim that the preservation of whiteness is crucial to the fight against racism, it attempts to demonstrate that pro-whiteness need not result in the deprecation of people of color. In his explanation of the value of the concept of whiteness, however, Outlaw implies a type of symmetry between white people and people of color that must be rejected because it functions to support white supremacy. In its differences from a transactional understanding of whiteness, Outlaw's account of the value of thinking of whiteness as preserved can helpfully illuminate the benefits of thinking of races as dynamically co-constituted.

Outlaw's primary concern is how one might promote "the recognition—even the celebration and nurturing—or racial and/or ethnic differences" without engaging in racism or invidious ethnocentricism.[18] Aligning himself with W. E. B. Du Bois, Outlaw argues that even though an understanding of race as biologically determined has no scientific validity, races should be conserved as distinct bio-cultural groups.[19] There are at least two related reasons for doing so, according to Outlaw. First, human beings have a need for order in their lives, and grouping individuals into races, or "raciation," provides this.[20] Such grouping does not entail the valorization of one's group, a point to which I will return subsequently. Outlaw holds that, while raciation is not the only way in which humans can group themselves, it is a necessary and important "respons[e] to the need for life-sustaining and meaningfully acceptable *order* of various kinds (conceptual, social, political)" because biological factors play a role in human ordering.[21] Distinguishing physical features, such as the color of one's skin and the texture of one's hair, impact how humans group themselves because humans tend to be drawn to those who look like themselves and tend to want to produce descendents that are similar to them in physical appearance.[22]

Outlaw does not argue that biology determines the ways in which human beings are raciated, because physical characteristics always combine with cultural characteristics to produce racial groups. As Outlaw explains,

> raciality is *not* wholly and completely fixed by biological factors, but only partially so. Biological factors do not *determine* raciality, but in complex interactions with environmental, cultural, and social factors and processes they provide certain boundary conditions and possibilities that affect raciation in terms of the development of distinctive gene pools from which are derived physical and biologically conditioned characteristics shared in certain frequencies by members of various groups.[23]

On Outlaw's account, physical factors alone never produce race. Rather, they interact—or transact, one might say—with environmental, cultural, and social factors to constitute raciation. But the complexity of raciation does not eliminate the distinctive role that physical characteristics play in its constitution. For Outlaw, to the extent that human organisms continue to group themselves on likeness of physical appearance, race will be a means by which humans structure themselves and the world.

According to Outlaw, without such order it is difficult for people to have meaningful individual or social identities or to manage expectations and behavior in a social setting. Lack of order tends to result in personal and social chaos, and the accompanying desperate attempts to reestablish an order that can provide life with structure and meaning.[24] The lack of meaningful individual or social identities and resulting difficulties managing expectations and behavior can produce racism among other things, such as sexism.[25] Outlaw's position implies that the "angry white man" syndrome can be viewed as an understandable psychological response on the part of men whose life structures of race and gender have been undercut and who see no possible order to take their place. This explanation would not excuse or condone their anger and the damage that it can produce; rather, it would acknowledge the constitutive role that race and gender play in the ordering of oneself and one's world. For Outlaw, the failure to appreciate the bio-cultural factors that racially (and sexually) constitute persons in a group is to promote invidious opposition between groups. On his terms, the preservation of the distinctiveness of racial (and sexual) groupings can be important to the elimination of the racism (and sexism) that result from a lack of life-sustaining order.

Outlaw also argues for the preservation of the distinctiveness between races because racial differences allegedly enrich everyone. As Outlaw claims, "the continued existence of discernable race- and ethnie-based communities of meaning is highly desirable *even if, in the very next instant, racism and perverted, invidious ethnocentrism in every form and manifestation would disappear forever*"[26] without them. According to Outlaw, human society would be impoverished if it were composed of only one race. The rich differences in art, literature, food, bodily gestures and styles, language and dialect, and philosophies and world views—just to name a few—that people of different races can bring to each other through their transaction are likely to be lost if raciation disappears. Just as W. E. B. Du Bois urged more than 100 years ago and Alain Locke stressed in the first half of the twentieth century, Outlaw asserts that racial diversity is beneficial to human beings of all races because different races have different "messages" to give to each other.[27] According to Outlaw, this helps explain why, after many years of reproduction, members of the human species have not all become the same light khaki color. Although racism and fear of miscegenation have played, and continue to play, a role in the maintenance of distinct races, discernible boundaries between racial groups do not exist merely because of racism. As Outlaw claims, racial boundaries exist also because of "bio-cultural group attachments and practices that are conducive to human survival and well-being."[28]

Outlaw's emphasis on the importance of racial grouping for human flourishing goes beyond supporting raciation; it extends to arguing for the attitudes and behavior characterized by what Outlaw calls racialism. While at times Outlaw speaks of raciation and racialism interchangeably, they are conceptually distinct and have different implications for whiteness. Raciation is the grouping of people into races; racialism is the valorization of one's own racial group.[29] Raciation is independent of racialism, whereas racialism necessarily includes raciation. Both must be distinguished from explicit racism, which seeks the subordination and exploitation of other racial groups that are seen as inferior to one's own. Neither raciation nor racialism is or need become racist, according to Outlaw.[30] He argues that one can and should valorize one's race because it provides the meaning and order necessary to the flourishing of human life. It is a deeply felt existential need. Doing so, however, does not require hostile opposition to or the deprecation of other racial groups. In Outlaw's view, taking pride in one's race does not necessarily establish racial hierarchies of superiority and inferiority.

Outlaw extends his claims about raciation and racialism to all racial groups, that of white people included. He makes this clear when he asks, "how might we work to conserve 'colored' populations and subgroupings (*and white is a color, as well*), races and ethnies, without making it easier for racialism and ethnocentrism to 'go imperial'?"[31] Outlaw implies symmetry between white and black people when it comes to their ability to affirm their race in noninvidious ways. As do people of color, white people have a legitimate existential need to conserve and valorize their race, and their pride in being white is not necessarily linked to racism or to attempts to dominate other racial groups.[32] Outlaw's position provocatively suggests that, without white pride on the part of white people, racism against people of color will be difficult to eliminate. According to Outlaw, white people who lack a way of ordering their life around their race in a meaningful way are likely to suffer from the chaotic disorientation that can contribute to vicious reactions against other races.

People do need meaningful ways to structure their lives, including ways that involve grouping together with people who are similar. What counts as similar in any given context, however, must be understood genealogically because it has a complex history that has made it what it is. Similarity is an economically, socially, culturally, and politically constituted concept. It is a product of selective emphasis, not a fixed, given category. For this reason, appeals to similarity tend to raise more questions than they answer. Why have some specific traits or characteristics, such as that of race, come to constitute a similarity across people's various differences? What are the effects of recognizing racial similarity rather than other instances of similarity in different situations? Grouping into races is not the only way by which people have gathered and continue to gather with others who are similar, and it may not always deserve encouragement. Understanding the historical factors that have led to racial grouping opens up the possibility that, at some point in the future, raciation may no longer be a meaningful way by which to structure human life.

Further, even though people require meaningful ways of ordering their lives, order need not and should not be understood as inflexible. It is not the case that personal and social chaos must erupt if and when rigid binaries of white and nonwhite, man and woman, or heterosexual and homosexual are transformed into fluid categories that are open to ongoing reconfiguration. In response to Outlaw's claim that the lack of structures of order makes it difficult to manage people's expectations or behavior in a social setting, it should be pointed out that this is precisely why the notion of order needs to be problematized.[33] Because the management of expectations and behavior through "proper" social and personal ordering is one way that both institutional and psychologically internalized racism is effectively maintained, orderings cannot be affirmed indiscriminately. As organisms composed of habits, human beings are constituted by patterns of activity that provide order, but those patterns need not and should not be rigid and unyielding.

Race is neither an ahistorical similarity between people nor an inflexible ordering of human life. Nonetheless, raciation currently is inevitable in the United States and many other countries. Racial identity is an important part of most people's identity, even if not consciously realized as such and even when racial identification takes the form of challenging rigid distinctions between racial groups, as it does for many people of mixed race. For this reason, races should be conceived as distinct rather than as melted together in their transaction. Raciation must be recognized as a feature of today's world if there is to be any hope of transforming it. Doing so, however, need not promote or support racism, even when it is white people who assert their existence as a distinct racial group. Instead of constituting a claim of supremacy, identifying oneself as similar to another person because both are considered to be white can be an acknowledgment of the place one holds in a racially stratified society. Such acknowledgment is a crucial first step in white people's attempts to change their racial habits and their environment's racial customs.

The same cannot be said for racialism. The symmetry between white and nonwhite people suggested by Outlaw does not hold in the matter of valorizing one's race because, in a society built on white privilege, valorizing one's racial group has very different meanings for white and nonwhite people. For black people to affirm their race is generally for them to fight against the deprecation of blackness; it is for them to attempt to reject the hierarchy of white over black that has long existed and continues to exist. In contrast, for white people to affirm their race is generally for them to affirm that very hierarchy. It is for them to attempt to keep intact their position of superiority over nonwhite people. Ingroup favoritism has different implications depending on whether the group in question is oppressed or oppressing. In both cases, to favor one's own group is to discriminate against other groups, but that discrimination is invidious only in the case of a group that holds a disproportionate amount of power and authority in a particular society. In the case of a group that holds little power and authority or in the case that power and authority is distributed widely across groups, for a group to favor itself is not necessarily to dominate or oppress others.

Understanding race as transactional does not mean that all racial groups necessarily should be affirmed in the same way, as Outlaw suggests they should be. The concept of transaction supports raciation but not racialism. In the preservation of their whiteness, rather than affirm their racial identity, white people need to find ways to use their whiteness in antiracist ways. I distinguish "use" from "affirmation" although affirmation may seem to include use. I think it need not, however, because one can make productive use of something without liking or endorsing it. Even if use includes a degree of affirmation, using one's whiteness in antiracist ways is a particular kind of usage that undercuts affirmation in the positing of it. It is to use one's whiteness against itself. It is to acknowledge one's whiteness, rather than to deny or attempt to quickly abolish it, but to do so in such a way that leads to the elimination of the privilege it accords.

Although racial habits are currently too deeply engrained for white or other people simply to stop ordering their world along racial lines, white raciation need not mean a white favoritism whose flip side, because of the power and authority held by white people, is invidious discrimination against nonwhite people. Identifying oneself as white can instead mean that one uses the privilege accorded to one as white to fight against racism. Whether they like it or not, white people often are allowed entrance into various social institutions that nonwhite people are not, and their voices often are accorded more weight than those of nonwhite people. It is important that white people acknowledge the role that their whiteness plays in such privilege precisely for the purpose of using their greater access and voice to combat the racism that resulted in it.[34] White people's ordering their lives along racial lines is historically necessary today, and this is why the concept of whiteness should be thought of as preserved. But their ordering can take the form of using whiteness to fight against racism, rather than to affirm a white pride that is difficult to distinguish from the promotion of white supremacy.

White people can bring to their transactions with other races the distinctiveness of members of an oppressor race coming to honestly confront and attempt to change their domination over others. Instead of domination and oppression, white people can contribute a fallibility and a humbleness, a learning how to admit graciously that one was wrong, and an openness to risking one's identity in allowing it to be transformed in ways that one does not control. These traits can be found in the lives of those people other than white, of course. But these traits take on a distinctive meaning when manifested by white people, who historically have seen and often continue to see themselves as authoritative and in control. The particular meaning of these traits, in the case of white people, is that of arrogance dismantled, which is valuable to antiracist projects because ending racism requires white people to relinquish inflated images of themselves.

Because of the value of the dismantling of white people's arrogance, conceiving the distinctiveness of whiteness as transactionally preserved can have positive effects. Thinking of white people as melting into non-whiteness would mean the loss of an important opportunity for white people to address their past and current racism in productively antiracist ways. The large "stew" of people of various races—black, brown, yellow, red, and other nonwhite races in particular—can benefit from this particular contribution of white people to their transactions, if and when white people make it. Of course, there is no guarantee that they will. White people's transactions with people of color can just as easily support the domination of people of color as it can undermine it. But it also is possible for white people's transactions with people of other races to take the form of attempting to give antiracist meaning and content to their raciation, and when they do, the dynamical preservation of whiteness through transaction can work against, rather than for, white supremacy.

Finally, a brief word about the status of the suggestion that bodies should be understood as transactional. Does such a claim attempt to present the truth of what bodies really are? If "truth" here means an accurate mirroring of reality, I would say that this book instead presents a working hypothesis about bodies as transactional. Understood in a pragmatic rather than a positivist sense, the hypothesis of transactional bodies should be taken as a general guideline for feminist, pragmatist, phenomenological, genealogical, and other theoretical inquiries about bodies. It is a guideline to be adopted because of the beneficial effects of thinking of bodies in transaction with their environments. The present advantages of thinking of bodies as transactional do not mean, however, that the notion of transactional bodies is inviolable or immutable; future experiences likely will indicate a need to revise it. The hypothesis that bodies are transactional is "true" in a transactional sense of true only as long as working with such a conception of bodies promotes the flourishing of those bodies and the worlds with which they transact.

Conclusion

Thinking about bodies as transactional does not merely present a theory, even a fallible one, about what bodies are. It also redirects theorists' attention to the transactional relationship between bodies and their environments so that particular transactions might be improved. Pragmatism and feminism in particular come together nicely on this point: the notion of bodies as transactional requires that the transformation and improvement of concrete, lived experience be the goal of any philosophy of corporeal existence. Both pragmatism and feminism emphasize the ethical and political implications of particular transactions between bodies and environments and urge that energies should be placed on such ethical and political work. For that reason, bringing pragmatism and feminism together to think corporeal existence as transactional is a valuable endeavor.

The cross-fertilizing of pragmatism and feminism, along with phenomenological and genealogical philosophy, holds much promise for the future of pragmatism and feminism and for philosophy more generally. There are undoubtedly many topics beyond those examined here that would benefit from a pragmatist-feminist approach. My hope is that this book will contribute to the growing field of pragmatist feminism by encouraging a pluralist spirit within philosophy, a spirit in which more pragmatists learn from feminist, phenomenological, and genealogical philosophy and in which more feminist, phenomenological, and genealogical philosophers benefit from pragmatism. By putting pragmatism and feminism to work together on the reconstruction of philosophy, philosophy might better contribute to the flourishing of transactions of all organisms and their environments.

NOTES

INTRODUCTION

1. Dewey, *Knowing and the Known*, LW 16:119. Dewey is not well known for his eloquence, with good reason, so I take particular delight in this quote.

2. See Peter Reed, "Man Apart: An Alternative to the Self-Realization Approach," *Environmental Ethics*, Spring 1989, 11(1): 53–69, for an example of environmental philosophy that romanticizes nature as "wholly other" from humans; see also Ramachandra Guha, "Radical American Environmentalism and Wilderness Preservation: A Third World Critique," *Environmental Ethics*, Spring 1989, 11(1): 71–83, for a criticism of deep ecology's anthropocentrism/biocentrism dualism.

3. Dewey, *Art as Experience*, LW 10:64.

4. See Victor Kestenbaum's *The Phenomenological Sense of John Dewey: Habit and Meaning* (Atlantic Highlands, N.J.: Humanities Press, 1977) for one of the few works that reads Dewey as phenomenological.

5. See Charlene Haddock Seigfried, *Pragmatism and Feminism: Reweaving the Social Fabric* (Chicago: University of Chicago Press, 1996), 6–8, for a good summary of the general traits of pragmatism.

6. Seigfried's *Pragmatism and Feminism* is currently the only book-length monograph on the connections between pragmatism and feminism. See also Seigfried's edited works on pragmatism and feminism: *Feminist Interpretations of John Dewey* (University Park: Penn State University Press, forthcoming) and a special issue of *Hypatia* on pragmatism and feminism, volume 8(2), 1993. Other, article-length contributions to pragmatist feminism include the following (not an exhaustive list): Ann Clark, "The Quest for Certainty in Feminist Thought," *Hypatia* 1993, 8(3): 84–93; Eugenie Gatens-Robinson, "Dewey and the Feminist Successor Science Project," *Transactions of the C. S. Peirce Society*, Fall 1991, 27(4): 417–433; Lisa Heldke, "John Dewey and Evelyn Fox Keller: A Shared Epistemological Tradition," *Hypatia* 1987, 2(3): 129–140; Heather E. Keith, "Feminism and Pragmatism: George Herbert Mead's Ethics of Care," *Transactions of the C. S. Peirce Society*, Spring 1999, 35(2): 328–344; Felicia Kruse, "Luce Irigaray's *Parler Femme* and American Metaphysics," *Transactions of the C. S. Peirce Society*, Fall 1991, 27(4): 451–464; Marjorie C. Miller, "Feminism and Pragmatism," *Monist*, October 1992, 75(4): 445–457, and "Essence and Identity: Santayana and the Category 'Women'," *Transactions of the C. S. Peirce Society*, Winter 1994, 30(1): 33–50; Marcia Moen, "Peirce's Pragmatism as a Resource for Feminism," *Transactions of the C. S. Peirce Society*, Fall 1991, 27(4): 435–450; Charlene Haddock Seigfried, "John Dewey's Pragmatist Feminism," in *Reading Dewey: Interpretations for a Postmodern Generation*, ed. Larry A. Hickman (Bloomington: Indiana University Press, 1998).

7. Seigfried, *Pragmatism and Feminism*, 31–32.

8. Seigfried, *Pragmatism and Feminism*, 10.

9. Seigfried, *Pragmatism and Feminism*, 27–29.

10. Friedrich Nietzsche, *Thus Spoke Zarathustra*, trans. R. J. Hollingdale (New York: Viking Penguin, 1969), Preface 4, 6.

11. A notable exception to this observation is Louise M. Rosenblatt's *The Reader the Text the Poem: The Transactional Theory of the Literary Work* (Carbondale: Southern Illinois University Press, 1978), which uses Dewey's notion of transaction to develop reader-response theory.

I. LIVING ACROSS AND THROUGH SKINS

1. See Dewey, *Experience and Nature*, LW 1:154, for an example of Dewey's use of the term "interaction." Although the distinction between the *concepts* of interaction and transaction is present early in Dewey's philosophy, Dewey does not fully develop the distinction between the *terms* "interaction" and "transaction" until *Knowing and the Known* (LW 16:1–294), a work co-written with Arthur F. Bentley late in Dewey's career (1949). According to pragmatist scholar Thelma Levine, the field to which the concept of transaction has contributed most is philosophy of science (LW 16:xxxiii). See also Louise M. Rosenblatt, *The Reader the Text the Poem: The Transactional Theory of the Literary Work* (Carbondale: Southern Illinois University Press, 1978) for the use of the concept of transaction in literary criticism.

2. Dewey, *Knowing and the Known*, LW 16:144.

3. Dewey, *Knowing and the Known*, LW 16:119–120.

4. Dewey, *Experience and Nature*, LW 1:251.

5. Dewey, *Experience and Nature*, LW 1:25.

6. Dewey, *Art as Experience*, LW 10:20.

7. Charles Scott, *The Question of Ethics: Nietzsche, Foucault, Heidegger* (Bloomington: Indiana University Press, 1990).

8. According to Dewey, it also explains why aesthetic experience is possible. See Dewey, *Art as Experience*, LW 10:22.

9. Lawrence J. Hatab, *A Nietzschean Defense of Democracy: An Experiment in Postmodern Politics* (Chicago: Open Court, 1995), 207. See also Kristen Brown's use of curry for a food metaphor similar to that of stew in "Possible and Questionable: Opening Nietzsche's Genealogy to Feminine Body," *Hypatia*, Summer 1999, 14(3): 46–48. According to Brown, non-Western curry is a relation that "depicts each ingredient in a simultaneous role as agent and patient undergoing continual transmutation vis-à-vis the ingredients around it" (47). In a curry, "cumin, turmeric, and brown mustard simme[r] together [to] shape one another reciprocally" (48).

10. See Robert B. Westbrook, *John Dewey and American Democracy* (Ithaca: Cornell University Press, 1991), 212–214.

11. Dewey quoted in Westbrook, 213–214. The first bracketed addition is Westbrook's; the second bracketed addition is mine; the italics are Dewey's.

12. Dewey, "The Principle of Nationality," MW 10:289.

13. Thanks to Phillip McReynolds for providing this example.

14. Anzia Yezierska, a Polish immigrant to the United States with whom Dewey

had an unconsummated affair, experienced Dewey's person and educational philosophy as demanding the assimilation of immigrants into Anglo-Americanism. See Yezierska, *Salome and the Tenements* (Urbana: University of Illinois Press, 1995 [1923]) and *All I Could Never Be* (New York: Brewer, Warren and Putnam, 1932) for fictionalized accounts of Yezierska's relationship with Dewey.

15. Westbrook, *John Dewey and American Democracy*, 214.

16. Dewey, *Individualism, Old and New*, LW 5:122–123.

17. Elizabeth Spelman, *Inessential Woman: Problems of Exclusion in Feminist Thought* (Boston: Beacon Press, 1988), 114.

18. Spelman, *Inessential Woman*, 115, 123.

19. Dewey, *Experience and Nature*, LW 1:210.

20. Spelman, *Inessential Woman*, 122.

21. Spelman, *Inessential Woman*, 123.

22. The following analysis of Wendell's work is adapted from my review of *The Rejected Body: Feminist Philosophical Reflections on Disability* (New York: Routledge, 1996) in *The APA Newsletter on Feminism and Philosophy*, Spring 1999, 98(2): 99–101.

23. Wendell, *The Rejected Body*, 35.

24. Wendell, *The Rejected Body*, 35.

25. Wendell, *The Rejected Body*, 35, 45.

26. Wendell, *The Rejected Body*, 16.

27. Wendell, *The Rejected Body*, 37–39.

28. Wendell, *The Rejected Body*, 24.

29. One example of this pointed out to me by Ladelle McWhorter (private correspondence) is that many women are disabled when it comes to using heavy tools, equipment, and weapons. Because most of these items are made for people having larger bodies than do women, many women are rendered incapable of using them effectively. Many of these "disabilities" are being eliminated because some weapons and equipment companies now make versions of their products for smaller bodies.

30. Wendell, *The Rejected Body*, 33.

31. Dewey, *Experience and Nature*, LW 1:205.

32. Dewey, *Experience and Nature*, LW 1:195, emphasis in original.

33. Dewey, *Experience and Nature*, LW 1:195.

34. Dewey, *Experience and Nature*, LW 1:196.

35. Dewey, *Experience and Nature*, LW 1:198. Although Dewey tends to restrict to humans the class of animals who have mind, on his own terms some nonhuman animals must be included in it. The gorilla Koko, for example, communicates with humans via sign language.

36. Dewey, *Experience and Nature*, LW 1:230.

37. Dewey, *Experience and Nature*, LW 1:230, 233.

38. Dewey, *Experience and Nature*, LW 1:200.

39. Thanks to Vincent Colapietro (personal conversation) for providing this insight.

40. Dewey, *Experience and Nature*, LW 1:221. Dewey's claim about the bodily basis for mental life is very similar to that of Mark Johnson in *The Body in the Mind: The Bodily Basis of Meaning, Imagination, and Reason* (Chicago: University of Chicago Press, 1987).

41. Elizabeth Grosz makes this claim on page xx in *Volatile Bodies: Toward a Corporeal Feminism* (Bloomington: Indiana University Press, 1994).

42. See Dewey, *Experience and Nature*, LW 1:217.

43. Dewey, *Experience and Nature*, LW 1:217.

44. Dewey uses this example in "The Reflex Arc Concept in Psychology," EW 5:96–109. The example also demonstrates how Dewey's notion of habit, to be discussed subsequently, is not Skinnerian behaviorism, which operates with the atomistic concepts of stimulus and response.

45. Dewey, *Experience and Nature*, LW 1:221.

46. Dewey, *Experience and Nature*, LW 1:222.

47. Dewey, *Human Nature and Conduct*, MW 14:3.

48. Dewey, *Experience and Nature*, LW 1:66. On a similar note, see also "The Postulate of Immediate Empiricism," MW 3:162n7, where Dewey claims that "[i]n general, I think the distinction between -ive and -ed one of the most fundamental of philosophic distinctions, and one of the most neglected. The same holds of -tion and -ing."

49. Here I follow Bruce Wilshire's lead in "verbing" nouns, as Wilshire does when he characterizes "mind" as "minding," that is, as "the activity of body-mind organization itself and the world around and within it so that dominant needs are satisfied" ("Body-Mind and Subconsciousness: Tragedy in Dewey's Life and Work," in *Philosophy and the Reconstruction of Culture: Pragmatic Essays after Dewey*, ed. John J. Stuhr [Albany: State University of New York Press, 1993], 264). I prefer "bodying" to "embodying" because the term "embodiment" can connote a mind-body separation in which a mind comes to be "inside," or embodied in a body.

50. Dewey, *Human Nature and Conduct*, MW 14:75, note 1. While the distinction between the terms "instinct" and "impulse" is important for Dewey, he does not always maintain it, often using the two words as synonyms. This usage is a result of Dewey's attempt to modify the understanding of instinct so that the word means what is designated by impulse. Because Dewey uses the two terms interchangeably—and indeed, using "instinct" more often than "impulse" in *Human Nature and Conduct*—readers easily can mistakenly believe Dewey to be talking about organic energies as having given, unlearned meanings. They can take him to be operating with the very understanding of organic energies that he was attempting to overthrow. The pattern of deliberately using technical terms in novel ways to challenge traditional ideas in philosophy, only to be attacked for using those terms as they are traditionally understood, is common for Dewey. See Dewey's revised but unfinished introduction to *Experience and Nature* (LW 1:361–364) for similar problems he encountered with the term "experience."

51. Dewey, *Human Nature and Conduct*, MW 14:75, note 1.

52. Dewey, *Human Nature and Conduct*, MW 14:32; emphasis in original.

53. Dewey, *Human Nature and Conduct*, MW 14:21.

54. The example of posture, both here and in subsequent text, is taken from page 301 of my "Democracy and the Individual: To What Extent Is Dewey's Reconstruction Nietzsche's Self-Overcoming?" *Philosophy Today*, Summer 1997, 41(2): 299–312.

55. Dewey, *Human Nature and Conduct*, MW 14:51.

56. The use of "subconscious" rather than "unconscious" is deliberate here. Dewey suspected that the notion of the unconscious, particularly as developed in psychoanalysis, makes the Cartesian assumption of the existence of a separate psychic realm that is not formed through transaction with its social and other environments. See Dewey, *Human Nature and Conduct*, MW 14:61–62.

57. Dewey, *Human Nature and Conduct*, MW 14:49.

58. Dewey, *Human Nature and Conduct*, MW 14:49.

59. Dewey, *Human Nature and Conduct*, MW 14:24.

60. Dewey, *Human Nature and Conduct*, MW 14:28.

61. Dewey, *Human Nature and Conduct*, MW 14:51.

62. Dewey, *Experience and Nature*, LW 1:214.

63. Dewey, *Human Nature and Conduct*, MW 14:15.

64. Dewey, *Human Nature and Conduct*, MW 14:15, emphasis in original.

65. See Dewey, *Experience and Nature*, LW 1:178–180, for an excellent discussion of both the problematic and Dewey's own preferred ways of speaking of the ownership of experience, which is similar to the problematic and his preferred ways of speaking of the ownership of habits.

66. Dewey, *Human Nature and Conduct*, MW 14:15. See also Dewey, *Experience and Nature*, LW 1:180.

67. Dewey, *Human Nature and Conduct*, MW 14:43.

68. Michel Foucault, *Power/Knowledge: Selected Interviews and Other Writings, 1972–1977*, ed. Colin Gordon, trans. Colin Gordon, Leo Marshall, John Mepham, and Kate Soper (New York: Pantheon Books, 1980), 97, 98.

69. Dewey, *Human Nature and Conduct*, MW 14:68.

70. Dewey, *Human Nature and Conduct*, MW 14:44.

71. Dewey, *Human Nature and Conduct*, MW 14:43.

72. Dewey, *Human Nature and Conduct*, MW 14:68.

73. Dewey, *Art as Experience*, LW 10:251.

74. Dewey, *Human Nature and Conduct*, MW 14:255.

75. Dewey, *Human Nature and Conduct*, MW 14:65.

76. Dewey, *Human Nature and Conduct*, MW 14:65.

77. Vincent Colapietro's comments about bodily expressivity versus discursivity (private communication) helped me see this point.

78. George Butterworth, "An Ecological Perspective on the Origins of Self," in *The Body and the Self*, ed. José Luis Bermúdez, Anthony Marcel, and Naomi Elan (Cambridge, Mass.: MIT Press, 1995), 90–91. Evolutionary habit does not have to be thought of as fundamentally non- or precultural. In the case of humans, evolution happens in conjunction with cultural factors, which means that the habits provided by humans' evolutionary heritage are culturally configured, at least indirectly. Nor must an evolutionary habit be thought of as fixed and unchanging even though it admittedly could not be transformed significantly in an individual's lifetime.

79. See chapter 2 for more on the issue of discursivity.

80. Dewey, *Human Nature and Conduct*, MW 14:67.

81. Dewey, *Human Nature and Conduct*, MW 14:75.

2. DISCURSIVITY AND MATERIALITY

1. Foucault uses "discourse" in this broader way in *The History of Sexuality*, volume 1, trans. Robert Hurley (New York: Vintage, 1978).

2. John Stuhr (private conversation) brought this point to my attention. See his use of the term in Stuhr, *Genealogical Pragmatism: Philosophy, Experience, and Community* (Albany: State University of New York Press, 1997).

3. Thanks to Susan Schoenbaum (private conversation) for helping me see this point about the extradiscursive body.

4. See Judith Butler, "Foucault and the Paradox of Bodily Inscriptions," *The Journal of Philosophy*, 1989, 86(11): 601–607, and *Gender Trouble* (New York: Routledge, 1990), for arguments that Foucault at times speaks of a nondiscursive body even as his position denies the possibility of doing so. See also Ladelle McWhorter, "Culture or Nature: The Function of the Term 'Body' in the Work of Michel Foucault," *The Journal of Philosophy*, 1989, 86(11): 608–614, and especially "Bodies Against Desire: Foucault's Resistance to Sexual Subjectivity" in *The Limits of Desire: Passion, Play, and Perversion*, ed. Ellen L. McCallum and Judith Roof (forthcoming), and chapter 5 of *Bodies and Pleasures: Foucault and the Politics of Sexual Normalization* (Bloomington: Indiana University Press, 1999) for convincing arguments that Foucault does not "cheat" by positing a nondiscursive body.

5. For a criticism, from the perspective of evolutionary anthropology, of poststructuralist and postmodern understandings of the body as discursive, see Maxine Sheets-Johnstone, "Corporeal Archetypes and Power: Preliminary Clarifications and Considerations of Sex," *Hypatia*, 1992, 7: 39–76.

6. Carol Bigwood, "Renaturalizing the body (with the help of Merleau-Ponty)," *Hypatia*, 1991, 6(3): 59.

7. Bigwood, "Renaturalizing the body," 59.

8. Bigwood, "Renaturalizing the body," 59.

9. Bigwood, "Renaturalizing the body," 60.

10. Bigwood, "Renaturalizing the body," 60.

11. Bigwood, "Renaturalizing the body," 61.

12. Bigwood, "Renaturalizing the body," 57.

13. Bigwood, "Renaturalizing the body," 62.

14. Bigwood, "Renaturalizing the body," 66.

15. Tuana, "Re-fusing Nature/Nurture," in *Hypatia Reborn: Essays in Feminist Philosophy*, ed. Azizah Y. al-Hibri and Margaret A. Simons (Bloomington: Indiana University Press, 1990), 80–81.

16. Bigwood, "Renaturalizing the body," 69.

17. Bigwood, "Renaturalizing the body," 59.

18. Bigwood, "Renaturalizing the body," 60.

19. Bigwood, "Renaturalizing the body," 68.

20. Bigwood, "Renaturalizing the body," 69.

21. Eugene Gendlin, "The primacy of the body, not the primacy of perception," *Man and World*, 1992, 00: 342.

22. Gendlin, "The primacy of the body," 344, emphasis in original.

23. Gendlin, "The primacy of the body," 345.

24. Gendlin, "The primacy of the body," 341.

25. Gendlin, "The primacy of the body," 347, 349.

26. Gendlin, "The primacy of the body," 348.

27. Antoine Bechara, Hanna Darnasio, Daniel Tranel, and Antonio R. Damasio, "Deciding Advantageously Before Knowing the Advantageous Strategy," *Science,* February 28, 1997, 275: 1293–1295.

28. Gendlin, "The primacy of the body," 349, 341.

29. Gendlin, "The primacy of the body," 346.

30. Dewey, *Experience and Nature*, LW 1:143.

31. See chapter 1 for more on the term "bodying," which designates bodies as activities rather than as things.

32. David Michael Levin, "The Body Politic: The Embodiment of Praxis in Foucault and Habermas," *Praxis International*, 1989, 9(1/2): 112–132.

33. Dewey, *The Study of Ethics: A Syllabus*, EW 4:312–313.

34. Gendlin, "The primacy of the body," 343.

35. Gendlin, "The primacy of the body," 343.

36. Gendlin, "The primacy of the body," 344.

37. Judith Butler, *Bodies That Matter: On the Discursive Limits of "Sex"* (New York: Routledge, 1993), 69.

38. Butler, *Bodies That Matter*, 68.

39. Butler, *Bodies That Matter*, 69.

40. Dewey, *The Quest for Certainty*, LW 4:19.

41. Dewey, *The Quest for Certainty*, LW 4:195.

42. Dewey, *Experience and Nature*, 324.

43. Maxine Sheets-Johnstone, "Corporeal Archetypes and Power," 155.

44. Butler, *Bodies That Matter*, 10.

45. Butler, *Bodies That Matter*, 68.

46. Butler, *Bodies That Matter*, 10.

47. Butler, *Bodies That Matter*, 67.

48. Dewey, *Experience and Nature*, LW 1:324.

49. Dewey, *Experience and Nature*, LW 1:324.

50. Dewey, *Experience and Nature*, LW 1:34.

51. Dewey, *Experience and Nature*, LW 1:34.

52. Butler, *Bodies That Matter*, 30.

53. Butler, *Bodies That Matter*, 9, emphasis in original; see also Butler, *Bodies That Matter*, 10.

54. Butler, *Bodies That Matter*, 3.

55. Butler, *Bodies That Matter*, 2.

56. Butler, *Bodies That Matter*, 29.

57. Butler, *Bodies That Matter*, 30.

58. Lois McNay makes a similar claim about Foucault's work, charging among other things that his work lacks any analysis of the concrete experiences of those who are subjects of power. See McNay, "The Foucauldian Body and the Exclusion of Experience," *Hypatia*, 1991, 6(3): 123–139.

59. On the epistemological focus of Butler's position, see Veronica Vasterling,

"Butler's Sophisticated Constructivism: A Critical Assessment," *Hypatia*, Summer 1999, 14(3): 17–38.

60. See, for example, Butler, *Bodies That Matter*, page xi.

61. Charlene Haddock Seigfried makes a similar point about pragmatist treatments of experience, although not with specific respect to the issue of the nondiscursive body. See Seigfried, "Weaving Chaos into Order: A Radically Pragmatic Aesthetic," *Philosophy and Literature*, 1990, 14(1): 108–109.

62. Susan Wendell, *The Rejected Body: Feminist Philosophical Reflections on Disability* (New York: Routledge, 1996), especially 133–138. The following analysis of Wendell's book is adapted from my review of it in *The APA Newsletter on Feminism and Philosophy*, Spring 1999, 98(2): 99–101.

63. Wendell, *The Rejected Body*, 136.

64. Wendell, *The Rejected Body*, 137.

65. Susan Bordo, *Unbearable Weight: Feminism, Western Culture, and the Body* (Berkeley: University of California Press, 1993).

66. Susan Bordo, "Bringing Body to Theory," in *Body and Flesh: A Philosophical Reader*, ed. Donn Welton (Malden: Blackwell, 1998).

67. Bordo, *Unbearable Weight*, 144–148.

68. Bordo, *Unbearable Weight*, 41.

69. Wendell, *The Rejected Body*, 85.

70. Wendell, *The Rejected Body*, 171.

71. Bordo, "Bringing Body to Theory," 94.

72. Bordo, "Bringing Body to Theory," 95.

73. Bordo, *Unbearable Weight*, 154–159.

3. COMMUNICATING WITH ANOTHER

1. This list is taken from my "Feminism and Phenomenology: A Reply to Silvia Stoller," *Hypatia*, Winter 2000, 15(1): 183–188.

2. See, for example, Jeffner Allen, "Through The Wild Region: An Essay in Phenomenological Feminism," in *Review of Existential Psychology and Psychiatry*, 1982, 18: 241–256; Judith Butler, "Sexual Ideology and Phenomenological Description: A Feminist Critique of Merleau-Ponty's Phenomenology of Perception," in *The Thinking Muse: Feminism and Modern French Philosophy*, ed. Jeffner Allen and Iris Marion Young (Bloomington: Indiana University Press, 1989); and Iris Marion Young, *Throwing Like a Girl and Other Essays in Feminist Philosophy and Social Theory* (Bloomington: Indiana University Press), especially 14–15 and 141–209.

3. The definition of ethical solipsism I provide here is taken from my "Feminism and Phenomenology."

4. Maurice Merleau-Ponty, *The Phenomenology of Perception*, trans. Colin Smith (Atlantic Highlands, N.J.: Humanities Press, 1962) 110, 111.

5. Merleau-Ponty, *The Phenomenology of Perception*, 156, 155.

6. Merleau-Ponty, *The Phenomenology of Perception*, 112.

7. Merleau-Ponty, *The Phenomenology of Perception*, 112.

8. Merleau-Ponty, *The Phenomenology of Perception*, 121.

9. Merleau-Ponty, *The Phenomenology of Perception*, 132, emphasis added.

10. Merleau-Ponty, *The Phenomenology of Perception*, 145.

11. Merleau-Ponty, *The Phenomenology of Perception*, 448.

12. Merleau-Ponty, *The Phenomenology of Perception*, 132.

13. Merleau-Ponty, *The Phenomenology of Perception*, 354, 348.

14. Merleau-Ponty, *The Phenomenology of Perception*, 348.

15. Merleau-Ponty, *The Phenomenology of Perception*, 361.

16. Merleau-Ponty, *The Phenomenology of Perception*, 354.

17. See Patrick L. Bourgeois and Sandra B. Rosenthal, "Role Taking, Corporeal Intersubjectivity, and Self: Mead and Merleau-Ponty," *Philosophy Today*, 1990, 34(2): 122–123.

18. Merleau-Ponty, *The Phenomenology of Perception*, 356.

19. Merleau-Ponty, *The Phenomenology of Perception*, 353.

20. Merleau-Ponty, *The Phenomenology of Perception*, 353–354.

21. Merleau-Ponty, *The Phenomenology of Perception*, 353.

22. This paragraph is adapted from my "Feminism and Phenomenology."

23. Merleau-Ponty, *The Phenomenology of Perception*, 353.

24. See chapter 1 for my use of the term "bodying," which designates bodies as activities rather than as things.

25. Merleau-Ponty, *The Phenomenology of Perception*, 354.

26. Here I adapt Elizabeth Spelman's caution that "[t]here are no short cuts through women's lives," from page 187 of Spelman's *Inessential Woman: Problems of Exclusion in Feminist Thought* (Boston: Beacon Press, 1988).

27. Dewey, *Experience and Nature*, LW 1:141, emphasis added.

28. On the suggestion that we start with our differences, that difference need not be seen as equivalent to the end of community, and that similarity is constituted rather than given, see Honi Fern Haber, *Beyond Postmodern Politics: Lyotard, Rorty, Foucault* (New York: Routledge, 1994), 113–134, and Spelman, *Inessential Woman*, especially page 13.

29. Spelman, *Inessential Woman*, 12.

30. Merleau-Ponty, *The Phenomenology of Perception*, 361.

31. As María C. Lugones notes, paying attention to the particularities of others must include the recognition that different particularities—such as gender, race, class, nationality, and so on—may affect people's understandings of each other in different ways. See Lugones, "On the Logic of Pluralist Feminism," in *Feminist Ethics*, ed. Claudia Card (Lawrence: University Press of Kansas, 1991), 41.

32. María C. Lugones, "Playfulness, 'World'-Traveling, and Loving Perception," *Hypatia* 2(2): 18.

33. Elizabeth McMillan makes a similar suggestion in "Female Difference in the Texts of Merleau-Ponty," *Philosophy Today*, 1987, 31: 366.

34. Lorraine Code, *Rhetorical Spaces: Essays on Gendered Locations* (New York: Routledge, 1995), 55.

35. Code makes a similar point in *Rhetorical Spaces*, 51.

36. Dewey, *Experience and Nature*, LW 1:141.

37. Lugones, "Playfulness, 'World'-Traveling, and Loving Perception," 17, emphasis in original.

38. Dewey, *Ethics*, LW 7: 270.

39. Dewey, *Ethics*, LW 7: 270.

40. Dewey, *Ethics*, LW 7: 270.

41. Bradford and Sartwell, "Voice Bodies/Embodied Voices," in *Race/Sex: Their Sameness, Difference and Interplay*, ed. Naomi Zack (New York: Routledge, 1997), 194–195.

42. Dewey, *Experience and Nature*, LW 1:141.

43. See Grosz, *Volatile Bodies*, 192, on the importance of finding a position that allows for one to be surprised by the other; see also Luce Irigaray, *An Ethics of Sexual Difference*, trans. Carolyn Burke and Gillian C. Gill (Ithaca: Cornell University Press, 1993), 72–82, on wonder's ability to prevent assimilation of the other into oneself.

44. Maurice Merleau-Ponty, *The Visible and the Invisible*, trans. Alphonso Lingis (Evanston: Northwestern University Press, 1968).

45. Merleau-Ponty, *The Visible and the Invisible*, 136, 139, 147.

46. Grosz, *Volatile Bodies*, 95.

47. Merleau-Ponty, *The Visible and the Invisible*, 133–134.

48. Merleau-Ponty, *The Visible and the Invisible*, 148.

49. I take the fabric image from Gary Brent Madison, *The Phenomenology of Merleau-Ponty*, trans. Gary Brent Madison (Athens: Ohio University Press, 1981), 174.

50. Madison, *The Phenomenology of Merleau-Ponty*, 175.

51. Because Merleau-Ponty died before completing *The Visible and the Invisible*, it may also seem unfair to criticize this work for what it lacks. My point nonetheless holds that his later work is missing an element important to feminism. Whether Merleau-Ponty would have provided it had he lived to finish this work, we unfortunately will never know.

52. See Irigaray, *An Ethics of Sexual Difference*, 151–184, for a different assessment of the problems in *The Visible and the Invisible*, one that is concerned about the "closed system" and "solipsistic relation to the maternal" set up by Merleau-Ponty in that work.

53. For further consideration of this claim, see my "The Racialization of Space: Toward a Phenomenological Account of Raced and Anti-Racist Spatiality," in *The Questions of Resistance*, ed. Steve Martinot (Atlantic Highlands, N.J.: Humanities Press, forthcoming), in which I indicate how Merleau-Ponty's standard of projective intentionality can promote white racist behavior.

54. Jim Garrison, "A Deweyan Theory of Democratic Listening," *Educational Theory*, Fall 1996, 46(4): 429–451.

4. RECONFIGURING GENDER

1. *Gender Trouble: Feminism and the Subversion of Identity* (New York: Routledge, 1990).

2. Namely, Butler's *Excitable Speech: A Politics of the Performative* (New York: Routledge, 1997).

3. This claim is suggested by *Excitable Speech* and made explicit in Butler's

"Performativity's Social Magic," in *Bourdieu: A Critical Reader*, ed. Richard Shusterman (Malden: Blackwell, 1999), 115, 126.

4. As chapter 2 makes clear, my claim that lived experience sometimes "overflows" the words used to describe it is not a claim that lived experience is non- or prediscursive.

5. See, for example, Judith Butler, *Gender Trouble;* Marilyn Frye, *The Politics of Reality: Essays in Feminist Theory* (Trumansburg, N.Y.: The Crossing Press, 1983); and Monique Wittig, *The Straight Mind and Other Essays* (Boston: Beacon Press, 1992).

6. Charlene Haddock Seigfried, *Pragmatism and Feminism: Reweaving the Social Fabric* (Chicago: University of Chicago Press, 1996), 212.

7. Foucault, *The Use of Pleasure*, trans. Robert Hurley (New York: Vintage Books, 1985).

8. Walter L. Williams, *The Spirit and the Flesh: Sexual Diversity in American Indian Culture* (Boston: Beacon Press, 1986).

9. Butler, *Bodies That Matter: On the Discursive Limits of "Sex"* (New York: Routledge, 1993), 94.

10. Butler, *Bodies That Matter*, 94.

11. Dewey, *Experience and Nature*, LW 1:64–65.

12. See chapter 1 on the term "bodying," which refers to bodies as activities rather than as things.

13. Dewey, *Human Nature and Conduct*, MW 14:25.

14. Dewey, *Human Nature and Conduct*, MW 14:30.

15. Nancy M. Henley, *Body Politics: Power, Sex, and Nonverbal Communication* (Englewood Cliffs: Prentice-Hall, 1977), 168–178.

16. Dewey, *Experience and Education*, LW 13:41.

17. Foucault, *The History of Sexuality*, volume 1, trans. Robert Hurley (New York: Vintage Books, 1978).

18. Dewey, *Human Nature and Conduct*, MW 14:211.

19. Dewey, *Human Nature and Conduct*, MW 14:115.

20. Michel Foucault, *Politics/Philosophy/Culture: Interviews and Other Writings, 1977–1984*, ed. Lawrence D. Kritzman (New York: Routledge, 1988), 36.

21. Dewey, *Human Nature and Conduct*, MW 14:135–136.

22. Dewey, *Human Nature and Conduct*, MW 14:49.

23. Dewey, *Human Nature and Conduct*, MW 14:47.

24. Butler never speaks of performativity in terms of habit in that particular work. She does, however, discuss performativity in terms of *habitus* in her more recent *Excitable Speech* and "Performativity's Social Magic."

25. Butler, *Gender Trouble*, 140, emphasis in original.

26. Butler, *Bodies That Matter*, x, emphasis in original.

27. Butler, *Bodies That Matter*, 95.

28. Butler, *Bodies That Matter*, 2, 94–95.

29. On this misunderstanding, see Butler, *Bodies That Matter*, x.

30. Butler, *Bodies That Matter*, 7. Butler makes a similar claim in her more recent "Performativity's Social Magic," 118.

31. Butler, *Bodies That Matter*, 15.

32. Butler, *Gender Trouble*, 147.

33. Butler, *Gender Trouble*, 145.

34. Butler, *Gender Trouble*, 148, emphasis in original.

35. Butler, *Gender Trouble*, 145.

36. Butler, *Bodies That Matter*, 237, emphasis in original.

37. Butler, *Bodies That Matter*, 237.

38. For a different concern about the negative effects of the rigidity of gender performativity and habits, see Butler, *The Psychic Life of Power: Theories in Subjection* (Stanford: Stanford University Press, 1997), especially chapters 5 and 6. There she suggests that rigid forms of gender produce melancholy because they preempt the grieving of the abandonment of homosexual attachments that is formative of gender.

39. Dewey, *Human Nature and Conduct*, MW 14:73.

40. Butler, *Excitable Speech*, 141–163.

41. Butler, *Excitable Speech*, 150, emphasis added.

42. Butler, *Excitable Speech*, 142.

43. Butler repeats her criticism of Bourdieu made in *Excitable Speech* in "Performativity's Social Magic," 118.

44. Butler, *Excitable Speech*, 153.

45. Butler, *Excitable Speech*, 155.

46. Butler, *Bodies That Matter*, 2. Butler also makes this sort of claim in "Performativity's Social Magic," 118.

47. Butler, "Performativity's Social Magic," 118.

48. Butler, *Excitable Speech*, 155.

49. For more on Butler's work in conjunction with the issue of discursivity, see chapter 2.

50. See Jacques Derrida, "Signature, Event, Context," in *Limited, Inc.*, ed. Gerald Graff, trans. Samuel Webster and Jeffrey Mehlman (Evanston: Northwestern University Press, 1988), 1–23.

51. Butler, *Bodies That Matter*, 2.

52. Butler, *Excitable Speech*, 161.

53. Butler, *Excitable Speech*, 159.

54. Butler, *Excitable Speech*, 161.

55. As Veronica Vasterling points out, Butler also suggests, but does not fully explicate, a similar position in *Bodies That Matter*. See Vasterling, "Butler's Sophisticated Constructivism: A Critical Assessment," *Hypatia*, Summer 1999, 14(3): 28.

56. Dewey, *Experience and Nature*, LW 1:66.

57. Dewey, *Human Nature and Conduct*, MW 14:89–90.

58. Dewey, *Human Nature and Conduct*, MW 14:90.

59. Dewey, *Human Nature and Conduct*, MW 14:73.

60. Dewey, *Human Nature and Conduct*, MW 14:90.

61. Dewey, *Human Nature and Conduct*, MW 14:214.

62. Butler, "Gender Trouble, Feminist Theory, and Psychoanalytic Discourse," in *Feminism/Postmodernism*, ed. Linda J. Nicholson (New York: Routledge, 1990), 339.

5. TRANSACTIONAL SOMAESTHETICS

1. Friedrich Nietzsche, *The Will to Power*, trans. Walter Kaufmann and R. J. Hollingdale, ed. Walter Kaufmann (New York: Vintage Books, 1967), section 229.

2. Friedrich Nietzsche, *The Gay Science*, trans. Walter Kaufmann (New York: Vintage Books, 1974), section 2, Nietzsche's preface, emphasis in original.

3. On this point, see Shannon Sullivan, "Democracy and the Individual: To What Extent Is Dewey's Reconstruction Nietzsche's Self-Overcoming?" *Philosophy Today*, Summer 1997, 41(2): 299–312.

4. Richard Shusterman, *Practicing Philosophy: Pragmatism and the Philosophical Life* (New York: Routledge, 1997). See also Shusterman, "Somaesthetics and the Body/Media Issue," *Body and Society*, 1997, 3(3): 33–49.

5. Shusterman, *Practicing Philosophy*, 175–177. Shusterman identifies two additional tasks for somaesthetic work: supplying philosophical skills and lending support to disciplines that explore our somatic experience, perhaps also investigating for itself nonverbal experiences in art and ethics; and critically examining and analyzing, in the role of cultural critic, the bodily practices of our culture. I will not directly address somaesthetics in these two senses although my discussion of somaesthetics has implications for both.

6. Friedrich Nietzsche, *Thus Spoke Zarathustra*, trans. R. J. Hollingdale (New York: Viking Penguin, 1969), Book I: pages 61, 62.

7. See Malcolm Pasley, "Nietzsche's Use of Medical Terms," in *Nietzsche: Imagery and Thought*, ed. Malcolm Pasley (London: Methuen, 1978), 123–158.

8. See Michel Haar, "Heidegger and the Nietzschean 'Physiology of Art,'" in *Exceedingly Nietzsche*, ed. David Farrell Krell and David Wood (New York: Routledge, 1988); David Michael Levin, *The Body's Recollection of Being: Phenomenological Psychology and the Deconstruction of Nihilism* (New York: Routledge, 1985), 34–35; and David Owen, "Nietzsche's Squandered Seductions: Feminism, the Body, and the Politics of Genealogy," in *The Fate of the New Nietzsche*, ed. Keith Ansell-Pearson and Howard Caygill (Brookfield: Avebury, 1993).

9. See Arifuku Kogaku, "The Problem of the Body in Nietzsche and Dogen," trans. Graham Parkes, in *Nietzsche and Asian Thought*, ed. Graham Parkes (Chicago: University of Chicago Press, 1991), 214–225.

10. See William T. Bluhm, *Force or Freedom? The Paradox in Modern Political Thought* (New Haven: Yale University Press, 1984), 216–217.

11. See Eric Blondel, *Nietzsche: The Body and Culture: Philosophy as a Philological Genealogy*, trans. Sean Hand (Stanford: Stanford University Press, 1991).

12. See Daniel W. Conway, "Disembodied Perspectives: Nietzsche contra Rorty," *Nietzsche-Studien*, band 21: 281–289.

13. Friedrich Nietzsche, *Twilight of the Idols/The Anti-Christ*, trans. R. J. Hollingdale (New York: Penguin Books, 1968), "The Four Great Errors," sections 3–7. See also Nietzsche, *Beyond Good and Evil*, in *Basic Writings of Nietzsche*, trans. and ed. Walter Kaufmann (New York: The Modern Library, 1968), sections 17–21.

14. Nietzsche, *The Twilight of the Idols*, "The Four Great Errors," section 3.

15. Nietzsche, *The Twilight of the Idols,* "The Four Great Errors," section 7, emphasis in original.

16. Friedrich Nietzsche, *On the Genealogy of Morals,* in *Basic Writings of Nietzsche,* trans. and ed. Walter Kaufmann (New York: The Modern Library, 1968), second essay.

17. Nietzsche, *The Twilight of the Idols,* "The Four Great Errors," section 7, emphasis in original.

18. Nietzsche, *The Will to Power,* section 314.

19. Nietzsche, *The Twilight of the Idols,* "The Four Great Errors," section 6.

20. Nietzsche, *The Will to Power,* section 229.

21. Nietzsche, *The Twilight of the Idols,* "The Four Great Errors," section 6.

22. Eric Blondel makes this mistake in his account of the body as a metaphor for interpretation. See Blondel, *Nietzsche: The Body and Culture,* especially pages 219 and 227. Kristen Brown makes a claim similar to mine when she argues that "[w]hile body as biology *only* is problematic, . . . body as symbolic *only* is also problematic." See Brown, "Possible and Questionable: Opening Nietzsche's Genealogy to Feminine Body," *Hypatia,* Summer 1999, 14(3): 54, emphasis in original.

23. Nietzsche, *The Will to Power,* sections 41–44.

24. Friedrich Nietzsche, *Ecce Homo,* in *Basic Writings of Nietzsche,* trans. and ed. Walter Kaufmann (New York: The Modern Library, 1968), "Why I Am So Clever," section 1.

25. Nietzsche, *Ecce Homo,* "Why I Am So Clever," section 2, emphasis in original.

26. Nietzsche, *Ecce Homo,* "Why I Am So Clever," section 1, emphasis in original.

27. Nietzsche, *Ecce Homo,* "Why I Am So Clever," section 10, emphasis in original.

28. Nietzsche, *The Will to Power,* section 41.

29. Nietzsche, *Ecce Homo,* "Why I Am So Clever," section 10, emphasis in original.

30. Nietzsche, *Ecco Home,* "Why I Am So Clever," section 1.

31. Nietzsche, *Ecce Homo,* "Why I Am So Clever," section 1, emphasis in original.

32. Nietzsche, *Ecce Homo,* "Why I Am So Clever," section 1.

33. Nietzsche, *The Will to Power,* section 532, emphasis in original.

34. Brian Domino, "Nietzsche and the Little Things," paper presented at Miami University, Oxford, Ohio, March 29, 1996.

35. For more on the term "bodying," which designates bodies as activities rather than as things, see chapter 1.

36. See, for example, Simone de Beauvoir, *The Second Sex,* trans. H. M. Parshley (New York: Vintage, 1989); bell hooks, *Ain't I A Woman? Black Women and Feminism* (Boston: South End Press, 1981); Genevieve Lloyd, *The Man of Reason: "Male" and "Female" in Western Philosophy* (Minneapolis: University of Minnesota Press, 1984); and Elizabeth Spelman, *Inessential Woman: Problems of Exclusion in Feminist Thought* (Boston: Beacon Press, 1988), chapter 5.

37. Elizabeth V. Spelman, "Woman as Body: Ancient and Contemporary Views," *Feminist Studies,* Spring 1982, 8(1): 114, 115.

38. I refer here to the quote from Nietzsche's *The Will to Power* that heads this chapter.

39. See, for example, Michel Foucault, *The Use of Pleasure,* volume 2 of *The History of Sexuality,* trans. Robert Hurley (New York: Vintage Books, 1985), 95–139, on Greek free males; and Shusterman *Practicing Philosophy,* 30–36, on Foucault himself.

40. Jacqueline Scott makes this point in "Nietzsche and the Problem of Women's Bodies," paper presented at the meeting of the Eastern Division of the American Philosophical Association, Philadelphia, December 28, 1997. See also Kelly Oliver, *Womanizing Nietzsche: Philosophy's Relation to the "Feminine"* (New York: Routledge, 1995) and Luce Irigaray, *Marine Lover of Friedrich Nietzsche,* trans. Gillian C. Gill (New York: Columbia University Press, 1991). For examples of Nietzsche's use of metaphors of pregnancy and maternity, see *On the Genealogy of Morals,* sections 16 and 19.

41. Nietzsche, *Ecce Homo,* "Why I Write Such Good Books," section 5; *Beyond Good and Evil,* sections 127, 232, 239.

42. Nietzsche, *Beyond Good and Evil,* section 239.

43. Nietzsche, *Beyond Good and Evil,* section 145, emphasis in original.

44. Nietzsche, *Beyond Good and Evil,* section 234, emphasis in original.

45. Nietzsche, *On the Genealogy of Morals,* Third Essay, section 20, emphasis in original.

46. Nietzsche, *The Will to Power,* section 532.

47. This paragraph draws from page 300 of my "Democracy and the Individual: To What Extent Is Dewey's Reconstruction Nietzsche's Self-Overcoming?"

48. Nietzsche, *Thus Spoke Zarathustra,* Book One, page 61; *Beyond Good and Evil,* section 12.

49. Nietzsche, *Thus Spoke Zarathustra,* Book One, pages 61–62.

50. I am reluctant to call Nietzsche's position on the body a dynamic monism, as Kristen Brown has done (Brown, "Possible and Questionable," 39, 51). While the qualifier "dynamic" suggests a reciprocal relationship between body and mind, the term "monism" problematically undercuts that suggestion by connoting a substance metaphysics that admits of no multiplicity. Although Brown does not use the word "transactional," I think the term captures better than does "dynamic monism" the account of the body that she wishes to put forth with her metaphor of curry.

51. Nietzsche, *The Will to Power,* section 786.

52. Matthais F. Alexander, *The Use of the Self: Its Conscious Direction in Relation to Diagnosis, Functioning and the Control of Reaction* (New York: E. P. Dutton, 1932). The book of Dewey's to which I refer, and in which explicit references to Alexander's work can be found, is *Human Nature and Conduct,* MW 14.

53. Architecture professor and Alexander Technician Galen Cranz makes this point in her cultural-somatic critique of the chair. See Cranz, *The Chair: Rethinking Culture, Body, and Design* (New York: W. W. Norton and Company, 1998).

54. Alexander, *The Use of the Self*, 39.

55. Alexander, *The Use of the Self*, 53, emphasis in original.

56. See Cranz, *The Chair*, 107–115, for a discussion of this point with regard to the body-damaging practice of sitting in chairs.

57. On "stuckness," see Nietzsche, *Beyond Good and Evil*, section 41. See also Nietzsche, *Human, All Too Human: A Book for Free Spirits*, trans. R. J. Hollingdale (New York: Cambridge University Press, 1986), section 427.

58. Nietzsche, *Human, All Too Human*, section 483.

59. Alexander, *The Use of the Self*, 57.

60. Sandra Bartky, *Femininity and Domination: Studies in the Phenomenology of Oppression* (New York: Routledge, 1990), chapter 7.

61. Bartky, *Femininity and Domination*, 119.

62. Bartky, *Femininity and Domination*, especially chapter 5, and Susan Bordo, *Unbearable Weight* (Berkeley: University of California Press, 1993).

63. I take the term "pseudodemocracy" from Frances Maher, "My Introduction to 'Introduction to Women's Studies': The Role of the Professor's Authority in the Feminist Classroom," in Gail E. Cohee, Elisabeth Daumer, Theresa D. Kemp, Paula M. Krebs, Sue A. Lafky, and Sandra Runzo, eds., *The Feminist Anthology: Pedagogies and Classroom Strategies* (New York: Teachers College Press, 1998), 29–30.

64. Susan Bordo analyzes this sort of situation in *Unbearable Weight*, pages 99–134.

65. Nietzsche, *Thus Spoke Zarathustra*, "Of the Bestowing Virtue," page 100.

6. TRANSACTIONAL KNOWING

1. Friedrich Nietzsche, *The Gay Science*, trans. Walter Kaufmann (New York: Vintage Books, 1974), section 2, Nietzsche's preface.

2. Susan Bordo's work on Descartes makes this point in a powerful way. See *The Flight to Objectivity: Essays on Cartesianism and Culture* (Albany: State University of New York Press, 1987).

3. Thomas Nagel and Nicholas Rescher have argued in favor of objectivism out of this concern. See Nagel, *The Last Word* (New York: Oxford University Press, 1997), and Rescher, *Objectivity: The Obligations of Impersonal Reason* (Notre Dame: University of Notre Dame Press, 1997).

4. Sandra Harding, *The Science Question in Feminism* (Ithaca: Cornell University Press, 1986), 191.

5. Harding, *Whose Science? Whose Knowledge? Thinking from Women's Lives* (Ithaca: Cornell University Press, 1991), 276.

6. Sandra Harding, "How the Women's Movement Benefits Science: Two Views," *Women Studies International Forum*, 1989, 12(3): 279; *Whose Science? Whose Knowledge?* 286–287; "Rethinking Standpoint Epistemology: 'What Is Strong Objectivity'?" in *Feminist Epistemologies*, ed. Linda Alcoff and Elizabeth Potter (New York: Routledge, 1993), 54.

7. Sandra Harding, "Rethinking Standpoint Epistemology," 150–151.

8. Harding, *Whose Science? Whose Knowledge?* 122–123, emphasis added.

9. Harding, *Whose Science? Whose Knowledge?* 152.

10. Harding, *Whose Science? Whose Knowledge?* 286.

11. Harding, *Whose Science? Whose Knowledge?* 149, 151.

12. Harding, *Whose Science? Whose Knowledge?* 150.

13. Harding, *Whose Science? Whose Knowledge?* 150.

14. Harding, *Whose Science? Whose Knowledge?* 152.

15. Donna Haraway levels precisely this criticism at earlier formations of Harding's standpoint theory. See Haraway cited in Martha McCaughey, "Redirecting Feminist Critiques of Science," *Hypatia* 1993, 8(4): 77.

16. Susan Hekman's charge to this effect can be found in McCaughey, "Redirecting Feminist Critiques of Science," 77.

17. Harding, *Whose Science? Whose Knowledge?* 273.

18. Harding, *Whose Science? Whose Knowledge?* xi.

19. Harding, *Whose Science? Whose Knowledge?* 59.

20. Harding, *Whose Science? Whose Knowledge?* 187.

21. Sandra Harding, "Comment on Hekman's 'Truth and Method: Feminist Standpoint Theory Revisited': Whose Standpoint Needs the Regimes of Truth and Reality?" *Signs: Journal of Women in Culture and Society*, 1997, 22(2): 383.

22. Harding, *Whose Science? Whose Knowledge?* 106n.

23. Jane Flax, "Postmodernism and Gender Relations in Feminist Theory," in *Feminism/Postmodernism*, ed. Linda J. Nicholson (New York: Routledge, 1990), 56.

24. Haraway's criticism can be found in McCaughey, "Redirecting Feminist Critiques of Science," 77.

25. Nancy C. M. Hartsock, "The Feminist Standpoint: Developing the Ground for a Specifically Feminist Historical Materialism," in *Discovering Reality*, ed. Sandra Harding and Merrill B. Hintikka (Boston: D. Reidel Publishing Company, 1983), 288.

26. Hartsock, "The Feminist Standpoint," 304.

27. Harding, *Whose Science? Whose Knowledge?* 185.

28. Harding, "After the Neutrality Ideal: Science, Politics, and 'Strong Objectivity,'" *Social Research*, 1992, 59(3): 586–587.

29. Thus, in note 12 of page 171 of her "From Aperspectival Objectivity to Strong Objectivity: The Quest for Moral Objectivity," *Hypatia* 12(1), Jennifer Tannoch-Bland misses the central thrust of Daniel Conway's criticism of Harding in her response to him (see Conway, "*Das Weib an sich:* The slave revolt in epistemology," in *Nietzsche, Feminism and Political Theory*, ed. Paul Patton [New York: Routledge, 1993]). While Tannoch-Bland is correct that Harding claims that the oppressed can help us gain not a completely pure, but a pure*r*, picture of the world, Conway is right that this claim "fails to take the 'postmodern turn' " precisely because it still operates with a notion of pure truth as its standard for objectivity (Tannoch-Bland partially quoting Conway, 171).

30. Harding, *Whose Science? Whose Knowledge?* 126, 127.

31. Susan Hekman makes a similar point in "Truth and Method: Feminist Standpoint Theory Revisited," *Signs: Journal of Women in Culture and Society*, 1997, 22(2): 354.

32. Conway, "*Das Weib an sich*," 121; Conway, "*Circulus Vitiosus Deus?* The

Dialectical Logic of Feminist Standpoint Theory," *Journal of Social Philosophy*, 1997, 28(1): 69.

33. Charlene Haddock Seigfried, *Pragmatism and Feminism: Reweaving the Social Fabric* (Chicago: University of Chicago Press, 1996), 152.

34. Sandra Harding, "Comment on Hekman's 'Truth and Method,'" 382. Susan Hekman's criticism to which Harding is responding in this quote can be found in Hekman's "Truth and Method."

35. Hekman rightly makes this reply to Harding in "Reply to Hartsock, Collins, Harding, and Smith," *Signs: Journal of Women in Culture and Society*, 1997, 22(2): 399.

36. For more on the claim that without something other than political grounds for privileging women's claims, feminist standpoint theory collapses into relativism, see McCaughey, "Redirecting Feminist Critiques of Science"; Conway, *"Das Weib an sich"*; and Conway, *"Circulus Vitiosus Deus?"*

37. Harding, *Whose Science? Whose Knowledge?* 239.

38. Harding, *Whose Science? Whose Knowledge?* 239.

39. Rorty, *Philosophy and the Mirror of Nature* (Princeton: Princeton University Press, 1979).

40. Dewey, "Does Reality Possess Practical Character?" MW 4:138n. See also Dewey, *Experience and Nature*, LW 1:308.

41. Dewey, *How We Think*, MW 6:236–241.

42. Dewey, *Human Nature and Conduct*, MW 14:202.

43. Dewey, *Experience and Education*, LW 13:13, 19.

44. Dewey, "The Problem of Truth," MW 6:66. See also "The Unfinished Introduction" to *Experience and Nature*, LW 1:331, where Dewey defines experience as "the complex of all which is distinctively human."

45. This is especially true in Dewey's writings on animal experimentation. See Dewey, "The Ethics of Animal Experimentation," LW 2:98–103.

46. For some of the implications of pragmatism for environmental philosophy, see Andrew Light and Eric Katz, eds., *Environmental Pragmatism* (New York: Routledge, 1996).

47. Dewey, "The Problem of Truth," MW 6:45.

48. Dewey, "A Short Catechism Concerning Truth," MW 6:10.

49. Jennifer Tannoch-Bland suggests that such a notion of correspondence can be retained; see "From Aperspectival Objectivity to Strong Objectivity," page 167.

50. Charlene Haddock Seigfried, "Like Bridges without Piers: Beyond the Foundationalist Metaphor," in *Antifoundationalism Old and New*, ed. Tom Rockmore and Beth J. Singer (Philadelphia: Temple University Press, 1992), 153.

51. Dewey, *Ethics*, LW 7:296.

52. On the self's becoming what it loves, see Jim Garrison, *Dewey and Eros: Wisdom and Desire in the Art of Teaching* (New York: Teachers College Press, 1997).

53. As Michael Goldman shows, Rorty's nonfoundationalism buys into the false dichotomy of either fixed, unchanging standards or arbitrary conventions, resting on the latter horn of the dilemma. See Goldman, "Rorty's New Myth of the Given," *Metaphilosophy*, 1988, 19(2):105–112.

54. See McCaughey, "Redirecting Feminist Critiques of Science," 78, and

Cassandra L. Pinnick, "Feminist Epistemology: Implications for Philosophy of Science," *Philosophy of Science*, 1994, 61:656.

55. Daniel W. Conway suggests that Haraway's postmodern feminist epistemology agrees that the standpoint of the oppressor must be included in refashioned notions of objectivity. See Conway, *"Das Weib an sich,"* 117.

56. Code, *Rhetorical Spaces: Essays on Gendered Locations* (New York: Routledge, 1995).

57. Judith Butler raises this issue when remarking on Laclau and Mouffe's radical democracy. See Butler, *Bodies That Matter: On the Discursive Limits of "Sex"* (New York: Routledge, 1993), 193.

58. Daryl Davis, *Klan-Destine Relationships: A Black Man's Odyssey in the Ku Klux Klan* (Far Hills, N.J.: New Horizon Press, 1998).

59. For an explanation of the reasons for Dewey's democratic commitments, see Shannon Sullivan, "Democracy and the Individual: To What Extent Is Dewey's Reconstruction Nietzsche's Self-Overcoming?" *Philosophy Today*, Summer 1997, 41(2): 299–312.

60. Phyllis Rooney cites Code in Rooney, "Feminist-Pragmatist Revisions of Reason, Knowledge, and Philosophy," *Hypatia*, 1993, 8(2):19.

61. Donna Haraway makes a similar claim about the construction of knowledge when she says that "accounts of a 'real' world do not, then, depend upon a logic of 'discovery' but on a power-charged social relation of 'conversation'" ("Situated Knowledges," 593).

62. Code, *Rhetorical Spaces*, 55.

63. For more on a transactional understanding of communication, see chapter 3.

64. See Judith Grant, "I Feel Therefore I Am: A Critique of Female Experience as the Basis for a Feminist Epistemology," *Women and Politics*, 1987, 7(3): 99–114, for an overview and critique of the foundational treatment of experience in some feminist philosophy.

65. Seigfried, *Pragmatism and Feminism*, 153.

66. Seigfried, *Pragmatism and Feminism*, 213.

67. Jaggar, "Globalizing Feminist Ethics," *Hypatia*, Spring 1998, 13(2):16.

68. Frances A. Maher and Mary Kay Thompson Tetreault, *The Feminist Classroom* (New York: Basic Books, 1994), 128, 140, 150.

69. I discuss transaction as it pertains to teaching in Shannon Sullivan, "Teaching as a Pragmatist: Relating Non-Foundational Theory and Classroom Practice," *Teaching Philosophy*, December 1997, 20(4): 401–419.

70. Seigfried, *Pragmatism and Feminism*, 154.

71. Dewey, *Human Nature and Conduct*, MW 14:77.

72. Dewey, *Human Nature and Conduct*, MW 14:77.

73. Dewey, *Human Nature and Conduct*, MW 14:115.

74. For a discussion of the adequacy of Dewey's appeal to nonviolent methods of resolution, see Charlene Haddock Seigfried, "John Dewey's Pragmatist Feminism," in *Reading Dewey: Interpretations for a Postmodern Generation*, ed. Larry A. Hickman (Bloomington: Indiana University Press, 1998).

75. It also suggests that we tease out those of other standpoint theorists, such as Evelyn Fox Keller, as well. Keller suggests a move toward pragmatist feminism

when she explicitly rejects a "copy" theory of truth for the position that "some representations are clearly better (more effective) than others" because of "the practices they facilitate" (Keller cited in Alan Soble, "Gender, Objectivity, and Realism," *The Monist* 1994, 77(4):522–523). Because she gives only political and not also epistemic reasons for preferring some practices over others, she is open to criticism that her criterion of "better" begs the question (Soble, "Gender, Objectivity, and Realism," 523). A transactional notion of truth would allow Keller to effectively support her criterion of "better" against those such as Soble's and, just as importantly, do so without slipping back, as Keller occasionally does, into claims that science includes "maximally reliable (even if not [completely] faithful) representation[s] of nature" (Soble, "Gender, Objectivity, and Realism," 525).

76. Harding, *Whose Science? Whose Knowledge?* 142, 144.

77. Harding, "Comment on Hekman's 'Truth and Method,'" 387.

78. Harding, "Comment on Hekman's 'Truth and Method,'" 387.

CONCLUSION

1. Dewey, *Knowing and the Known*, LW 16:119–120.

2. Dewey, *Art as Experience*, LW 10:19.

3. As Charles Mills explains, "contemporary 'critical race theory' . . . adds the adjective ["critical"] specifically to differentiate itself from essentialist [and racist] views of the past" (*The Racial Contract* [Ithaca: Cornell University Press, 1997], 126).

4. On this point, see Dewey, "The Principle of Nationality," MW 10:289.

5. Ignatiev, "Abolitionism and the White Studies Racket," *Race Traitor*, Winter 1999, 10: 3–7.

6. Ignatiev, "Abolitionism and the White Studies Racket," 4.

7. Ignatiev, "Abolitionism and the White Studies Racket," 7.

8. Samuel L. Gaertner, John F. Dovidio, Brenda S. Banker, Mary C. Rust, Jason A. Nier, Gary R. Mottola, and Christine M. Ward, "Does White Racism Necessarily Mean Antiblackness? Aversive Racism and Prowhiteness," in *Off White: Readings on Race, Power, and Society*, ed. Michelle Fine, Lois Weis, Linda C. Powell, and L. Mun Wong (New York: Routledge, 1997), 167–178. My subsequent discussion of psychological forms of racism should not be taken to mean that they are more important than other forms of racism, such as institutional racism and the racism built into the authorization of those who may speak and produce knowledge. A similar point about the equally adverse effects of anti-blackness and "egalitarian" prowhiteness could be made in the case of these other forms of racism.

9. Gaertner et al., "Does White Racism Necessarily Mean Antiblackness?" 168.

10. Gaertner et al., "Does White Racism Necessarily Mean Antiblackness?" 169.

11. Gaertner et al., "Does White Racism Necessarily Mean Antiblackness?" 172–173.

12. Gaertner et al., "Does White Racism Necessarily Mean Antiblackness?" 173.

13. Kwame Anthony Appiah explicitly holds the position that Ignatiev suggests, that is, that the concept of race should be abandoned because biologistic accounts

of race have been debunked. See Appiah, "The Conservation of 'Race,'" *Black American Literature Forum*, Spring 1989, 23(1): 37–60.

14. See chapter 1 for more on the term "bodying."

15. I say "currently" because the ethnic groups considered white in the United States have changed over the years. To take one case in point, the Irish have not always counted as white, as made clear in Noel Ignatiev's *How the Irish Became White* (New York: Routledge, 1995).

16. Mills, *The Racial Contract*, 125.

17. Ignatiev, "Abolitionism and the White Studies Racket," 7.

18. Lucius T. Outlaw, *On Race and Philosophy* (New York: Routledge, 1996), 4, 137.

19. For Du Bois's specific argument, see William Edward Burghardt Du Bois, "The Conservation of Races," in *African-American Social and Political Thought, 1850–1920*, ed. Howard Brotz (New Brunswick: Transaction Publishers, 1992).

20. For work in cognitive psychology and psychological anthropology that supports this claim, see Lawrence A. Hirschfeld, *Race in the Making: Cognition, Culture, and the Child's Construction of Human Kinds* (Cambridge, Mass.: MIT Press, 1996).

21. Outlaw, *On Race and Philosophy*, 8, emphasis in original.

22. Outlaw, *On Race and Philosophy*, 17.

23. Outlaw, *On Race and Philosophy*, 170, emphasis in original.

24. Outlaw, *On Race and Philosophy*, 15, 20.

25. Outlaw does not discuss sex or gender in connection with his point about order, but his arguments concerning race suggest an extension to them.

26. Outlaw, *On Race and Philosophy*, 157, emphasis in original. "Ethnie" is Outlaw's term for ethnic groups.

27. Outlaw, *On Race and Philosophy*, 157. See also Du Bois, "The Conservation of Races," and Alain Locke, "The Contribution of Race to Culture," in *The Philosophy of Alain Locke: Harlem Renaissance and Beyond*, ed. Leonard Harris (Philadelphia: Temple University Press, 1989).

28. Outlaw, *On Race and Philosophy*, 13.

29. Outlaw, *On Race and Philosophy*, 18.

30. Outlaw, *On Race and Philosophy*, 8.

31. Outlaw, *On Race and Philosophy*, 21, emphasis added.

32. Outlaw, "Race, Social Identity, and Human Dignity," paper presented at the Sixteenth International Social Philosophy Conference, Philadelphia, July 15, 1999.

33. Outlaw, *On Race and Philosophy*, 15, 20.

34. For more on using whiteness as a tool against racism, see Shannon Sullivan, "The Racialization of Space: Toward a Phenomenological Account of Raced and Anti-Racist Spatiality," in *The Questions of Resistance*, ed. Steve Martinot (Atlantic Highlands, N.J.: Humanities Press, forthcoming).

BIBLIOGRAPHY

Alexander, Matthais F. 1932. *The Use of the Self: Its Conscious Direction in Relation to Diagnosis, Functioning and the Control of Reaction*. New York: E. P. Dutton.

Allen, Jeffner. 1982. "Through The Wild Region: An Essay in Phenomenological Feminism." *Review of Existential Psychology and Psychiatry* 18: 241–256.

Allen, Jeffner and Iris Marion Young, eds. 1989. *The Thinking Muse: Feminism and Modern French Philosophy*. Bloomington: Indiana University Press.

Appiah, Kwame Anthony. 1989. "The Conservation of 'Race.'" *Black American Literature Forum* 23(1): 37–60.

Bartky, Sandra. 1990. *Femininity and Domination: Studies in the Phenomenology of Oppression*. New York: Routledge.

Bechara, Antoine, Hanna Darnasio, Daniel Tranel, and Antonio R. Damasio. 1997. "Deciding Advantageously Before Knowing the Advantageous Strategy." *Science* 275: 1293–1295.

Bigwood, Carol. 1991. "Renaturalizing the body (with the help of Merleau-Ponty)." *Hypatia* 6(3): 54–73.

Blondel, Eric. 1991. *Nietzsche: The Body and Culture: Philosophy as a Philological Genealogy*. Trans. Sean Hand. Stanford: Stanford University Press.

Bluhm, William T. 1984. *Force or Freedom? The Paradox in Modern Political Thought*. New Haven: Yale University Press.

Bordo, Susan. 1987. *The Flight to Objectivity: Essays on Cartesianism and Culture*. Albany: State University of New York Press.

——. 1993. *Unbearable Weight: Feminism, Western Culture, and the Body*. Berkeley: University of California Press.

——. 1998. "Bringing Body to Theory." In *Body and Flesh: A Philosophical Reader*, ed. Donn Welton. Malden: Blackwell Publishers.

Bourgeois, Patrick L. and Sandra B. Rosenthal. 1990. "Role Taking, Corporeal Intersubjectivity, and Self: Mead and Merleau-Ponty." *Philosophy Today* 34(2): 117–128.

Bradford, Judith and Crispin Sartwell. 1997. "Voice Bodies/Embodied Voices." In *Race/Sex: Their Sameness, Difference and Interplay*, ed. Naomi Zack. New York: Routledge.

Brown, Kristen. 1999. "Possible and Questionable: Opening Nietzsche's Genealogy to Feminine Body." *Hypatia* 14(3): 39–58.

Butler, Judith. 1989a. "Foucault and the Paradox of Bodily Inscriptions." *The Journal of Philosophy*, 86(11): 601–607.

——. 1989b. "Sexual Ideology and Phenomenological Description: A Feminist Critique of Merleau-Ponty's *Phenomenology of Perception*." In *The Thinking Muse: Feminism and Modern French Philosophy*, ed. Jeffner Allen and Iris Marion Young. Bloomington: Indiana University Press.

———. 1990. *Gender Trouble*. New York: Routledge.

———. 1993. *Bodies That Matter: On the Discursive Limits of "Sex."* New York: Routledge.

———. 1997a. *Excitable Speech: A Politics of the Performative*. New York: Routledge.

———. 1997b. *The Psychic Life of Power: Theories in Subjection*. Stanford: Stanford University Press.

———. 1999. "Performativity's Social Magic." In *Bourdieu: A Critical Reader*, ed. Richard Shusterman. Malden: Blackwell.

Butterworth, George. 1995. "An Ecological Perspective on the Origins of Self." In *The Body and the Self*, ed. José Luis Bermúdez, Anthony Marcel, and Naomi Elan. Cambridge, Mass.: MIT Press.

Clark, Ann. 1993. "The Quest for Certainty in Feminist Thought." *Hypatia* 8(3): 84–93.

Code, Lorraine. 1995. *Rhetorical Spaces: Essays on Gendered Locations*. New York: Routledge.

Conway, Daniel W. 1992. "Disembodied Perspectives: Nietzsche contra Rorty." *Nietzsche-Studien* band 21: 281–289.

———. 1993. "*Das Weib an sich:* The slave revolt in epistemology." In *Nietzsche, Feminism and Political Theory*, ed. Paul Patton. New York: Routledge.

———. 1997. "*Circulus Vitiosus Deus?* The Dialectical Logic of Feminist Standpoint Theory." *Journal of Social Philosophy* 28(1): 62–76.

Cranz, Galen. 1998. *The Chair: Rethinking Culture, Body, and Design*. New York: W. W. Norton and Company.

Davis, Daryl. 1998. *Klan-Destine Relationships: A Black Man's Odyssey in the Ku Klux Klan*. Far Hills, N.J.: New Horizon Press.

Derrida, Jacques. 1988. "Signature, Event, Context." In *Limited, Inc.*, ed. Gerald Graff, trans. Samuel Weber and Jeffrey Mehlman. Evanston: Northwestern University Press.

Dewey, John. (See List of Abbreviations)

———. 1894. *The Study of Ethics: A Syllabus*. EW 4:219–362.

———. 1896. "The Reflex Arc Concept in Psychology." EW 5:96–109.

———. 1905. "The Postulate of Immediate Empiricism." MW 3:158–167.

———. 1908. "Does Reality Possess Practical Character?" MW 4:125–142.

———. 1910a. "A Short Catechism Concerning Truth." MW 6:3–11.

———. 1910b. *How We Think*. MW 6:177–356.

———. 1911. "The Problem of Truth." MW 6:12–68.

———. 1917. "The Principle of Nationality." MW 10:285–291.

———. 1922. *Human Nature and Conduct*. MW 14.

———. 1925. *Experience and Nature*. LW 1.

———. 1926. "The Ethics of Animal Experimentation." LW 2:98–103.

———. 1929. *The Quest for Certainty*. LW 4.

———. 1929–1930. *Individualism, Old and New*. LW 5:41–123.

———. 1932. *Ethics*. LW 7.

———. 1934. *Art as Experience*. LW 10.

———. 1938. *Experience and Education*. LW 13:1–62.

———. 1949. *Knowing and the Known.* LW 16: 1–294.

Domino, Brian. 1996. "Nietzsche and the Little Things." Paper presented at Miami University, Oxford, Ohio, March 29.

Du Bois, William Edward Burghardt. 1992 [1897]. "The Conservation of Races." In *African-American Social and Political Thought, 1850–1920,* ed. Howard Brotz. New Brunswick: Transaction Publishers.

Flax, Jane. 1990. "Postmodernism and Gender Relations in Feminist Theory." In *Feminism/Postmodernism,* ed. Linda J. Nicholson. New York: Routledge.

Foucault, Michel. 1978. *The History of Sexuality.* Vol. 1, trans. Robert Hurley. New York: Vintage.

———. 1980. *Power/Knowledge: Selected Interviews and Other Writings, 1972–1977,* ed. Colin Gordon; trans. Colin Gordon, Leo Marshall, John Mepham, and Kate Soper. New York: Pantheon Books.

———. 1985. *The Use of Pleasure.* Vol. 3 of *The History of Sexuality,* trans. Robert Hurley. New York: Vintage.

———. 1988. *Politics/Philosophy/Culture: Interviews and Other Writings, 1977–1984,* ed. Lawrence D. Kritzman. New York: Routledge.

Gaertner, Samuel L., John F. Dovidio, Brenda S. Banker, Mary C. Rust, Jason A. Nier, Gary R. Mottola, and Christine M. Ward. 1997. "Does White Racism Necessarily Mean Antiblackness? Aversive Racism and Prowhiteness." In *Off White: Readings on Race, Power, and Society,* ed. Michelle Fine, Lois Weis, Linda C. Powell, and L. Mun Wong. New York: Routledge.

Garrison, Jim. 1996. "A Deweyan Theory of Democratic Listening." *Educational Theory* 46(4): 429–451.

———. 1997. *Dewey and Eros: Wisdom and Desire in the Art of Teaching.* New York: Teachers College Press.

Gatens-Robinson, Eugenie. 1991. "Dewey and the Feminist Successor Science Project." *Transactions of the C. S. Peirce Society* 27(4): 417–433.

Gendlin, Eugene T. 1992. "The primacy of the body, not the primacy of perception." *Man and World* 00: 341–353

Goldman, Michael. 1988. "Rorty's New Myth of the Given." *Metaphilosophy* 19(2): 105–112.

Grant, Judith. 1987. "I Feel Therefore I Am: A Critique of Female Experience as the Basis for a Feminist Epistemology." *Women and Politics* 7(3): 99–114.

Grosz, Elizabeth. 1994. *Volatile Bodies: Toward a Corporeal Feminism.* Bloomington: Indiana University Press.

Guha, Ramachandra. 1989. "Radical American Environmentalism and Wilderness Preservation: A Third World Critique." *Environmental Ethics* 11(1): 71–83.

Haar, Michel. 1988. "Heidegger and the Nietzschean 'Physiology of Art.'" In *Exceedingly Nietzsche,* ed. David Farrell Krell and David Wood. New York: Routledge.

Haber, Honi Fern. 1994. *Beyond Postmodern Politics: Lyotard, Rorty, Foucault.* New York: Routledge.

Haraway, Donna. 1988. "Situated Knowledges: The Science Question in Feminism and the Privilege of Partial Perspective." *Feminist Studies* 14(3): 575–599.

Harding, Sandra. 1986. *The Science Question in Feminism*. Ithaca: Cornell University Press.

———. 1989. "How the Women's Movement Benefits Science: Two Views." *Women's Studies International Forum* 12(3): 271–283.

———. 1991. *Whose Science? Whose Knowledge? Thinking from Women's Lives.* Ithaca: Cornell University Press.

———. 1992. "After the Neutrality Ideal: Science, Politics, and 'Strong Objectivity.'" *Social Research* 59(3): 567–587.

———. 1993. "Rethinking Standpoint Epistemology: 'What Is Strong Objectivity'?" In *Feminist Epistemologies*, ed. Linda Alcoff and Elizabeth Potter. New York: Routledge.

———. 1997. "Comment on Hekman's 'Truth and Method: Feminist Standpoint Theory Revisited': Whose Standpoint Needs the Regimes of Truth and Reality?" *Signs: Journal of Women in Culture and Society* 22(2): 382–391.

Hartsock, Nancy C. M. 1983. "The Feminist Standpoint: Developing the Ground for a Specifically Feminist Historical Materialism." In *Discovering Reality*, ed. Sandra Harding and Merrill B. Hintikka. Boston: D. Reidel Publishing Company.

Hatab, Lawrence J. 1995. *A Nietzschean Defense of Democracy: An Experiment in Postmodern Politics*. Chicago: Open Court.

Hekman, Susan. 1997a. "Truth and Method: Feminist Standpoint Theory Revisited." *Signs: Journal of Women in Culture and Society* 22(2): 341–365.

———. 1997b. "Reply to Hartsock, Collins, Harding, and Smith." *Signs: Journal of Women in Culture and Society* 22(2): 399–402.

Heldke, Lisa. 1987. "John Dewey and Evelyn Fox Keller: A Shared Epistemological Tradition." *Hypatia* 2(3): 129–140.

Hirschfeld, Lawrence A. 1996. *Race in the Making: Cognition, Culture, and the Child's Construction of Human Kinds*. Cambridge, Mass.: MIT Press.

hooks, bell. 1981. *Ain't I a Woman? Black Women and Feminism*. Boston: South End Press.

Ignatiev, Noel. 1995. *How The Irish Became White*. New York: Routledge.

———. 1999. "Abolitionism and the White Studies Racket." *Race Traitor* 10: 3–7.

Irigaray, Luce. 1991. *Marine Lover of Friedrich Nietzsche*, trans. Gillian C. Gill. New York: Columbia University Press.

———. 1993. *An Ethics of Sexual Difference*, trans. Carolyn Burke and Gillian C. Gill. Ithaca: Cornell University Press.

Jaggar, Alison M. 1998. "Globalizing Feminist Ethics." *Hypatia* 13(2): 7–31.

Johnson, Mark. 1987. *The Body in the Mind: The Bodily Basis of Meaning, Imagination, and Reason*. Chicago: University of Chicago Press.

Keith, Heather E. 1999. "Feminism and Pragmatism: George Herbert Mead's Ethics of Care." *Transactions of the C. S. Peirce Society* 35(2): 328–344.

Kestenbaum, Victor. 1977. *The Phenomenological Sense of John Dewey: Habit and Meaning*. Atlantic Highlands, N.J.: Humanities Press.

Kogaku, Arifuku. 1991. "The Problem of the Body in Nietzsche and Dogen," trans. Graham Parkes. In *Nietzsche and Asian Thought*, ed. Graham Parkes. Chicago: University of Chicago Press.

Kruse, Felicia. 1991. "Luce Irigaray's *Parler Femme* and American Metaphysics." *Transactions of the C. S. Peirce Society* 27(4): 451–464.

Levin, David Michael. 1985. *The Body's Recollection of Being: Phenomenological Psychology and the Deconstruction of Nihilism.* New York: Routledge

———. 1989. "The Body Politic: The Embodiment of Praxis in Foucault and Habermas." *Praxis International* 9(1/2): 112–132.

Light, Andrew and Eric Katz, eds. 1996. *Environmental Pragmatism.* New York: Routledge.

Lloyd, Genevieve. 1984. *The Man of Reason: "Male" and "Female" in Western Philosophy.* Minneapolis: University of Minneapolis Press.

Locke, Alain. 1989 [1930]. "The Contribution of Race to Culture." In *The Philosophy of Alain Locke: Harlem Renaissance and Beyond,* ed. Leonard Harris. Philadelphia: Temple University Press.

Longino, Helen. 1993. "Subjects, Power and Knowledge: Description and Prescription in Feminist Philosophies of Science." In *Feminist Epistemologies,* ed. Linda Alcoff and Elizabeth Potter. New York: Routledge.

Lugones, María C. 1987. "Playfulness, 'World'-Traveling, and Loving Perception." *Hypatia* 2(2): 3–19.

———. 1991. "On the Logic of Pluralist Feminism." In *Feminist Ethics,* ed. Claudia Card. Lawrence: University Press of Kansas.

Madison, Gary Brent. 1981. *The Phenomenology of Merleau-Ponty,* trans. Gary Brent Madison. Athens: Ohio University Press.

Maher, Frances A. 1998. "My Introduction to 'Introduction to Women's Studies': The Role of the Professor's Authority in the Feminist Classroom." In *The Feminist Anthology: Pedagogies and Classroom Strategies,* ed. Gail E. Cohee, Elisabeth Daumer, Theresa D. Kemp, Paula M. Krebs, Sue A. Lafky, and Sandra Runzo. New York: Teachers College Press.

Maher, Frances A., and Mary Kay Thompson Tetreault. 1994. *The Feminist Classroom.* New York: Basic Books.

McCaughey, Martha. 1993. "Redirecting Feminist Critiques of Science." *Hypatia* 8(4), 72–84.

McWhorter, Ladelle. 1989. "Culture or Nature? The Function of the Term 'Body' in the Work of Michel Foucault." *The Journal of Philosophy* 86(11): 608–614.

———. 1999. *Bodies and Pleasures: Foucault and the Politics of Sexual Normalization.* Bloomington: Indiana University Press.

———. Forthcoming. "Bodies against Desire: Foucault's Resistance to Sexual Subjectivity." In *The Limits of Desire: Passion, Play, and Perversion,* ed. Ellen L. McCallum and Judith Roof.

Merleau-Ponty, Maurice. 1962. *The Phenomenology of Perception,* trans. Colin Smith. Atlantic Highlands, N.J.: Humanities Press.

———. 1968. *The Visible and the Invisible.* trans. Alphonso Lingis. Evanston: Northwestern University Press.

McMillan, Elizabeth. 1987. "Female Difference in the Texts of Merleau-Ponty." *Philosophy Today* 31: 359–366.

McNay, Lois. 1991. "The Foucauldian Body and the Exclusion of Experience." *Hypatia* 6(3): 123–139.

Miller, Marjorie C. 1992. "Feminism and Pragmatism." *Monist* 75(4): 445–457.

———. 1994. "Essence and Identity: Santayana and the Category 'Women.'" *Transactions of the C. S. Peirce Society* 30(1): 33–50.

Mills, Charles W. 1997. *The Racial Contract*. Ithaca: Cornell University Press.

Moen, Marcia. 1991. "Peirce's Pragmatism as a Resource for Feminism." *Transactions of the C. S. Peirce Society* 27(4): 435–450.

Nagel, Thomas. 1997. *The Last Word*. New York: Oxford University Press.

Nelson, Lynn Hankinson. 1993. "Epistemological Communities." In *Feminist Epistemologies*, ed. Linda Alcoff and Elizabeth Potter. New York: Routledge.

Nietzsche, Friedrich. 1967. *The Will to Power*, trans. Walter Kaufmann and R. J. Hollingdale; ed. Walter Kaufmann. New York: Vintage Books.

———. 1968a. *Beyond Good and Evil*. In *Basic Writings of Nietzsche*, trans. and ed. Walter Kaufmann. New York: The Modern Library.

———. 1968b. *Ecce Homo*. In *Basic Writings of Nietzsche*, trans. and ed. Walter Kaufmann. New York: The Modern Library.

———. 1968c. *On the Genealogy of Morals*. In *Basic Writings of Nietzsche*, trans. and ed. Walter Kaufmann. New York: The Modern Library.

———. 1968d. *Twilight of the Idols/The Anti-Christ*, trans. R. J. Hollingdale, N.Y.: Penguin Books.

———. 1969. *Thus Spoke Zarathustra*, trans. R. J. Hollingdale. New York: Viking Penguin.

———. 1986. *Human, All Too Human: A Book for Free Spirits*, trans. R. J. Hollingdale. New York: Cambridge University Press.

Oliver, Kelly. 1995. *Womanizing Nietzsche: Philosophy's Relation to the "Feminine."* New York: Routledge.

Outlaw, Lucius T., Jr. 1996. *On Race and Philosophy*. New York: Routledge.

———. 1999. "Race, Social Identity, and Human Dignity." Paper presented at the Sixteenth International Social Philosophy Conference, Philadelphia, July 15.

Owen, David. 1993. "Nietzsche's Squandered Seductions: Feminism, the Body, and the Politics of Genealogy." In *The Fate of the New Nietzsche*, ed. Keith Ansell-Pearson and Howard Caygill. Brookfield: Avebury.

Pasley, Malcolm. 1978. "Nietzsche's Use of Medical Terms." In *Nietzsche: Imagery and Thought*, ed. Malcolm Pasley. London: Methuen.

Pinnick, Cassandra L. 1994. "Feminist Epistemology: Implications for Philosophy of Science." *Philosophy of Science* 61: 646–657.

Reed, Peter. 1989. "Man Apart: An Alternative to the Self-Realization Approach." *Environmental Ethics* 11(1): 53–69.

Rescher, Nicholas. 1997. *Objectivity: The Obligations of Impersonal Reason*. Notre Dame: University of Notre Dame Press.

Rockmore, Tom, and Beth J. Singer, eds. 1992. *Antifoundationalism Old and New*. Philadelphia: Temple University Press.

Rooney, Phyllis. 1993. "Feminist-Pragmatist Revisions of Reason, Knowledge, and Philosophy." *Hypatia* 8(2): 15–37.

Rorty, Richard. 1979. *Philosophy and the Mirror of Nature*. Princeton: Princeton University Press.

Rosenblatt, Louise M. 1978. *The Reader the Text the Poem: The Transactional Theory of the Literary Work*. Carbondale: Southern Illinois University Press.

Scott, Charles E. 1990. *The Question of Ethics: Nietzsche, Foucault, Heidegger.* Bloomington: Indiana University Press.

Scott, Jacqueline. 1997. "Nietzsche and the Problem of Women's Bodies." Paper presented at the meeting of the Eastern Division of the American Philosophical Association, Philadelphia, December 28.

Seigfried, Charlene Haddock. 1990. "Weaving Chaos into Order: A Radically Pragmatic Aesthetic." *Philosophy and Literature* 14(1): 108–116.

———. 1992. "Like Bridges without Piers: Beyond the Foundationalist Metaphor." In *Antifoundationalism Old and New,* ed. Tom Rockmore and Beth J. Singer. Philadelphia: Temple University Press.

———. 1996. *Pragmatism and Feminism: Reweaving the Social Fabric.* Chicago: University of Chicago Press.

———. 1998. "John Dewey's Pragmatist Feminism." In *Reading Dewey: Interpretations for a Postmodern Generation,* ed. Larry Hickman. Bloomington: Indiana University Press.

Seigfried, Charlene Haddock, ed. 1993. *Hypatia* 8(2). Special Issue: Feminism and Pragmatism.

———. Forthcoming. *Feminist Interpretations of John Dewey.* University Park: Penn State University Press.

Sheets-Johnstone, Maxine. 1992. "Corporeal Archetypes and Power: Preliminary Clarifications and Considerations of Sex." *Hypatia* 7: 39–76.

Shusterman, Richard. 1997a. *Practicing Philosophy: Pragmatism and the Philosophical Life.* New York: Routledge.

———. 1997b. "Somaesthetics and the Body/Media Issue." *Body and Society* 3(3): 33–49.

Soble, Alan. 1994. "Gender, Objectivity, and Realism." *The Monist* 77(4): 509–530.

Spelman, Elizabeth V. 1982. "Woman as Body: Ancient and Contemporary Views." *Feminist Studies* 8(1): 109–131.

———. 1988. *Inessential Woman: Problems of Exclusion in Feminist Thought.* Boston: Beacon Press.

Stuhr, John J. 1997. *Genealogical Pragmatism: Philosophy, Experience, and Community.* Albany: State University of New York Press.

Stuhr, John J., ed. 1993. *Philosophy and the Reconstruction of Culture: Pragmatic Essays after Dewey.* Albany: State University of New York Press.

Sullivan, Shannon. 1997a. "Democracy and the Individual: To What Extent Is Dewey's Reconstruction Nietzsche's Self-Overcoming?" *Philosophy Today* 41(2): 299–312.

———. 1997b. "Teaching as a Pragmatist: Relating Non-Foundational Theory and Classroom Practice." *Teaching Philosophy* 20(4): 401–419.

———. 1999. Review of *The Rejected Body: Philosophical Feminist Reflections on Disability* by Susan Wendell. *The APA Newsletter on Feminism and Philosophy* 98(2): 99–101.

———. 2000. "Feminism and Phenomenology: A Reply to Silvia Stoller." *Hypatia* 15(1): 182–188.

———. Forthcoming. "The Racialization of Space: Toward a Phenomenological Account of Raced and Anti-Racist Spatiality." In *The Questions of Resistance,* ed. Steve Martinot. Atlantic Highlands, N.J.: Humanities Press.

Bibliography

Tannoch-Bland, Jennifer. 1997. "From Aperspectival Objectivity to Strong Objectivity: The Quest for Moral Objectivity." *Hypatia* 12(1): 155–178.

Tuana, Nancy. 1990. "Re-fusing Nature/Nurture." In *Hypatia Reborn: Essays in Feminist Philosophy*, ed. Azizah Y. al-Hibri and Margaret A. Simons. Bloomington: Indiana University Press.

Vasterling, Veronica. 1999. "Butler's Sophisticated Constructivism: A Critical Assessment." *Hypatia* 14(3) 17–38.

Welton, Donn, ed. 1998. *Body and Flesh: A Philosophical Reader*. Malden: Blackwell Publishers.

Wendell, Susan. 1996. *The Rejected Body: Feminist Philosophical Reflections on Disability*. New York: Routledge.

Westbrook, Robert B. 1991. *John Dewey and American Democracy*. Ithaca: Cornell University Press.

Wilshire, Bruce. 1993. "Body-Mind and Subconsciousness: Tragedy in Dewey's Life and Work." In *Philosophy and the Reconstruction of Culture: Pragmatic Essays after Dewey*, ed. John J. Stuhr. Albany: State University of New York Press.

Yezierska, Anzia. 1932. *All I Could Never Be*. New York: Brewer, Warren and Putnam.

———. 1995 [1923]. *Salome of the Tenements*. Urbana: University of Illinois Press.

Young, Iris Marion. 1990. *Throwing Like a Girl and Other Essays in Feminist Philosophy and Social Theory*. Bloomington: Indiana University Press.

INDEX

SHANNON SULLIVAN is Assistant Professor of Philosophy and Women's Studies at the Pennsylvania State University.